C++ FOR REAL PROGRAMMERS

Revised Edition

LIMITED WARRANTY AND DISCLAIMER OF LIABILITY

C++ FOR REAL PROGRAMMERS

JEFF ALGER
Microsoft Corporation
Redmond, WA

AP PROFESSIONAL
AP PROFESSIONAL is a division of Academic Press

Boston   San Diego   New York
London   Sydney   Tokyo   Toronto

AP Professional
An Imprint of ACADEMIC PRESS
A Division of HARCOURT BRACE & COMPANY

This book is printed on acid-free paper ⊗

Academic Press
525 B Street, Suite 1900, San Diego, CA 92101-4495
1300 Boylston Street, Chestnut Hill, MA 02167

United Kingdom Edition published by
ACADEMIC PRESS LIMITED
24-28 Oval Road, London NW1 7DX

Library of Congress Cataloging-in-Publication Data
Alger, Jeff.
    C++ for real programmers / Jeff Alger. – 2nd ed.
        p. cm.
        Includes index.
        ISBN 0-12-049942-8 (alk. Paper).
        ISBN 0-12-049943-6 (disk)
    1. C++ (Computer program language) I. Title.
    QA76.73.C153A43 1998
    005.13'--dc21   97-35352
                             CIP

Printed in the United States of America
  98 99 00 IP 9 8 7 6 5 4 3 2 1

Contents

Contents

Contents

Acknowledgments

As with any book, thanks are due to more people than can be gathered into any single list. A book is much more than a bunch of pages with funny black marks all over them. It is one part altruism, one part ego, and one part primal scream. Above all, it is a significant portion of an author's life and that of his family. My deepest thanks to my wife, Cindy, and sons Nick, JJ, and Bobby for their patience, support, and acceptance of all those times that Daddy couldn't come out and throw the ball around.

If patience is a virtue, some of the most virtuous people I know work at AP Professional. I am indebted to all of you for supporting the idea of this book from the start and keeping just the right level of pressure on to get it done. Now that I think of it, perhaps I had the easy part — while I rest, you are now stuck with the job of selling it!

Special thanks to John Trudeau at Apple Computer, who first encouraged me to get what to that point were random thoughts and experiences down on paper in the form of a seminar for advanced C++ programmers. I'm not sure whether to direct thanks or my sincerest apologies to the many students who had to live through the early versions of that course before it finally started to take shape.

Many people over the years have influenced my thinking about C++ and object-oriented programming. A few that spring to mind are Neal Goldstein, Larry Rosenstein, Eric Berdahl, John Brugge, Dave Simmons, and Dave Buell. None of you are responsible for anything in this book that you disagree with but may freely claim credit for anything you first planted in my psyche.

My thanks also extend to my new colleagues at Microsoft Corporation, who hired me anyway at a time when this book was "nearly complete," which meant that the first 90 percent was done and only the second 90 percent remained. I did not have my Microsoft hat on when I wrote this book, so please don't get upset with them for anything I've said herein. This book was started and substantially completed before I went to work there and has not been contributed to, reviewed by, or approved by anyone at Microsoft.

James Coplien, we've never met, but your book *Advanced C++ Programming Styles and Idioms* was and remains a big influence on my thinking. It is very hard to blaze trails, but your book did an exceptional job of opening up the subject of advanced C++ usage. I hope we'll see more authors following in your footsteps.

Finally, I want to thank Bjarne Stroustrup for inventing such a weird language. Simple, consistent languages like Smalltalk are boring to write about or even to think about. If C++ didn't have all those backwaters and strange rules, it wouldn't be such fertile soil for authors, consultants, and other assorted gadflies like yours truly. Bjarne, I like your language — really, I do — but in the same way Churchill loved democracy: it's the worst object-oriented language ever invented ... except for all the others.

I'm Sorry ... Sort Of

I also want to take this opportunity to apologize to all the people I've offended in the course of writing this book. I have no idea who you are, but I found out the hard way through two articles published in IEEE *Computer* magazine how many people get upset when one makes light of a *serious* subject like C++. If you are among them, I'm sorry to have offended your sensibilities. Not sorry enough to lose any sleep over it, but a little.

I don't claim original authorship of any ideas in this book. If you see something in here that you or someone else invented, feel free to claim that you said it first — I won't argue. Advanced C++ usage has always been more of a trade than a profession, learned by apprenticeship and the sharing of ideas with others rather than through formal education, so there are no really authoritative sources to go to to track down who said what when. My overriding interest in writing this book is to bring as many people up to speed as quickly and painlessly as possible — footnotes are not a high priority. If anyone feels slighted by this approach, you too have my sincerest apologies and are hereby invited to write a book of your own.

On the other hand, I have taken bold liberties in applying new names to old but confusing concepts, and I feel not the slightest twinge of regret at having done so. This is in the grand tradition of the C++ community, which has renamed virtually all object-oriented concepts, among them *subclass* ("derived class"), *superclass* ("base class"), *method* ("member function"), and *inheritance* ("derivation"). Even such age-old C concepts as bit shifting are not sacred to the C++ naming police. If you object to new names for old ideas, used in the interest of clarity, you're programming in the wrong language, buddy.

I have done everything possible to verify that all the code fragments in this book and on the accompanying floppy disk work as they should, but some errors undoubtedly have slipped through the net. Act as if even *reading* any of them might be enough to make your programs crash and burn horribly — test, test, and test some more before using them in your own programs. Remember: my objective in this book is to illustrate idioms and concepts, not to ship a class library. The idioms are all sound, but beyond that you're on your own.

Jeff Alger

January 1998

SECTION 1   *Introduction and Review*

This section answers the critical question "Why did the author bother to write yet another book about C++?" and then follows with a roller-coaster-paced review of advanced features of the language. This is all in preparation for the material in later sections, so skim or read for detail, according to your comfort with the backwaters of C++ syntax.

CHAPTER 1

Why Yet Another Book About C++?

At last count, there are at least 2,768,942 books about C++ on the market, along with training classes, multimedia-based self-help courses, magazines, and C++ cocktail parties galore. But throughout, there is a depressing sameness. Browsing the C++ section of a bookstore is sort of like browsing the accounting section; the books all basically cover the same material and differ only in how many pounds they weigh and how many colors they use for charts and tables. By my count, 2,768,940 of those other books are for beginners, are for one particular compiler, or are reference works on C++ syntax. For those who already know the language and are looking to advance to the next level, this is frustrating and expensive; you have to pick a chapter here and a section there in order to find something you don't already know. For those who have already achieved C++ guru status, it's a waste of time.

This book is different. For one thing, I assume you already know C++. You probably have a couple of years or more of C++ programming and designing under your belt. You're probably a hotshot programmer, maybe so good that you no longer introduce yourself at those cocktail parties as a Programmer; your title is drawn from the words *Senior, Architect, Designer, Lead*, and *Software*, in no particular order. You know an overloaded function isn't one of those C++ cocktail parties, an overloaded operator doesn't work for the phone company, and a collection class isn't a seminar on how to raise money for charity. You probably have a copy of Stroustrup's *Annotated C++ Reference Manual*, cite it frequently by its acronym, ARM, in casual conversation, and don't bother to explain to anyone who doesn't already know that you're talking about a book, not a limb.

If this is you, welcome; come on in. An alternative title for this book might be *C++: The Way of the Gurus.* This is different from the C++ you see described in books about the basics. More than any other language I know, C++ at this level is not so much a language as a subculture with idioms, tricks, and standard architectural concepts not readily apparent from the language itself. This language-within-a-language is seldom talked about in books and magazines. Most C++ programmers rediscover its tricks for themselves, thinking they've invented something really clever, only to discover later that, as the talent scout said to the man juggling monkeys, "It's been done." Others are fortunate enough to apprentice to a C++ master, but there aren't enough masters to go around. This book is an attempt to provide a third path to true C++ enlightenment: self-study. Second, this book is for those who have already reached that lofty plateau but want companionship, lively conversation, and the occasional brain teaser.

The Zen of C++

C++ is a language learned in stages. Only when the last stage is reached does it all finally start to make sense, to combine into a Zen that unifies the otherwise scattered tricks and syntax. I think of learning C++ as being like rising up in an elevator. Ding! Second floor. C++ is a more reasonable C, strongly typed as long as you don't fool around too much and, hey, how about those nifty //

comments? All those C programmers who didn't want to go into management needed a career path, and Bjarne Stroustrup, bless his soul, dreamed up a doozy.

Ding! Third floor. C++ is a decent-but-not-great object-oriented programming language. It's not Smalltalk, but hey, what do you expect from a language that runs so blindingly fast? C++ is the Cobol of the 1990s, politically correct and sure to get your project funded by top management. Heck, they might even double your budget if you mention C++ often enough in your proposal. That's just as well, because no one really knows how to estimate and manage C++ projects, and as to tools, say, lot of weather we're having, isn't it?

Ding! Top floor, everybody out. Hey, where did everyone go? Sure is drafty up here. C++ is really yacc++, not so much a language as a way of creating your own languages. It is elegant not for its simplicity — like *jumbo shrimp*, the terms *C++* and *simple* grate on the ears when used in the same sentence — but for its potential. Lurking behind every gnarly design problem is a clever idiom, a nice twist to the language that makes the problem melt away like the Wicked Witch of the West without her umbrella. That idiom solves the problem as elegantly as a *real* language like Smalltalk or Lisp would, but without causing smoke to rise from your CPU and the stock of companies that manufacture memory chips to rise on Wall Street. C++ isn't a language — it's an experience, a mind-altering drug.

There's that word again, *elegant*. There is a Zen to designing for C++: you have to stop trying so hard to be elegant in order to achieve true elegance. C is very much a next-generation C. It compiles efficiently and runs fast. It has a very conventional block-structured grammar and an abbreviated syntax for commonly used forms, such as i++. There are nouns, verbs, adjectives, and lots of slang, such as

```
cout<<17<<endl<<flush;
```

C++ programmers have been cowed into embarrassment by the language purists. The purists think that a language built on nothing more than atoms and parentheses is the height of modern civilization. To the syntax terrorists, making it nearly impossible to visually distinguish a simple variable from a function call from a macro is a surefire crowd-pleasing feat of prestidigitation. Gee, folks, if you're so smart, why aren't you rich? In real life, the crowds only pay to see languages in which different ideas *look* different. The "simple, consistent" languages have never gained much of a following outside academia, while block-structured languages have drawn the masses. Why should this surprise anyone? Computer languages have to be learned and read, and for that they use the same gray matter we use to learn and remember natural languages. Quick, can you name one natural language without nouns and verbs and with parentheses all over the place? I thought not. Everything we know about linguistics predicts that learning time will be shorter and reading comprehension and retention higher for computer languages with all those supposedly "bad" properties. i++ really *is* more readable by any verifiable measure than i := i+1, and people really do have an easier time reading x = 17+29 than something like (setq x (+17 29)). This has nothing to do with the design of the programming language and everything to do with how *we* are designed. C++ is ugly in large part because we are ugly. Once you learn to know and love its quirks and stop worrying about mathematical consistency, you are on the road to elegance in C++. What makes C++ readable is proudly and forthrightly admitting to the reader that there are a lot of different concepts buried on the page.

Like Lisp, Smalltalk, and other dynamic languages — and unlike C — C++ provides the hooks needed to manipulate the low-level behavior of the compiler. You can make up your own data types and fool the compiler into adopting them as its own progeny. You can control how functions are called, how data members are accessed, how memory is allocated and deallocated, and how and when things get initialized and cleaned up, all without sacrificing efficiency or type safety (often). Unlike those other languages, a

C++ program will merrily crash and burn if you use this power the wrong way. Even if it doesn't, your fellow programmers might if you don't find a way to make your design intent clear by using just the right idiom for a complicated design. Daedalus and his son, Icarus, escaped imprisonment on Crete by making wings out of feathers and wax. Daedalus, the master architect and inventor, soared to distant shores. His brash son flew too close to the sun and crashed into the sea. Hmm, now that I think of it, maybe that's not such a good analogy. Daedalus was the designer of the Labyrinth, which was so complicated that people either died looking for a way out or became lunch for the Minotaur. Perhaps a more contemporary analogy will do. Every time you use those low-level C++ features, it's like the bumbling detective Sledge Hammer from the 1980s TV series saying to the compiler, "Trust me, I know what I'm doing." The compiler rolls its eyes and plays along.

C++ is intriguing because of its inherent contradictions: it is powerful because of tools that are easily abused. It provides an extensible programming environment without compromising space or speed. It is elegant in one set of hands while dangerous in others, simple and complex at the same time. After years of using it, you still can't make up your mind whether to admire it or walk away in disgust. Yet, the truly expert know the concepts that underlie the language that tip the scales in its favor. These concepts are not readily apparent but are learned by applying the language to a wide variety of problems over a period of years. Certain architectural paradigms go best with specific features of the language. If you mismatch the two, the result is chaos. If you get the right combination, the result is, well, elegant.

Three Great Ideas in C++

So much can be written about advanced C++ usage that it's hard to know where to begin. Have you ever seen one of those pictures that looks at first like a random pattern but slowly reveals itself as an elephant or spiral or whatever after you stare at it for a while? Suddenly the dots and blots make sense when they can be seen as part of a unifying theme. That's one of the most frustrating things about learning C++ architectures and idioms. There seems to be a huge bag of random tricks and no rules as to how and when to use them. This book illuminates the elephant. There are lots of ways to organize advanced C++ thinking, but this book collects them into a few simple themes.

- indirection
- homomorphic class hierarchies
- memory spaces

Each of these is supported by specific syntax and features of C++, and all work together to solve an amazing variety of problems. There are lots of other design principles and tricks that one could make a case for including in this book, but these three categories, taken together, organize a very large subset into a coherent framework.

In this first section, you will find a review of many of the important sideshows in the C++ syntactic circus. Many C++ programmers have little experience with overloaded operators, for example, even though they may have "book knowledge" of how they work. I have found that an amazing proportion of C++ programmers have never used templates or exception handling, and few really understand how to use iostreams beyond simple calls to cout and cin. Section 1 is an attempt to level the playing field, filling in the gaps in your C++ knowledge in preparation for the game. Feel free to read for depth, browse, or skip parts of Section 1 depending on your knowledge of C++ minutae.

The term *indirection* covers a wide variety of individual topics, but the concept is the same throughout: some client object makes a request of a second object, which turns right around and delegates the work to a third object. The object in the middle is where the indirection takes place. Some might argue that this is almost the dictionary definition of delegation, one of the bulwarks of object-oriented design, but in C++ the idioms one uses with this concept and the language support for it go beyond what is considered delegation in other languages. I use the term *pointer* a lot in this book; in fact, the term occurs in every chapter. Pointers in C++ can do a lot. They can determine where in memory, on disk, or in the network the object pointed to resides; when it gets destroyed; whether it may be updated or is read-only; even whether it exists or is simply an assignable location in some abstract memory space — all without the active cooperation of the pointee, which may be completely oblivious to all this surrounding grubby, low-level activity. Pretty heavy stuff, but built from a bunch of very simple idioms.

A lot has been written about how to design class hierarchies, much of it is quite useful and much of it "just emulates real-world objects" trash. Most of the arguments could be applied equally to any other object-oriented language, and I have no intention of cluttering up a book on C++ with my own views on general object-oriented design. However, there is a specific kind of derivation, *homomorphic*, that is amazingly useful in conjunction with C++-specific features. In a homomorphic class hierarchy, all derived classes obtain their public interface from some ancestral base class. In fact, the mother of all base classes is usually as pure as the driven snow: it has no data members, and all of its member functions are pure virtuals. In C++, there are many powerful design and programming idioms that go along with this concept.

The idea of a *memory space* has to do with more than just managing memory. In C++, you can overload operators new and delete to determine where objects are created and how they are destroyed. You can also create abstract collections in which it is not always evident when you are dealing with a real object and when you are dealing with an abstraction for one. Those spear tips you see coming over the ridge are the new distributed object-oriented frameworks from companies like Microsoft, Apple, and Taligent. These require that you rethink some basic notions about where objects reside and how they can be moved about, subjects I lump into the memory space category. Memory spaces are useful for determining the type of an object at run time, something sorely lacking in C++. Yes, we'll talk about handling memory, but there is much more to this section.

How to Read This Book

This book is not a manual full of prescriptions for handling specific problems. It is a book of ideas and challenges. I will have succeeded if, when you reach the end, you feel that your workbench of C++ design tools has been expanded; I make no attempt to tell you how and when to use those tools.

It is impossible to thoroughly teach all the material in any one chapter without first teaching all the others, but I've done my best to organize things in such a way that material is immediately usable by the end of each chapter, yet the chapters build on one another to slowly build up the mental elephant from the tusks, ears, trunk, and feet. Once you are done, the material is also organized so that this book can be used as a reference, a sort of personal and very much abridged dictionary of C++ tricks and idioms.

My years of teaching and using C++ have taught me that even experienced C++ programmers often have gaps in their background; the remainder of this section levels the playing field. It is not an introduction to the language, but is closer to a C++ edition of Trivial Pursuit focused on material that will be of use in later chapters. Chapter 2 is a pell-mell run-through of the language. Chapter 3 is about templates, a subject only slowly becoming important as more compilers support it. Chapter 4 discusses exception handling using the proposed ANSI standard, together with a few comments about the sort of nonstandard exception handling encountered in the real world.

Section 2 is all about pointers: dumb, smart, smarter, master, and insufferably brilliant. This is the foundation stone upon which everything else in the book is built, and I feel strongly that every reader will benefit from it.

Section 3 deals with the design and implementation of types and class hierarchies in C++. It focuses on one particular brand of class hierarchy, the homomorphic variety. Class objects, exemplars, and other assorted curiosities are also discussed. Most readers will want to read all this material, but you can feel free to browse and pick and choose. And just when you thought you'd heard all there is to say about pointers, they'll pop up once again in the context of homomorphic type hierarchies.

Section 4 tackles head-on everyone's nightmare subject in C++: memory management. The discussion ranges from the naive to the profound to the ridiculously overengineered, but the emphasis throughout is on problems a C++ programmer might encounter and ways to leverage language features to solve them. I consider the early chapters in this section to be essential to leading a happy and fulfilled C++ life, but if you don't care, for example, about scavenging garbage collectors, I would suggest that you do something more productive with your time than reading the last couple of chapters.

A Few Words About Coding Style

Specifically, three words: I don't care. Is that few enough? If people spent half as much time designing their programs or, better yet, working with their users, as they spend worrying about where those }'s belong, the whole industry would be a lot more productive. I do care that teams be consistent, but in my twenty years in the industry I have yet to see the book or style guide that can best a one-hour meeting of the team at the start of the project. I also have yet to see the book on coding style that can turn an undisciplined programmer's code into something readable; in fact, style guides are sometimes used as an excuse for not paying close enough attention to whether the program, when read, actually makes sense. Most to the point, I have yet to see one programmer convince another that she is right when styles clash, so arguments on this topic are a waste of time.

I do have my own conventions and style, but for the most part I'm going to go out of my way to use a little bit of all the various styles I've seen. The focus in this book is on idioms, not placement of }'s or how you capitalize things. I hope that by doing so, I'll offend everyone equally.

I have also taken liberties with inline member functions, particularly virtual ones. The politically correct way to do an inline member function is like this.

```
class Foo {
public:
    void MemberFn();
};
inline void Foo::MemberFn()
{
...
}
```

Throughout this book, you will see this listed as

```
class Foo {
public:
    void MemberFn() {...}
};
```

I have even shown virtual member functions in line, even though many compilers won't accept that syntax, and those that do sometimes don't handle it properly. The reason for all this is space. If I made all these inlines separate, this would be a much larger book with more page breaks in the middle of listings. So don't take inlines too seriously.

Settle into an easy chair, turn on some good music, put a cup of tea at your elbow, and enjoy!

CHAPTER 2

C++ Syntax and Trivia

In the years I've been teaching C++, I've found that the vast majority of C++ programmers, even experienced ones, have little experience with certain features of the language. The features vary from person to person, but given the complexity and depth of C++, just about everyone needs some level of review. Call this chapter and the succeeding two an attempt to level the playing field before we plunge into the really interesting stuff. This chapter isn't a replacement for the *Annotated Reference Manual* or any other reference work, and I won't cover the complete language specification. Instead, I'll review those language features that tend to be least understood or incorrectly understood. Grab hold of your hats and hang on for the quickest ride through advanced C++ syntax you've ever had!

Variables and Constants

I won't belabor the basics of variables, but there are a couple of issues that deserve some review: constness and heap versus stack based objects.

Const

Const is one of those overloaded terms in C++ that takes on different meanings in different contexts. Yes, there is a common thread among them, but you still must memorize the special cases. ⌐

Const Variables. If you declare something to be const, it can't be changed. Once it is defined, you can't change its value or allow it to be passed as an argument to a function that doesn't swear not to change it either. Here is a simple const integer.

```
const int j=17; // An integer constant
j = 29; // Illegal, cannot change the value
const int i; // Illegal, must have an initial value
```

The third line is nonsense, since it asks the compiler to define a variable with an arbitrary value that can never be changed, a bizarre sort of generator of random integer constants. More generally, you have to tell the compiler what constructor to use. Were i to come from some nontrivial class, the declaration of a const instance would require that you specify the constructor and its arguments. An int is just a degenerate case, since const int j=17; is really the same as int j(17);.

Once you tell the compiler something is supposed to be const, it suddenly wakes up and starts looking, not just for actual errors, but for potential errors as well. Once something is known to be const, the compiler won't allow you to use it in any non-const context, even if your six-year-old daughter could look at the code and prove there is no possible error.

```
const i=17;
int& j=i; // Illegal, since you might later change j
```

It doesn't matter whether or not you actually change the value pointed to by j; what matters is that the compiler will assume that you might be tempted, and it removes that temptation altogether. Another way of putting this is that constness is a property of the variable, not the object, and a const value cannot be pointed to by a non-const variable.

Const and #define. The following two lines are *not* equivalent.

```
const int i=17;
#define i 17
```

The first is a variable with a specific location in memory storing its value, the second a macro. The distinction is usually unimportant except for the extra machine cycle or two chewed up every time you access the const variable. However, if the variable is a global and its type is some nontrivial class with a constructor, the distinction occasionally becomes critical. See "Global Variables" later in this chapter for more details.

Enum Constants. Enums haven't been used all that much in C for a simple reason: The symbols for the constants have global scope and clutter up the name space in a hurry. In C++, that isn't much of a problem, since the symbols are scoped to the enclosing class or struct.

```
class Foo {
public:
    enum Status { kOpen=0, kClosed };
};
// In your code
Foo::Status s = Foo::kOpen;
```

Notice that the type name and the symbols must both be explicitly scoped. This means that you can reuse the symbols kOpen and kClosed for other purposes elsewhere in your code. Enum symbols are treated as macros by the compiler, unlike const variables. This can be important when you initialize global variables, as discussed later in this chapter.

Pointer to Const. Pointers aren't quite as simple, since there are two values involved: the address and the contents at that address. In this example, p is a pointer to a constant value; the address contained in the pointer can be changed, but the contents of that address cannot.

```
const int* p;
int i=17;
p = &i; // Legal
*p = 29; // Illegal
```

This extends to structs and objects as well.

```
class foo {
public:
    int x;
};
const foo* f = new foo;
f->x = 17; // Illegal, can't assign to members
```

Const Pointer. A const pointer is the opposite: The address itself cannot be changed, but the contents assigned to that address may be changed.

```
int i=17;
int j=29;
int* const p; // Illegal! Must have an initial value
int* const p1 = &i; // OK
*p1 = 29; // Legal, can change the pointee
p1 = &j; // Illegal
```

Const Pointer to Const. Basically, you can't do much of anything with a const pointer to const (say that three times fast). This is a constant address of a constant value.

```
int i=17;
int j=29;
const int* const p; // Illegal, need initial address
```

```
const int* const p1 = &i; // Correct
*p1 = 29; // Illegal
p1 = &j; // Illegal
```

Const Arguments to Functions. A const argument to a function must obey the same rules as any other constant variable.

```
void f(const int* p)
{
    *p = 17; // Illegal
    int i=29;
    p = &i; // Legal, but why would you want to?
}
// Somewhere deep in your code
int i=17;
f(&i); // OK, actual argument doesn't have to be const
```

Note that the argument used to call the function doesn't have to be const. That is strictly up to the receiving end. Passing by reference requires the same treatment as passing by address.

```
void f(const int& p)
{
    p = 17; // Illegal
    int i=29;
    p = i; // Still (barely) legal  ?
}
int i=17;
f(i); // OK
```

Non-const Arguments to Functions. If the formal argument to a function is declared to be non-const, the actual argument used with a specific call must also be non-const.

```
void f(int*);
int i=17;
const int* p = &i;
const int j=29;
f(&i); // OK, because i is not const
f(p); // Illegal
f(&j); // Also illegal because j is const
```

```
{
    int i;
    foo f(constructor_args);
    // About to exit - destructors of i and f called
}
```

Stack-based objects live as long as the enclosing code block. When that code block exits scope, the destructor is automatically called. Obviously, taking the address of a stack-based object is chancy unless you can absolutely, positively prove that it won't be used after the object leaves scope. Something like the following is always to be considered dangerous until proven otherwise.

```
{
    int i;
    foo f;
    SomeFunction(&f);
}
```

There is no way to prove, without peering inside SomeFunction(), that this is safe. SomeFunction might well pass the address along, perhaps storing it in a nearby data member, where Murphy's Law guarantees that it will be used sometime after f has been destroyed. Even if your oh-so-careful examination of SomeFunction reveals that the address isn't kept around after the call, it is a certainty, right up there with death and taxes, that some junior programmer a year from now will modify SomeFunction to hold on to that address just a couple of machine instructions too long and KABOOM! Better to avoid the problem altogether by not passing the address of a stack-based object in the first place.

Allocating on the Heap. To allocate an object on the heap, use operator new.

```
foo* f = new foo(constructor_args);
```

This looks simple enough. operator new allocates the object and calls the appropriate constructor on the basis of arguments passed. But when is the object destroyed? That is a subject deep enough to occupy about one-third of this book, so we won't try to get into design strategies here. For the moment, the answer is "When someone invokes operator delete on its address." The object will not be automatically removed from memory; you must explicitly tell the program when to trash it.

Pointers and References. A common source of confusion arises when you associate pointers with heap-based objects. In fact, the two have nothing to do with one another. You can take the address of a stack-based object and you can dereference the address of a heap-based object. You can create a reference to either.

```
{
    foo f;
    foo* p = &f;
    f.MemberFn(); // Uses the object itself
    p->MemberFn(); // Uses its address
    p = new foo;
    foo& r = *p; // A reference to the object
    r.MemberFn(); // Same as p->MemberFn()
}
```

As you can see, use of . versus -> depends on the variables, not on any property of the objects themselves. While we're at it, the politically correct terminology for these operators (. and ->) is *member selector operators*. If you call them "dot" and "arrow" at one of those C++ cocktail parties, everyone will turn and stare at you and in a remote corner someone will drop a glass on the floor.

Drawbacks of Stack-Based Objects. If you use operator delete on a stack-based object and you are really lucky, your program will crash and burn. If you are unlucky, as most of us are, your program will act like an angry lover: It will do crazy things to random parts of memory but not tell you why it's mad at you. You see, in most implementations of C++, operator new stuffs a couple of hidden bytes above the address it returns. Those bytes contain the size of the block it allocated. That way, operator delete always knows how much space following the address should be reclaimed. Stack-based objects are allocated without calling operator new, however, and don't have those extra nuggets of information. If you call operator delete on a stack-based object, therefore, it grabs whatever happens to live above your variable on the stack and treats it as a byte count.

So far, we've identified at least two good reasons to avoid stack-based objects unless you have a really, really good excuse for using them:

1. If you take the address of a stack-based object, that address may be retained and used after the object has left scope.
2. If you take the address of a stack-based object, that address may be handed over to operator delete.

A good rule for stack-based objects, then, is: *Never take their address or addresses of their members.*

Advantages of Stack-Based Objects. On the other hand, allocating objects on the stack is blindingly fast, as fast as the compiler can allocate other automatic variables like integers. Operator new, at least the default version, has to chew up a few machine cycles deciding exactly where the space is to come from and leaving all the right information around to reclaim the space later. Performance is one of the big reasons people choose to allocate on the stack. Later on, we'll show that there are plenty of ways to speed up operator new, so this isn't as compelling a reason as at first it might appear.

The fact that a stack-based object is automatically deleted is the second big advantage, so much so that it is common for people to create little helper stack-based classes that wrap heap-based objects. The following amusing little curiosity wraps a heap-based Foo with a stack-based PFoo. Its constructor allocates a Foo; its destructor deallocates it. If you're not familiar with conversion operators, refer to that section of this chapter; basically, operator Foo*() allows a PFoo to be used anywhere a Foo* could have been used, such as in the call to g().

```
class PFoo {
private:
    Foo* f;
public:
    PFoo() : f(new Foo) {}
    ~PFoo() { delete f; }
    operator Foo*() { return f; }
}
void g(Foo*);
{
    PFoo p;
    g(p); // Invokes operator Foo*() to convert
    // p is destroyed and, in turn, the Foo
}
```

Note that this class isn't completely safe, since the address returned by operator Foo*() will become invalid after the enclosing PFoo is deleted. We'll fix that later.

We'll be revisiting this sort of chicanery at great length. The point here is that stack-based objects can be very useful simply because you don't have to manually delete them. In due course, we'll show that even heap-based objects can be automatically deleted, but those techniques are very complex and not really for everyday use.

There is one more advantage to stack-based objects if you are lucky enough to have ANSI-compliant exception handling. If an exception occurs as the stack is unwound, the destructors of stack-based objects are called automatically. The same is not true of heap-based objects. This can make a real mess of your heap. At the risk of sounding like a broken record, I'll say that this too will be dealt with later.

Scopes and Functions

One of the big improvements of C++ over C is in the features for limiting the scope of a symbol. This is a two-edged sword, as the rules for scoping can get a little hairy at times. C++ also adds the concept of function overloading and, by extension, operator overloading. Presumably you are familiar with the basics, so this ten-minute tour will be limited to some of the nooks and crannies of functions and scopes.⌋

Scopes

A scope is established by any of the following:

- a class
- a struct
- a union
- a code block
- the global name space

Symbols declared within a scope apply only within that scope. Those symbols are not limited to enums and simple variables. Structs, classes, and functions can also be defined within a specific scope.

Classes. A class in C++ is more than a data structure. It is equivalent to the idea of a module in other programming languages, a way to divide the set of symbols in an orderly way.

```
class Foo {
public:
    static int y; // A global variable
    static void GFn(); // A global function
    int x; // A member variable
    Foo(); // A constructor
    void Fn(); // A member function
    typedef int (*IntFn)(); // A type
    enum Status { kOpen=0, kClosed }; // Another type
    struct Bar { // A nested struct
        int a;
        int b;
        static void BarFn();
        };
```

```
private:
    void Hn();
};
```

This code fragment shows several variations on the theme of classes. y is a global variable and GFn() is a global function, except that their names are scoped to Foo. They can be accessed by name from within any member function of Foo, but must be accessed using the scope resolution operator :: elsewhere.

```
Foo::Foo()
{
    GFn(); // We are already in the scope of Foo
}
void f()
{
    Foo::GFn(); // Scope resolution needed
}
```

Similarly, the typedef IntFn, the enum Status, and even the nested struct Bar are accessible without scope resolution within a member function of Foo, but they require scope resolution elsewhere. The syntax for scope resolution can get a little frightening if nested types are publicly visible, as is the case for Bar here.

```
Foo::Bar b;
Foo::Bar::BarFn();
```

For this reason, nested structs are usually either trivial or non-public.

x, Foo(), and Fn() are all members of the class and make sense only in the context of a specific instance of the class. They are all accessible using the member selector operators . and ->. It is a little-known fact — including among C++ compiler-writers, as I have found out the hard way — that it is also legal to invoke a static member function or access a static data member using the member selector operators. The following is legal, though so confusing to the poor folks who have to read your code that you should only do it on your last day on a job.

```
Foo f;
f.GFn(); // Same as Foo::GFn();
```

Structs. A struct in C++ should really be called AAC — "almost-a-class." You can do anything with a struct that you can do with a class. For example, you can derive from a struct; declare public, private, and protected sections; and declare virtual member functions. However, the default rules are a little different: The default visibility is public so that all those C programs out there that use structs don't have to be massively changed in order to fit through the C++ meat grinder.

That's the theory, but let's get real. Would you really want to show your face after declaring a struct that used multiple inheritance and had virtual member functions? In practice, structs are used in place of classes only when the following conditions are met:

- There are no virtual member functions.
- The struct is not derived from anything other than perhaps another struct.
- Nothing is derived from the struct, except perhaps another struct.

The "in" crowd of C++ programmers tends to use structs only to represent tidy little bundles of data with trivial member functions. In particular, structs are commonly used when a C++ object must be bitwise compatible with some external data structure, particularly one defined as a C struct. It is perfectly OK to declare constructors and non-virtual member functions, especially trivial inlines, since those do not create a vtable that would compromise bitwise compatibility.

Unions. Unions in C++ are pretty much the same as they are in C. They are a sop to those who want to save a few bytes by layering several different data structures on top of one another. Unions may have non-virtual member functions, including constructors and destructors, but there are some pretty severe restrictions otherwise:

- Members of a union may not have constructors, although the union itself may.
- A union may not be derived from anything.
- Nothing may derive from a union.
- Destructors of members are not called, although the destructor of the union itself, if present, is called.

Because unions and derivation don't mix, it doesn't make sense to declare virtual member functions or protected members. You are allowed to declare members private or public. Basically, unions are only useful when you really have to conserve space, when you aren't going to derive from or to the union, and when there won't be any virtual member functions or constructors. That is to say, they aren't very useful at all.

Code Blocks. There isn't anything to say about code blocks that you don't already know from C or that we haven't already discussed in regard to stack-based objects.

The Global Name Space. C++ global name spaces are so complicated that I half expect to see the C++ compiler come walking down the aisle swinging incense and chanting while it compiles globals. Let's keep it as simple as we can. Global *types* are scoped to the file in which they are declared. Global *variables* and *functions* are in addition subject to linkage rules that span source files. Consider the following situation.

```
// in Foo.cpp
typedef int Symbol;
// In Bar.cpp
typedef void (*Symbol)();
```

There is no conflict here, unless you are perverse enough to #include one .cpp file in the other. The symbol Symbol is known to the compiler only within the source files in which it is encountered, so it may be used in different ways in different source files. The following is not legal because now the symbol represents a variable and not just a type. The variable name must be unique across all files submitted to the linker.

```
// In Foo.cpp
int Symbol;
// In Bar.cpp
void (*Symbol)();
```

The only exception to this is function overloading, discussed in the next section. Obviously, it will be common to run into name conflicts in a reasonably large project with multiple programmers working independently in different source files. Using static members is one solution; declaring globals to be static is another. If a variable or function is declared to be static, it is defined only within that source file.

```
// In Foo.cpp
static int Symbol;
// In Bar.cpp
static void (*Symbol)();
```

The keyword static tells the compiler to make sure the linker doesn't confuse the two uses of the same symbol as long as the source files don't compile together; two different variables will be generated.

Any symbol declared in global name space may be accessed with the scope resolution operator :: by forgetting to provide a scope.

```
::Fn(); // Call a global function of that name
int x = ::i; // Assign the value of a global variable
::SomeType y; // Use a globally declared type
```

Explicit scope resolution always overrides any locally defined symbols, such as those in a code block or class.

Overloading

C++ allows you to recycle your function names in many different ways. Classes are one way to carve up the function name space: Functions with the same name in unrelated classes mean different things. Function overloading carries on this grand tradition of partitioning function name spaces by allowing you to reuse a function name multiple times within a single scope.

Arguments. Two functions with the same name are not considered the same if they differ in the number, order, or type of their arguments.

```
void Fn();
void Fn(int);
void Fn(long); // OK if long and int are different sizes
int Fn(int); // Illegal - differs only in return type
int Fn(char*); // OK, differs in arguments
void Fn(int, char*);
void Fn(char*, int); // OK, args are in different order
void Fn(char* s, int x, int y=17); // OK, 3 args not 2
Fn("hello",17); // Error - matches 2 signatures
```

As long as the arguments are different, the compiler doesn't complain if you change the return type. Default initializers such as y=17 are allowed at the point that the function is declared, even though they may prove ambiguous when someone actually tries to use the function, as in the last line of this example.

Const. A const function that otherwise has the same arguments as a non-const function is still a different function. The compiler will call the const or non-const version according to the type of the variable pointing or referring to the object.

```
class Foo {
public:
    void Fn();
    void Fn() const; // A different function!
};
Foo* f = new Foo;
f->Fn(); // Calls non-const version
const Foo* f1 = f;
f1->Fn(); // Calls const version
```

Visibility

C++ has an elaborate — some would say too elaborate — set of rules for determining when things that are plainly in front of your face are visible and when you should wink and turn a blind eye. The basic rules of public, protected, and private symbols in a class or struct are so basic that I won't belabor them here. The following is my shortlist of all-time confusing subjects regarding visibility in C++.

Private Derivation. When you privately derive from a base class, all of its protected and public members become private to the derived class; members of the private base class are not republished to clients of the derived class. They are only accessible from within member functions of the base class and member functions of the derived class, or within friends of the derived class.

It is also illegal to typecast a derived class as one of its private base classes or to expect the compiler to do so.

```
class Mixin {
private:
    int x;
protected:
    int y;
public:
    Mixin();
    void A();
};
class Foo : private Mixin {…};
class Bar : public Foo {…};
```

The data member x is visible only within member functions of Mixin: the constructor and A(). The data member y is visible only within member functions of Foo, as is the member function Mixin::A(). None of the members of Mixin are visible at all within derived classes of Foo, such as Bar in this fragment. Any friend of Foo would see x and A(), but a friend of Bar would not.

Redeclaring Members. It doesn't come up very often, but it is legal to redeclare a virtual member function to have different visibility than it has in the base class.

```
class Foo {
protected:
    virtual void Fn();
};
class Bar : public Foo {
public:
    virtual void Fn();
};
```

Fn() was protected in Foo, but the override is declared to be public. This is not possible with non-virtual member functions or data members. When you redeclare a data member or non-virtual member function, it shadows the base class version.

```
class Foo {
private:
    int x;
public:
    void Fn();
};
class Bar : public Foo {
private:
    int x; // A second data member with the same name
public:
    void Fn(); // A second member function
};
// In client code
Bar *b = new Bar;
b->Fn(); // Calls Bar::Fn()
Foo* f = b; // Legal, because Foo is a public base class
f->Fn(); // Calls Foo::Fn()
```

There are two distinct data members with the same local name, x. Whenever you are within the scope of Foo, the symbol x will get Foo::x. In the scope of Bar, x means Bar::x. This is obviously going to be terribly confusing if x is public or protected, but no ambiguity can result as long as x is private. Fn() shows the havoc that results from shadowing a public or protected member function. A good C++ compiler will issue a warning when you try to shadow a protected or public member.

Visibility of Overloaded and Virtual Member Functions. If a member function is non-virtual in the base class, it is a bad idea to make it virtual in the derived class. It won't behave like a virtual member function and will confuse the bejabbers out of anyone trying to read your code. Looking at it the other way around, it is surprising but true that the keyword virtual is only required in the base class. If virtual is left out in the derived class, the compiler is supposed to treat the derived class version as if it were declared virtual anyway. I like to call this sort of compiler logic DWIMNWIS (pronounced "dwimnis"): "Do what I mean, not what I say." C++ is so generally lacking in this sort of logic that when it occasionally pops up it seems out of place, as in this rule. In this example, Bar::Fn() is called by both pointers.

```
class Foo {
public:
    virtual void Fn();
};
class Bar : public Foo {
public:
    void Fn(); // Treated as virtual anyway
};
Bar* b = new Bar;
b->Fn(); // Calls Bar::Fn()
Foo* f = b;
f->Fn(); // Also calls Bar::Fn()
```

There are two good reasons not to pull this sort of shenanigan. First, the compiler may not implement this properly, in which case the second call is to Foo::Fn(). Second, your colleagues will probably trash your office after wrestling with your code all night trying to figure out why you chose to make Fn() virtual in one place and not in another.

If you create a member function with the same name but a different signature in a derived class, it shadows *all* base class signatures for that function, but only within the scope of the derived class. Confused? You're not alone.

```
class Foo {
public:
    virtual void Fn();
    virtual void Fn(char*);
};
class Bar {
public:
    virtual void Fn(int); // Legal but unadvisable
};
```

Some junior programmer probably stayed up really late thinking up this architecture. Here's what happens, blow by blow:

- If you try to call Fn() from a Bar*, you only have access to the one signature, void Fn(int). *Both base class versions are shadowed and inaccessible from a* Bar*.

- If you typecast a Bar* to a Foo*, you can now call both signatures declared in Foo but not the signature void Fn(int). Furthermore, there is no override, because the signature of Bar::Fn() is not the same as the base class version. In other words, the keyword virtual doesn't make any difference the way this code is set up.

If you are ever tempted to do something like this, get up from your chair, walk slowly around the block a few times, take a deep breath, then sit down at your desk and choose a different design. If you overload, override either all or no signatures of the overloaded function. Never override a subset of the signatures and never add new signatures in a derived class unless you override all signatures of the base class function. If that's too confusing, just remember it this way: If you have to ask, it's probably not a good idea.

Friend. Any class can declare just about anything else to be a friend. A friend is compiled normally, except that all protected and private members of the class-it-is-a-friend-of are visible as if the friend were a member function of the class. Functions, both global and member, may be declared friends. Classes may also be declared friends of other classes; in that case, all of the friend's member functions can "see" all members of the class-it-is-a-friend-of.

```cpp
class Foo;
class BarBar {
public:
    int Fn(Foo*);
};
class Foo {
friend void GlobalFn(); // Friendly global function
friend class Bar; // Friendly class
friend int BarBar::Fn(Foo*); // Friendly member function
friend class DoesNotExist; // See discussion below
private:
    int x;
    struct ListNode {
        ListNode* next;
        void* datum;
        ListNode() : next(NULL), datum(NULL) {}
    } head;
protected:
    int y;
public:
    void G();
};
void GlobalFn()
{
    Foo* f = new Foo;
    f->x = 17; // Legal because of friendship
}
class Bar {
private:
    Foo* f;
public:
    Bar() : f(new Foo) {}
    void WalkList();
};
void Bar::WalkList()
```

```
{
    Foo::ListNode* n = f->head.next;
    for (;n != NULL; n = n->next)
        cout << n->datum << endl;
}
int BarBar::Fn(Foo* f)
{
    return f->x;
}
```

It is conventional to declare friends first, before any other members and before use of public, protected, or private. This is because friend is not affected by the normal visibility rules of public, private, and protected; something either is a friend or it isn't. All of the code fragments that follow Foo are legal. They are all friends and have access to all members, including private ones, of Foo. The truly interesting line in this example is the one declaring a nonexistent class DoesNotExist to be a friend. Curiously enough, this will never generate a compiler warning or error. Friend declarations are ignored at the time Foo is compiled. They are only used when the friend is compiled. If the friend doesn't exist, the compiler stays fat, dumb, and happy.

Types and Operators

While the features discussed in this section may seem a random jumble, they all revolve around the idea of abstract data types.

Constructors

Constructors may be thought of in either of two ways: as a function that initializes an object or in the mathematical sense as a mapping from the constructor arguments to the domain of the class. I prefer to think of them in the latter context; otherwise it becomes difficult to avoid permanently crossing your eyes when you try to understand certain other language features, such as conversion operators.

The rules for constructors are very complex, but every C++ programmer needs to know them thoroughly or be doomed to spend at least three all-night debugging sessions per year.

No-Argument Constructors. If your class provides a constructor that takes no arguments, that constructor is used by default in these three circumstances.

```
class Foo {
public:
    Foo();
};
class Bar : public Foo { // 1. Base class
public:
    Bar();
};
class BarBar {
private:
    Foo f; // 2. Data member
};
Foo f; // 3. Instance of Foo created
Foo* f1 = new Foo; // 3. Same as previous line
```

Assuming that Bar's constructor does not specify some other constructor of Foo in its member initialization list (see the next section), the no-argument constructor of Foo will be called every time someone creates an instance of Bar. Similarly, unless f appears in the member initialization list of BarBar's constructor, the no-argument constructor of Foo will be used. Finally, any time an instance of Foo is created without specifying a constructor, the no-argument constructor is used by default.

Constructors with Arguments. Constructors are like any other function in that they can be overloaded; you can declare as many constructor signatures as you want. The only real differences between constructor signatures and those of normal functions are that constructors return no values and may not be declared const. If you declare any constructors that accept arguments but do not declare a no-argument constructor, the compiler will no longer allow construction of the class, even as a base of some other class, using a no-argument constructor.

```
class Foo {
public:
    Foo(char*);
};
Foo f; // Illegal - no no-argument constructor!
class Bar : public Foo {
public:
    Bar();
};
Bar::Bar()
{ // Error! No no-argument constructor for Foo
}
```

Member Initialization Lists. To get around these problems, C++ once more dips into its bag of :'s to create the member initialization list. This is a comma-separated list of constructor specifications following the signature of a constructor and before its code block.

```
class Foo {
public:
    Foo(char*);
};
class Bar : public Foo {
public :
    Bar(char*);
};
class BarBar {
private:
    Foo f;
    int x;
public:
    BarBar();
};
Bar::Bar(char* s) : Foo(s) {...}
BarBar::BarBar() : f("Hello"), x(17) {...}
```

In the constructor of Bar, the member initialization list is used to initialize the base class Foo. The compiler figures out which constructor to use on the basis of the signature implied by the actual arguments. In the absence of this member initialization list, there would be no way to construct a Bar, since the compiler would have no way to figure out what value to pass to the constructor of the base class Foo. In the constructor of BarBar, the member initialization list is used to initialize — that is, call constructors of — data members f and x. We wrote the constructor this way and not

```
BarBar::BarBar() : f("Hello")
{
    x = 17;
}
```

because unless the compiler is exceedingly clever, the first version is slightly more efficient. In the second version, the data member x is first initialized to 0 (a standard requirement of C++) using the default no-argument constructor of int, then is assigned the value 17 within the code block. The first version does only the one initialization and therefore saves a machine cycle or two. The difference here is trivial, since x is an int, but were it a more complex class with a no-argument constructor and overloaded assignment, the difference could be enough to make the user glance at her watch.

Member initialization lists are required whenever you have a base class or data member that does not have a no-argument constructor; specifically, it has one or more constructors that take arguments but no user-defined no-argument constructor. A member initialization list is optional when all base classes and data members either have no constructors or have a user-defined no-argument constructor.

Order of Construction. If a class does not provide any constructors, it is still initialized as if the compiler had provided a no-argument constructor for you. That no-argument constructor invokes the no-argument constructors of classes and data members. The order of construction is well defined whether you are using default or overloaded constructors, no-argument, or constructors with arguments:

1. Base class constructors are invoked in the order in which the base classes appear in the derivation list (the other colonized, comma-separated list in which you declare your base classes).

2. Constructors of data members are then invoked in the order in which the data members are declared in the class declaration.

3. Once all base classes and data members have been constructed, the code block of your own constructor is executed.

This logic is applied recursively. Thus, the first base class of the first base class of the first base class, and so on, is the first class to be constructed. This order is irrespective of the order of your member initialization lists. (Were this not the case, the order of construction might be different for different overloaded constructors. This would make it difficult for the compiler to guarantee that destructors would be called in the reverse order of constructors.)

Copy Constructors. There is a special constructor signature that defines the copy constructor.

```
class Foo {
public:
    Foo(const Foo&);
};
Foo::Foo(const Foo& f)...
```

The copy constructor is used to make copies of objects. This can occur in a surprising variety of circumstances.

```
void Fn(Foo f) {...}
void Gn(Foo& f) {...}
Foo f;
Foo f1(f);
Foo f2 = f; // Construction, not assignment!
Fn(f); // Invokes copy constructor to pass by value
const Foo f3;
Gn(f3); // Copy constructor used to make non-const copy
```

Let's look at this code carefully. The statement Foo f1(f); is clearly creating a new instance of Foo and using another Foo as an argument. This is always legal as long as Foo has no pure virtual member functions. It doesn't matter whether you have declared your own copy constructor; if not, the compiler will supply one for you. It doesn't matter whether Foo has other user-defined constructors; a copy constructor is *always* available, unlike no-argument constructors.

The statement Foo f2 = f; may look like assignment because of the =, but it is really an alternative way to invoke the copy constructor. The way to tell the difference between assignment and initialization is to ask yourself, "Has the object previously been constructed, or is it being created as part of the statement?" If it already exists, you are dealing with assignment. If it is being newly created, as in this case, you are dealing with a copy constructor.

The call to Fn() passes a copy of Foo by value. The copy constructor is used to make the temporary copy, which lives only as long as Fn() executes. At that time, the destructor of the copy is called to clean it up.

The call to Gn() is probably a mistake, and a good compiler will give you a stern lecture on C++ style by saying something like "Temporary non-const copy created — why don't you learn how to program, you idiot!" At least, that's the way compilers usually treat *me*. The problem is that the argument is passed by reference, but the actual argument is const and the formal argument is not. Any changes you make to the argument within Gn will be made to the copy, not to the original.

The default copy constructor provided by the compiler uses a well-defined sequence to invoke the copy constructors of base classes and data members.

1. Copy constructors of base classes are invoked in the order in which they are declared in the derivation list.
2. Copy constructors of data members are invoked in the order in which they are declared in the class declaration.

This logic is applied recursively, so the first base class of the first base class, and so on, is the first class copied. Does this sound familiar? The order is the same as for any other constructor.

Unlike other constructors, the compiler is proud and jealous where copy constructors are concerned. If you overload (why it isn't called *overriding* is beyond me) the copy constructor for a given class, the compiler picks up its ball and bat and goes home, figuratively speaking. Unless you explicitly invoke the copy constructors of base classes and data members in the member initialization list of your own copy constructor, the compiler will use the *no-argument constructor* to initialize base classes and members. You read that right.

```
class Foo {...};
class Bar : public Foo {
private:
    Foo f;
public:
    Bar(const Bar&);
};
// Probably wrong
Bar::Bar(const Bar& b)
{ // Oops! No member initialization list
    // No-argument constructors of base class and
    // data member will be used!
}
// Probably right
Bar::Bar(const Bar& b) : Foo(b), f(b.f) {...}
```

The first copy constructor makes the compiler really, really angry, so angry it won't even tell you that it's thrown your good china in the trash. It will use the no-argument constructor of Foo to initialize the base class and the data member. In 99 cases out of 100 that's not what you want; you want base classes and data members to be copied, too. The second version is probably correct. The base class and data member appear in the member initialization list, explicitly invoking their copy constructors (b gets cast to type Foo by the compiler in the expression Foo(b)).

There are situations in which you want the compiler's default tantrum, such as this serializing base class, which assigns a unique serial number to each derived object.

```
class Serialized {
private:
    static int NextSerialNumber;
    int serialNumber;
public:
    Serialized(const Serialized&);
    Serialized();
    int SerialNumber();
};
// In Serialized.cpp
int Serialized::NextSerialNumber = 0;
Serialized::Serialized()
: serialNumber(NextSerialNumber++)
{
}
Serialized::Serialized(const Serialized&)
: serialNumber(NextSerialNumber++)
{
}
int Serialized::SerialNumber()
{
    return serialNumber;
}
```

We really don't care which constructor — no-argument or copy — the compiler chooses when it compiles a derived class, because we've overloaded both to do the same thing.

Private and Protected Constructors. It is common to declare constructors to be protected in order to prevent users from instantiating the class. When a constructor is private, only member functions and static member functions of the class may create stack-based instances or use operator new with the class, at least with that constructor. When a constructor is protected, a user may create instances of the derived class, since the constructor of the base class may be "called" from the constructor of the derived class. OK, it's a stretch of the imagination, but those are the semantics. The problem with this logic is that it isn't foolproof. If a constructor is protected, any member function of either the base or derived class may instantiate the base class, including static member functions of either.

```
class Foo {
protected:
    Foo();
};
class Bar : public Foo {
public:
    Foo* Fn();
};
Foo* Bar::Fn()
{
    return new Foo; // Works despite your best efforts
}
```

You may have thought that Foo was an abstract class that couldn't be instantiated, but surprise! There is a hole big enough to drive a truck through. Friends of Foo and Bar are also allowed to instantiate Foo. The only ironclad way to ensure that a class cannot be instantiated is to give it at least one pure virtual member function.

Anonymous Instances. An anonymous instance is an object that ... well, you'll see.

```
struct Point {
    int X;
    int Y;
    Point(int x, int y) : X(x), Y(y) {}
};
double distance(Point p)
{
    return sqrt(double(p.X)*double(p.X)
                + double(p.Y)*double(p.Y));
}
double d = distance(Point(17,29));
```

The argument to distance() is the anonymous instance. We didn't assign a variable to keep track of it. An anonymous instance lives only as long as it takes to evaluate the expression in which it occurs.

Anonymous instances are usually associated with simple structs like Point, but they may be used with any class.

Initializing Global Objects. The rules for determining the order in which global objects are constructed are complicated enough if you read the language specification. They are virtually unpredictable (a little C++ pun) if you take into account the vagaries of commercial C++ compilers. According to the language specification, constructors of global objects, including static data members of classes and structs, are supposed to be called, but many compilers do not do this. If you are lucky enough to have a compiler that thinks constructors are important to global variables, the order in which globals are constructed is limited only by the compiler writer's imagination. Here are the only rules you are supposed to be able to count on:

1. All global variables are initialized to 0 before any processing takes place.
2. Objects enclosed in a global structure or array are constructed in the order in which they appear in that structure or array.
3. Each global object is constructed before it is first used by any program code. The compiler determines whether everything gets initialized before main() is called or whether initialization is deferred to the first use.
4. Global objects appearing in the same "translation unit" (generally a .cpp file) are initialized in the order in which they appear in that unit. The net effect of this and of rule 3 is that initialization may be done unit by unit, as each unit is first used.

That's it. The following seemingly innocuous sequence of global declarations is actually at the whim of the compiler. It may produce the intended result, or it may crash and burn.

```
// In file1.cpp
Foo foo;
Foo* f = &foo;
// In file2.cpp
extern Foo* f;
Foo f1(*f); // Use copy constructor
```

If all this were in the same source file, there would be no problem. Foo* f = &foo; is safe because globals within the same source file are guaranteed (snicker) to be initialized in the order they are defined. In other words, foo has already been constructed by the time you get to this statement. However, there is no way to guarantee that the globals in file1.cpp will be initialized before the globals in file2.cpp. If file2.cpp gets set up first, *f* will have a value of 0 — the same as NULL on most machines — and dereferencing it will cause smoke to rise from your program.

The best advice is to not count on the order of initialization of .cpp files. One standard trick to manage this is to define a global in your .h file that maintains a static data member containing a count of how many .cpp files have been initialized. On a transition from 0 to 1, call a function that initializes all the globals in the library .cpp file. On a transition from 1 to 0, destroy everything in that .cpp file.

```
// In Library.h
class Library {
private:
    static int count;
    static void OpenLibrary();
    static void CloseLibrary();
public:
    Library();
    ~Library();
};
static Library LibraryDummy;
inline Library::Library()
{
    if (count++ == 0)
        OpenLibrary();
}
```

```
inline Library::~Library()
{
    if (--count == 0)
        CloseLibrary();
}
// In Library.cpp
int Library::count = 0; // Done before any processing
int aGlobal;
Foo* aGlobalFoo;
void Library::OpenLibrary()
{
    aGlobal = 17;
    aGlobalFoo = new Foo;
}
void Library::CloseLibrary()
{
    aGlobal = 0;
    delete aGlobalFoo;
    aGlobalFoo = NULL;
}
```

This takes a little getting used to. What's happening here is that the .h file is being compiled with many of other .cpp files, one of which is Library.cpp. There's no telling in what order the globals that appear in those .cpp files will be initialized. Each, however, will have its own static copy of LibraryDummy. Each time a .cpp file that includes Library.h is initialized, the count is incremented by LibraryDummy's constructor. On exit from main() or when exit() is called, the .cpp files will deallocate their globals and decrement the count through LibraryDummy's destructor. The constructor and destructor guarantee that OpenLibrary() and CloseLibrary() are called exactly once.

This trick is attributed to many different people, but the prototypical example of it is in the iostreams library. The problem is solved there by initializing all those large data structures used by the library exactly once and only when needed.

Destructors

Destructors are invoked whenever a stack-based object leaves scope, including anonymous instances and temporary objects created by the compiler or when a heap-based object is submitted to operator delete. The following facts about destructors are not widely enough known.

Order of Invocation. Destructors are guaranteed to be invoked in the exact reverse order of constructors. That means that the body of the object's destructor is the first to be executed, then the destructors of data members in reverse order of their appearance in the class declaration, then base classes starting with the last one in the derivation list and ending with the first base of the first base, and so forth.

Destruction of Globals. If the discussion of order of initializing globals still has your head spinning, there is good news. It is guaranteed, assuming your friendly local compiler writer has done her homework, that destructors of globals will be called in exactly the reverse order of construction, whatever that may have been.

Globals are destroyed whenever main() exits scope or when the function exit() is called.

Non-virtual Destructors. C++ uses the type of the variable that points to your object to determine which destructor to call. If the type of the pointer is base*, you are hosed unless the destructor of the class is virtual.

```
class Foo {
public:
    ~Foo();
};
class Bar : public Foo {
private:
    int* numbers;
public:
    Bar() : numbers(new int[17]) {...}
```

```
    ~Bar();
};
Bar* b = new Bar;
delete b; // Calls Bar::~Bar()
Foo* f = new Bar;
delete f; // Yikes! Calls Foo::~Foo()!
```

When f is deleted, the array pointed to by the data member numbers becomes a sort of Flying Dutchman, doomed to sail forever through memory. Declaring both destructors virtual avoids this problem; no matter what type of pointer is used (except, of course, a void*), the starting point for destruction is Bar::~Bar().

Another and much more insidious problem with non-virtual destructors occurs when you start doing your own memory management. The compiler tells your overloaded operator to delete the size of the thing being deleted, but surprise! That size may not be correct if the destructor is non-virtual. Imagine the look on the face of your memory management code when it is told that the object is only 20 bytes when it is really 220! C++ compilers brag about this sort of thing over a brewsky after work.

The bottom line is, unless your class or struct has no derived classes or you have a really, really compelling reason to do otherwise, make your destructors virtual. Do not pass Go; do not collect $200.

Directly Invoking Destructors. This won't make a whole lot of sense until we start talking about custom memory management, but it is possible to directly invoke a destructor without going through operator delete. It is a function like any other.

```
class Foo {
public:
    ~Foo();
};
Foo* f = new Foo;
f->Foo::~Foo();
```

We'll make use of this later. For now, just store it away someplace in your C++ collection.

Assignment

Assigning one object to another is serious business in C++. That's why the language imposes so many weird rules, to make sure you stay awake and concentrate on your code.

Syntax and Semantics of Assignment. Assigning one object to another involves using the = sign.

```
Foo f;
Foo f1;
f1 = f;
```

The third line is where the assignment takes place. If f and f1 were integers or something similarly simple, explaining this line of code would be very straightforward: the contents of the memory referred to by f are copied over the memory referred to by f1. Sigh. It's not quite so simple in C++ when Foo is a non-trivial class. In this example, the compiler is providing a default member operator=, which is invoked to do the actual copying. As with copy constructors, you can either sit back and let the compiler do the heavy lifting, or you can provide your own operator=. You might not like the results produced by the default version, as when the destructor of the class deallocates memory.

```
class String {
private:
    char* s;
public:
    String(char*);
    ~String();
    void Dump(ostream& os);
};
String::String(char* str) : s(NULL)
{
    if (str == NULL) { // NULL means the empty string
        s = new char[1];
        *s = '\0';
        }
    else {
        s = new char[strlen(str)+1];
```

```
        strcpy(s, str);
        }
}
String::~String()
{
    delete s;
}
void String::Dump(ostream& os)
{
    os<<"\""<<s<<"\"";
}
String* s1 = new String("Hello");
String* s2 = new String("Goodbye");
s2 = s1;
delete s1; // Oops, storage is gone (snicker)
s2->Dump(cout); // Gotcha! Ha ha ha ha!
delete s2; // Stop it! You're killing me! Ha ha ha ha!
```

What the compiler does by default is to copy the contents of s2->s
over the contents of s1->s. The value of the pointer, not the string
pointed to, is copied, so after the assignment we've got two big
problems. Two different objects point to the same spot in memory,
and no one points to the copy of "Good-bye" set up by the statement
String* s2 = new String("Goodbye");. It gets worse immediately; when s1
is deleted, its destructor deallocates the storage pointed to by s1.
But that storage is still pointed to by s2->s. The data you'll get when
you try to print out s2->s will look like a stock ticker on caffeine.
When you get around to deleting s2, the comedy of errors gets even
more uproarious, because the memory manager tries to recover
space that has already been recovered. C++ is such a riot!

Of course, the same problem exists when you make copies. The
default copy constructors for pointers copy the pointer, not the
pointee. For this reason, copy constructors and operator= are usually overloaded together.

Assignment Versus Initialization. I know, we've already talked
about the difference between initialization and assignment, but it's
so critical I'll say it again. If the object on the left-hand side of the =

has previously been constructed, the = means assignment. If the object on the left-hand side of the = is being constructed for the first time, we're talking construction and constructors. The first use of = in this example is initialization, and it results in a call to the copy constructor. The second is assignment and invokes operator=.

```
Foo f;
Foo f1 = f; // Initialization; f1 doesn't exist yet
f1 = f; // Assignment; f1 was previously constructed
```

Default Assignment. Like the default copy constructor, the default operator= has a well-defined behavior. And like the copy constructor, which recursively invoked other copy constructors, the default operator= does more than simply copy bits from one object image to another. Here is the default sequence:

1. Assign base classes in the order in which they appear in the derivation list. This will use the base class's overloaded operator= or, if it is not overloaded, the default operator=.

2. Assign data members in the order in which they appear in the class declaration. This uses any overloaded operator= for the data members if present or the default operator= otherwise.

These rules are applied recursively. As with constructors, the first base of the first base of the first base, etc., is assigned first.

Overloading Operator=. Overloading operator= is like overloading any other operator. For the moment, the signature of operator= in which we are interested is X& X::operator=(const X&).

```
class String {
private:
    char* s;
public:
    String(char*);
    ~String();
    String(const String&); // Might as well fix this too
    String& operator=(const String&);
    void Dump(ostream& os);
};
```

```
String::String(char* str) : s(NULL)
{
    if (str == NULL) { // NULL means the empty string
        s = new char[1];
        *s = '\0';
        }
    else {
        s = new char[strlen(str)+1];
        strcpy(s, str);
        }
}
String::~String()
{
    delete s;
}
String::String(const String& s1) : s(NULL)
{
    s = new char[strlen(s1.s)+1];
    strcpy(s, s1.s);
}
String& String::operator=(const String& s1)
{
    if (this == &s1) return *this;
    delete s; // Deallocate prior value
    s = new char[strlen(s1.s)+1];
    strcpy(s, s1.s);
    return *this;
}
void String::Dump(ostream& os)
{
    os<<"\""<<s<<<<"\"";
}
```

The copy constructor and operator= both now make copies of the other guy's string, rather than simply copying the address. The destructor is now safe, and all is well with the world.

The definition of operator= here is a generic boilerplate you should commit to memory (yours, not the computer's):

1. Make sure the assignment is not something like x = x;. If the left- and right-hand sides are both the same object, you don't have to do anything. If you don't trap this special case, the next step will cleanly wipe out the value before you can get to the strcpy.

2. Delete any prior storage.

3. Copy the value.

4. return *this;

operator= returns *this to allow nested assignment like a = b = c. In C++, as in C, an assignment expression has as its value the value assigned. The expression groups right-to-left, as in a = (b = c).

Now for the bad news. As with copy constructors, when you over-load operator=, C++ picks up its ball and bat and goes home in a huff. If you overload operator=, you must take over responsibility for assigning data members and base classes; by default, the base classes and data members of the left-hand side remain unchanged.

Assigning Data Members. In some cases, data members will be native data types, such as ints, that can be assigned using the compiler's operator=. In other cases, such as the String class, data members must be manually copied. In the remaining cases, the data members are of some non-trivial class. The best way to handle such data members is to assign them. The compiler then figures out whether there is an overloaded operator= for the data member or whether it should use its own default logic.

```
class Foo {
public:
    Foo& operator=(const Foo&);
};
class Bar {
public:
    // No overload of operator=
};
class FooBar {
private:
    Foo f;
    Bar b;
```

```
public:
    FooBar& operator=(const FooBar&);
};
FooBar& FooBar::operator=(const FooBar& fb)
{
    if (this == &fb) return *this;
    f = fb.f; // Uses overloaded Foo::operator=
    b = fb.b; // Uses default operator=
    return *this;
}
```

Using this technique, you really don't care whether the data member has an overloaded operator=. That's what you have a compiler for.

Assigning Base Classes. Assigning base classes involves a bit of syntactic chicanery. If you've never seen it, you might fumble for quite a while before stumbling on the right combination. Here it is.

```
class Foo {...};
class Bar : public Foo {
public:
    Bar& operator=(const Bar&);
};
Bar& Bar::operator=(const Bar& b)
{
    if (this == &b) return *this;
    this->Foo::operator=(b); // Huh?
    return *this;
}
```

The other things that might occur to you, such as *((Foo*)this)=b;, will not work; trust me. They all create temporary copies. This syntax works because the compiler knows how to promote a Bar to a Foo as an argument. This syntax works whether or not you have overloaded Foo::operator=. If you didn't overload it, it is still there nonetheless, and you can call it by its fully scoped name Foo::operator=.

Other Signatures for operator=. operator= is not limited to just this one signature. You can overload operator= to take any other argument type that you like as its right-hand side. What makes the signature X& X::operator=(const X&) special is that the compiler provides a default version and uses this signature as part of its default recursive assignment algorithm.

```
class String {
// As before
public:
    String& operator=(const String&); // Normal
    String& operator=(char*); // Overload
    String& operator=(int); // Calls atoi()
};
```

In this code fragment, we have created several overloads of operator= for various data types on the right-hand side. The second one avoids having to construct a temporary String from a char* just long enough to assign it to the left-hand side. The third performs a different sort of conversion. Only the first, however, overloads — that is, replaces — the default version.

Overloading Operators

One of the nice things about C++ is that you can add to the meanings of operators. This can improve the readability of your code, since you don't have to make up silly function names like "Add" when a + would be perfectly obvious. However, in my experience there are two problems with operator overloads: They are easily abused and can turn your code into mush, and most people have never used them anyway. This isn't an exhaustive list of all the operators you can munge, but it should help set the stage for the material later in the book.

The Functional Form of Operators. There are two ways to think of an operator like +: either as a special syntactic form or as a function. In C++, the functional form is always the keyword 'operator' followed by the operator symbol.

```
class Foo {...};
Foo x, y, z;
z = x + y; // Infix (normal) form
z = operator+(x,y); // Non-member function form
z = x.operator+(y); // Member function form
```

The last three lines are conceptually equivalent, although in practice you would define either a member or non-member operator, but not both. For binary operators, the operator appears between the arguments in the infix form. In the non-member function form, the two arguments are passed to the global function. In the member function form, the object whose operator is being called is the left-hand side of the operator, and the argument is the right-hand side. Unary operators such as ! and - can also be overloaded. The non-member form takes one argument, and the member form takes no argument (the object to the left of the . or -> is the subject of the operation).

You are not allowed to redefine any of the built-in operators, such as integer addition. The way the compiler enforces this is to require that at least one argument to each overloaded operator be a user-defined type, usually a class. You are restricted to the operators already defined for C++. I've wanted to add an operator$%^& during many all-night debugging sessions, but C++ is adamant on the subject.

Your overloaded operators derive their precedence and grouping properties from the built-in operators, so you can't, for example, change the left-to-right grouping order of operator+. There are no restrictions on the return type of an overloaded operator, and you can overload the same operator any number of times as long as the signatures remain unique.

Non-member Overloads. Overloading a non-member operator involves defining a global function.

```
class String {
friend String operator+(const String&, const String&);
private:
    char* s;
```

```
public:
    // Constructors & etc.
};
String operator+(const String& s1, const String& s2)
{
    char* s = new char[strlen(s1.s)+strlen(s2.s)+1];
    strcat(s,s1.s,s2.s);
    String newStr(s);
    delete s;
    return newStr;
}
String s1="Hello";
String s2="Goodbye";
String s3 = s1 + s2;
```

Other than the funny function name, the overloaded function really doesn't look any different from any other global function. In case you were wondering, this is really what friend was invented for. If we didn't declare operator+ to be a friend, it wouldn't have access to the data member s. This would leave us on the horns of a dilemma: Provide a way for everyone in the world to access the char* or choose a much less efficient implementation that would require copying the string every time it is accessed. Conceptually, this operator+ is really part of the bundle of functionality that comes with the String library, so it isn't as outrageous as it seems to make it a friend and turn over the keys to String's internal structure.

Any operator may be overloaded as a non-member function with the exception of conversion operators, =, [], (), and ->, all of which must be overloaded as member functions.

Member Overloads. The syntax is similar for member overloads, except that the function becomes a member function with one less argument than the non-member version.

```
class String {
private:
    char* s;
```

```
public:
    // Constructors & etc.
    String operator+(const String&) const;
};
String String::operator+(const String& s1) const
{
    char* s = new char[strlen(s1.s)+strlen(s2.s)+1];
    strcat(s,s1.s,s2.s);
    String newStr(s);
    delete s;
    return newStr;
}
String s1="Hello";
String s2="Goodbye";
String s3 = s1 + s2;
```

Any operator may be overloaded as a member operator. If operators can be overloaded as either members or non-members, which one should you choose? The answer is to use the member overload unless you have a specific reason to use a non-member overload. These are the most common reasons to use a non-member overload:

1. The first argument is a basic type like an int or double.
2. The first argument is a type defined in an off-the-shelf library you don't want to modify.

Member overloads are found by the compiler by examining the left-hand side of a binary operator and the sole argument to a unary one. If your type is the one on the right, you're out of luck if you use a member overload. The most common example of a non-member overload is operator<< for the ostream library.

```
ostream& operator<<(ostream& os, const String& s)
{
    os<<str.s; // Assumes this function is a friend
    return os;
}
```

This must be a non-member overload since your type, String, is on the right-hand side. That is, unless you want to tear into the off-the-shelf iostream.h headers and add a member overload for your String class to the ostream class. I thought not.

A footnote: the above may not work with your compiler if strlen and strcat are sloppily declared, as they often are, to take char*'s rather than const char*. You could decide it isn't worth it and declare the function to be non-const, but that seems a little severe. Better to "cast away" constness if you are absolutely sure the library function doesn't modify the argument and you are willing to put up with compiler warnings.

```
String String::operator+(const String& s1) const
{
    char* s = new char[strlen((char*)s1.s)
                       +strlen((char*)s2.s)+1];
    strcat(s,(char*)s1.s,(char*)s2.s);
    String newStr(s);
    delete s;
    return newStr;
}
```

See what happens when not everyone appreciates the value of constness?

Conversion Operators. A conversion operator is a special case. If a constructor maps from some other domain onto your own class, a conversion operator does the opposite: given an instance of your class, it produces some other data type.

```
class String {
private:
    char* s;
public:
    operator long(); // Uses atol to convert to a long
};
String::operator long()
{
    // Probably want to verify that string is numeric
    // and within the range of a long integer here.
    return atol(s);
```

```
}
String s("1234");
long x = s; // Invokes operator long()
```

Conversion operators must be member operators. The nice thing about a conversion operator, as shown here, is that the compiler will usually figure out when to use it automatically. If it needs a long, it looks for an operator long(). If it needs a Foo, it looks for either a constructor of Foo accepting a String or an operator Foo() in String. This leads to an interesting question: If a conversion basically does the same thing as a constructor, why do we have both? Constructors are nice because they maintain the encapsulation of the class being built; a conversion operator building some other class would have to know a whole lot about that class. This is why constructors are generally the preferred way to convert from one type to another. But what if the type to be built is a basic type like an int? You can't just go mucking about in the compiler defining new constructors for int that know all about your user-defined types. At least, if you do, you shouldn't admit it. Only a conversion operator can automatically convert to a basic type. Even if the type being built isn't a basic type, it still may be part of a predefined library that you don't want to modify. Again, a conversion operator does the trick.

A conversion operator may be declared for any set of data types you like. They take no arguments, and the return type is implied by the operator name. As with any other operator, conversion operators may be const or non-const. In fact, it is common to provide both a const and a non-const version of the same operator. The const version is usually more efficient because the non-const version usually involves copying things so the original cannot be modified.

```
class String {
private:
    char* s;
public:
    operator const char*() const { return s; }
    operator char*();
```

```
};
String::operator char*()
{
    char* newStr = new char[strlen(s)+1];
    strcpy(newStr, s);
    return newStr;
}
```

Client code using the non-const version must take responsibility for deleting the duplicate.

Search Order and Ambiguity. If, during its rambling through your code, the C++ compiler finds an operator, it goes through the following logic in the given order to decide how to compile the code. The discussion assumes a binary operator, but the logic is the same for unary operators:

1. If both arguments are basic types, the built-in operator is used.
2. If the left-hand side is a user-defined type, the compiler looks for a member overload of that class for the entire signature of the operator subexpression. If one is found, it is used.
3. If all else fails, the compiler looks for a non-member overload.

Ambiguity can arise only if it exists within the class of the left-hand side or within the global space, never because of overlaps between a member overload and a non-member overload. Where ambiguity exists, the error message is deferred until you actually try to use the operator. This is the compiler's way of lulling you into a false sense of security, waiting until you start nodding off before hitting you with a baseball bat.

Virtual Operators. Member operators may be declared virtual like any other member functions. The compiler will dispatch to the overloaded operator of the left-hand side as for any member function. This is very useful in situations in which you are trying to set up a family of classes but publish only their common base class to the outside world. The syntax is simple, but the design principles get pretty thick. This is one of the main subjects of Section 3 of the book, so we won't go into the details here.

operator->. operator-> is different from other operators. Let's start with the basic syntax.

```
class Pointer {
private:
    Foo* f;
public:
    Pointer(Foo* foo) : f(foo) {}
    Foo* operator->() const { return f; }
};
Pointer p(new Foo);
p->MemberOfFoo();
```

This works, using p to indirectly invoke a member function of Foo. The compiler treats any pointer to a struct or class (a *-type variable) as a basic type, and there is a built-in operator-> for all basic pointer types. When the compiler sees a use of ->, it looks at the left-hand side; if it is pointer-to-struct or pointer-to-class, the built-in operator-> is used to access a member. If the left-hand side is a user-defined type, that type must overload operator->. The overload must return either a pointer-to-struct or pointer-to-class, or some other user-defined type that also overloads operator->. If the return value is a user-defined type, the compiler replaces the left-hand side with the return value from operator->, in this case a Foo*, and tries again until it ultimately comes up with a built-in pointer. Thus, the following double indirection also works.

```
class Pointer2 {
private:
    Pointer p;
public:
    Pointer(Foo* foo) : p(foo) {}
    Pointer operator->() const { return p; }
};
Pointer2 p(new Foo);
p->MemberOfFoo();
```

Here operator-> is evaluated three times:

1. Pointer2::operator-> returns a Pointer.
2. Pointer::operator-> then returns a Foo*.
3. The compiler treats the Foo* as a basic type and accesses its member function.

Unlike with any other operator, the return value is not under your control or even accessible to you once the operator function returns. It is used purely by the compiler. This concept — an object that masquerades as a pointer — is fundamental to the rest of this book.

operator[]. operator[] may be overloaded to take any single argument and return any type as its value.

```
class String {
private:
    char* s;
public:
    String(char*);
    char operator[](int n) const; // the nth character
};
char String::operator[](int n)
{
    // Do a range check here
    return s[n];
}
```

Because operator[] can take only one argument, anonymous instances are often used to simulate multidimensional arrays.

```
struct Index3 {
    int X,Y,Z;
    Index3(int x, int y, int z) : X(x), Y(y), Z(z) {}
};
class Array3D { // A 3-dimensional array of String
private:
    // Actual data structure here
public:
    String& operator[](const Index3&);
```

```
};
String s = anArray[Index3(17,29,31)];
```

Even though operator[] takes a single argument, this only moderately clumsy syntax allows you to set up an arbitrary number of pseudo-arguments.

operator(). Bet you didn't know this could be overloaded, did you? If you frequently have an inescapable urge to turn an object into a function, you may be coming mentally unglued and should seriously consider a career change. However, C++ will humor you in the meantime. The left-hand side of operator() is an object you want treated as if it were a callable function. The arguments to the operator are the formal arguments passed by the caller to that object-as-function.

```
class Function {
public:
    int operator() (char*);
};
int Function::operator() (char* s)
{
    cout<<"\""<<s<<"\"";
}
Function fn;
int x = fn("Hello"); // Prints "Hello" to cout
```

operator() can return any type and accept any arguments, obeying all the same rules as any other function. operator() can only be overloaded as a member function.

operator new. When you invent your own language, you get to invent your own rules as well, and one of the new rules in C++ is that an operator doesn't have to have a name consisting entirely of punctuation. operators new and delete are the specific exceptions. operator new is called whenever the compiler decides it is time to allocate a new object on the heap. *Object*, as used here, means any sort of heap-based storage, including ints, char*'s, etc., not just instances of your own classes. The default operator new has this interface:

```
void* operator new(size_t bytes);
```

The sole argument is the number of bytes of storage to allocate, the return value the address of that storage. operator new is not supposed to ever return NULL; instead, when it runs out of memory it throws an exception (see Chapter 4). The default implementation of operator new varies widely, from simple pass-throughs to malloc or calloc to custom memory management delivered with the compiler.

operator new can be overloaded as either a member or non-member function. If it is overloaded as a member function, it is inherited, so derived classes will be managed the same way as a base class that overloads operator new.

```
class Foo {
public:
    void* operator new(size_t bytes);
};
void* Foo::operator new(size_t bytes)
{
    if (bytes < MAXBYTES)
        // do custom allocation here on small blocks
    else return ::operator new(bytes);
}
```

It is obviously tricky to create portable code if everyone goes around overloading the global operator new, so in general a member overload is preferred. That brings an added bonus: you can still use the default operator new from within the member overload, as in the previous fragment. operator new can also be overloaded to take on additional signatures. While these additional signatures won't be called automatically by the compiler, they can be very useful in custom memory management, in which you control the selection of versions of operator new.

```
class Pool { // A custom memory pool
public:
    virtual void* Allocate(size_t bytes);
};
```

```
void* operator new(size_t bytes, Pool* p)
{
    return p->Allocate(bytes);
}
extern Pool* DefaultPool;
Foo* f = new(DefaultPool) Foo;
```

The extra arguments are placed after the new and before the class name Foo; they are passed along to the overloaded operator following the compiler-supplied size.

operator delete. operator delete is usually overloaded in tandem with operator new to perform some sort of custom memory management. There are two alternative interfaces you can use, either of which will be called automatically by the compiler when an object is deleted:

1. `void operator delete(void* address);`

2. `void operator delete(void* address, size_t bytes);`

The first version simply hands you the address of the block to deallocate; you have to peer into your own crystal ball to figure out how big that block is. The second version appears to hand you the size of the block to deallocate, but surprise! It may be smaller than the true size! The problems arise in situations like this:

```
class Foo {
private:
    int x;
public:
    ~Foo(); // Non-virtual destructor
};
class Bar : public Foo {
private:
    int y;
public:
    ~Bar();
};
Bar* b = new Bar;
delete b; // Size is correct
```

```
Foo* f = new Bar;
delete f; // Size is that of Foo, not Bar
```

The compiler figures out the size based on the destructor it calls. If the destructor is non-virtual and the type of the pointer is that of a base class, the base class destructor is called, so the size of the base class is used. There are three circumstances under which the size will be correct:

1. The destructor is virtual.
2. The type of the pointer is the actual type of the object.
3. The actual type is the same size as the pointer type.

The last of these will be true only if the derived class does not add any data members, and when either both or neither of the base and derived classes have any virtual member functions and, therefore, vtables pointers to store. Confused? Let's keep it simple: make your destructors virtual.

Like operator new, operator delete can be overloaded either as a member or non-member function. If it is overloaded as a member function, it is inherited. Unlike with operator new, you can't add more function signatures to operator delete; the two just described are the whole kit and kaboodle.

CHAPTER 3

Templates and Type Safety

Although the standards for templates were published quite a while ago, their use is still not very widespread. Of course, it's difficult to use something that your compiler doesn't support, which is probably the number-one reason most C++ programmers don't know how to use them. Thank goodness almost all the major compilers have now come into the twentieth century, so that is no longer a problem. That leaves understanding what they are, how to navigate through the syntactic minefield, and why you should care in the first place. This chapter is not just a review of syntax; it also covers the basics of type safety in C++, with a special focus on templates.

What Is a Template and Why Should You Care?

Here is the interface to a simple collection class, specifically a linked list:

```
class ListNode {
private:
    ListNode* next;
    void* data;
public:
    ListNode(void* d, ListNode* n=NULL)
        : next(n), data(d) {}
    ~ListNode() { delete next; }
    void* Data() { return data; }
    ListNode* Next() { return next; }
};
```

See anything wrong?

The Problems

First of all, there are all those void*'s, which you and I both know perfectly well are really something else. At some point in your client code, you'll be doing things like this:

```
for (ListNode* n = listHead; n != NULL; n = n->Next())
    f((Foo*)n->Data());
```

That is, you have to constantly typecast downward from void* to something specific. How can you be sure that the datum really is a Foo*? You're on your own in proving it, because when you typecast like this, the compiler throws up its hands and says, "I sure hope you know what you're doing." Maybe you are convinced that your use of the class is typesafe, but can you really guarantee that someone else won't do something stupid and put some other type into your collection? If you really believe that, I'd advise you to stay away from speculative investments and put your money in government-backed securities; you aren't destined to have much luck in this life.

A second problem is that the list nodes themselves don't know to what type they point. Suppose you want the list's destructor to delete the things pointed to by the list, not just the nodes. You can't hand a void* to operator delete and expect it to figure out which destructor to call.

Workarounds

One possible workaround is to insist that the objects in your collection all descend from a common ancestor. That is, you can replace all those void*'s with some base class-*. That imposes a little more discipline. If the base class destructor is virtual, at least we can rewrite the destructor of ListNode to take the contents of the list with it while committing suicide. But if that base class has derived classes, it's a sure bet you'll be back at work busily doing unsafe typecasts to those derived types.

Another workaround is to make your list type-specific. If you want to store a list of Foos, create a ListOfFoos collection class to hold them. That way, you won't have to do any typecasting if Foo doesn't have derived classes. But do you really want to create all those duplicate classes that differ only in the types they deal with? I know copy/paste is a major advance in text processing and text-manipulating scripts can propagate code in a hurry, but you'll still be left with a nagging headache of a maintenance problem if you decide to change the representation of all those lists.

In the past, people created #define macros to handle this sort of problem.

```
#define ListNode(Type) \
class ListNode##Type { \
private: \
    ListNode##Type* next; \
    Type* data; \
public: \
    ListNode##Type(Type* d, ListNode* n=NULL) \
        : next(n), data(d) {} \
    ~ListNode##Type() { delete next; } \
    Type* Data() { return data; } \
    ListNode##Type* Next() { return next; } \
};
```

The compiler, sensing a threat to its domain, will make loud, ugly noises if you forget a backslash, but this technique basically works if you are careful. The ## means "concatenation" and contributes to the ugliness, but you have to make sure the collection types all have distinct names, so get used to it. This technique isn't going to win you any Malcolm Baldridge quality awards in your company. If the member functions aren't inlines, you'll have to create more macros to implement them and make sure they only get implemented in one compilation unit. Some compilers have a problem with very lengthy macros. You can't nest #defines, so corecursive, typesafe data structures are out. Worst of all, if an error occurs anywhere in a macro, the debugger will fold its arms and tell you it occured *somewhere* in the macro, but won't tell you the specific line number.

Templates Are Glorified Macros

Enter the template, a glorified #define macroprocessor. Templates are nothing more or less than macros without all these limitations. They can be nested. You don't have to worry about duplicate definitions of their member functions. Most C++ source debuggers find the correct line number in the template when an error occurs. Size is not a problem. And you won't have to clutter up your beautiful code with all those \'s and ##'s.

Template Syntax

If you are going to use templates, you'd better get used to liberally sprinkling your conversation with the term *parameterized*. Templates can be used to create parameterized types — usually classes — and parameterized functions.

Parameterized Types

A parameterized type is a seemingly normal class declaration preceded by the magic incantation template <class Type>, where Type is a symbol of your own choosing while the rest is pure boilerplate. Everywhere that Type (or whatever you choose) occurs inside the following class declaration, it is treated as a macro to be substituted for when the class is used with a specific type. Here is the rewritten ListNode class, now a parameterized type.

```
template <class Type>
class ListNode {
private:
    ListNode<Type>* next;
    Type* data;
public:
    ListNode(Type* d, ListNode<Type>* n=NULL)
        : next(n), data(d) {}
    ~ListNode() { delete next; }
    Type* Data() { return data; }
    ListNode<Type>* Next() { return next; }
};
ListNode<Foo> list = new ListNode<Foo>(new Foo);
Foo* f = list->Data(); // Returns the correct type
```

Within the body of the class declaration, the formal parameter to the template becomes a placeholder. When the class is used, the actual parameter is substituted. The compiler literally generates the correct, typesafe source code as you use the template.

Parameterized Functions

A parameterized function is declared in exactly the same way, by preceding the function declaration with the template... boilerplate. You have to repeat the template syntax for both the declaration and the definition of the function. Remember that these are macros, so everything must be in the .h file. It won't work if you put the definition in a .cpp file, unless that is the *only* .cpp file in which the function is called.

```
// Declare the function
template <class Type>
Type* fn(Type* t);
// Define its implementation
template <class Type>
```

```
Type* fn(Type* t) {
    // Normal body code using Type as a macro parameter
}
Foo* f = fn<Foo>(new Foo);
```

The compiler generates the definition on demand, when the function is called. Now it is the function name that is parameterized, as opposed to a class name.

Parameterized Member Functions

Defining member functions is the same, except that you have to use more <'s and >'s. Let's change ListNode to not define its member functions in the class declaration.

```
template <class Type>
class ListNode {
private:
    ListNode<Type>* next;
    Type* data;
public:
    ListNode(Type* d, ListNode<Type>* n=NULL);
    ~ListNode();
    Type* Data();
    ListNode<Type>* Next();
};
template <class Type>
ListNode<Type>::ListNode
    (Type* d, ListNode<Type>* n=NULL)
    : next(n), data(d)
{
}
template <class Type>
ListNode<Type>::~ListNode()
{
    delete next;
}
template <class Type>
Type* ListNode<Type>::Data()
{
```

```
    return data;
}
template <class Type>
ListNode<Type>* ListNode<Type>::Next()
{
    return next;
}
```

Remember that this all has to be in the .h file, unless the member functions are only called from within the .cpp file in which they are defined. In that case, the definitions of the member functions must precede their first use.

When You Have to Supply a Parameter

All those <'s and >'s can get confusing because, as usual, C++ isn't totally consistent. Basically, you have to use <Type> everywhere except for three places in the declaration of a class or definition of a member function:

1. Following the word class at the top
2. When naming a constructor
3. When naming the destructor

Arguments to constructors and destructors must be parameterized, as must all uses of the class name other than in these three specific cases. You must always supply a parameter when you use a parameterized type or function. It would have been a lot easier on everyone if C++ simply required the parameter everywhere, but hey, this is C++, and besides, it saves a few characters of source code. In these three situations, the compiler can reasonably figure out what those missing characters should have been.

Templates with More Than One Parameter

It is possible to have a type with more than one parameter. It doesn't happen very often, and usually when I've seen such classes, I've had to sit down the author and have a long talk about factoring software.

Nevertheless, every now and then a legitimate use of multiargument templates comes along. The syntax is identical, except that in place of the <class Type>, you use a comma separated list like <class Type1, class Type2>. Finally, no, the parameter doesn't have to always be a class. It can be a struct or just about anything else, although classes seem to have a pretty strong lock on the parameter market.

Nested Parameterized Types — Not!

Sigh. Yes, it works, but please use this feature with caution. Not only are nested templates difficult to read, but they also generate gobs of code when they are expanded. Remember that each of the templates will be expanded when the outermost template is used.

```
template <class Type>
class B {...};
template <class Type>
class A {
    B<A<Type>>* member; // Yuck!
};
```

Look at that awful syntactic garbage. This is the sort of thing that happens when you nest parameterized types. We'll talk later about how to refactor this sort of code; for the moment, avoid it like the plague.

Derivation

You can derive parameterized classes from other classes, parameterized or not. You can also derive from a parameterized class; in that case, the derived class is parameterized by the same formal argument as the base class. The derived class may add more parameters, but that's like those people who used to hold contests to see who could cram the most APL code into a single line. In other words, don't do it. By far the most common of all these permutations is deriving a parameterized type from a nonparameterized one. We'll explore this and other ways of combining parameterized and simple types in the next section.

Combining Parameterized and Simple Types

Suppose you have a parameterized class that requires 1000 lines of code to implement all its member functions. Each time you use it with a new type, the compiler will merrily disgorge another 1000 lines of expanded code. Even at today's memory prices, that's a steep price to pay for type safety.

Suppose you are shipping a class library and you don't want to ship source, only interfaces. If your library contains parameterized functions, they'll have to be in the public .h file for all the world to see. Bummer.

Suppose someone hands you a perfectly good, but non-typesafe class or class library. Maybe it was written using a compiler that doesn't support templates, or maybe the author just didn't believe in templates. You want to "harden" the code by making it typesafe using templates. Do you really want to restructure everything, putting all the implementing code into .h files and changing the class declarations to use parameters and <>'s?

For all of these reasons, parameterized types are commonly combined with simple, nonparameterized types. When this is done, in 99 cases out of 100, the parameterized type "wraps" the simple type in a nice soft flannel typesafe blanket. The simple class isn't changed in the process — you just put your parameterized class in the middle between the unsafe class and the user. You can use several different techniques in these situations, and there are numerous idioms that have grown up around this idea.

Unsafe Types as Public Base Classes — Not!

Don't do it. Really. If you try to impose type safety in a publicly derived class, the client has full access to all that unsafe stuff in the base class. There are absolutely ingenious ways to shore up this technique, especially using techniques we'll discuss in later chapters, but they're right up there with building a suspension bridge out of bottle caps: brilliant engineering, wrong medium.

Unsafe Types as Private Base Classes

Ah, that's more like it. The easiest way to enforce type safety is to make the unsafe class a private base class of a typesafe template.

```
class UnsafeNode { // Same as ListNode above
private:
    UnsafeNode* next;
    void* data;
public:
    UnsafeNode(void* d, UnsafeNode* n);
    virtual ~UnsafeNode();
    UnsafeNode* Next();
    void* Data();
};
template <class Type>
class SafeNode : private UnsafeNode {
public:
    SafeNode(Type* d, SafeNode* n)
        : UnsafeNode(d,n) {}
    virtual ~UnsafeNode() { delete (Type*)Data(); }
    SafeNode* Next()
        { return (SafeNode*)UnsafeNode::Next(); }
    Type* Data() { return (Type*)UnsafeNode::Data(); }
};
```

This does the trick nicely. The base class is inaccessible from clients of the derived template. This sample illustrates another trick of the C++ name space. It isn't necessary to make up new member function names for Next() and Data() in the derived class just because they differ in return type; because neither is virtual, the derived version shadows the base class version from clients. Some compilers wave an accusing finger at you as they shadow base class members, but the warning is perfectly harmless if the derivation is private. After all the aggravation the compiler brings your way, it's nice to be able to throw some back from time to time.

One of the drawbacks of private derivation is that you have to manually republish any member functions of the base class that clients can still use in a typesafe way. This doesn't occur that often, and when it does, it is a small price to pay for the extra safety. The republishing technique is identical to what we did to Next() and Data(), except that the interface is identical to that of the private base class.

Unsafe Types as Data Members

The next way to combine two classes is through delegation: Make an instance of the unsafe class a data member of the parameterized class and delegate processing to it. You can impose type safety by not making the data member visible to the user. This isn't always a simple matter; often the wrapper has different semantics than the member.

Consider the previous UnsafeNode linked list example. Instead of deriving SafeNode privately from that class, suppose you make an UnsafeNode a data member of SafeNode. Given a SafeNode, you can no longer find the next SafeNode in the list! Try it. Each UnsafeNode points to another UnsafeNode, not to a SafeNode. One solution is to use different semantics for the wrapper and the wrappee.

```
// In SafeList.h
class UnsafeNode; // Forward declaration
template <class Type>
class SafeList { // Wraps UnsafeNode in a typesafe way
private:
    UnsafeNode* head;
public:
    SafeList() : head(NULL) {}
    ~SafeList();
    UnsafeNode* Cursor(); // For iteration
    Type* Next(UnsafeNode*&); // Advance to next item
    void DeleteAt(UnsafeNode*&); // Delete item at cursor
    void InsertFirst(Type*); // Insert as new list head
    void InsertBefore(UnsafeNode*&); // Before cursor
```

```
        void InsertAfter(UnsafeNode*&); // After cursor
};

// In SafeList.cpp
class UnsafeNode { // Same as ListNode above
private:
    UnsafeNode* next;
    void* data;
public:
    UnsafeNode(void* d, UnsafeNode* n);
    ~UnsafeNode();
    UnsafeNode* Next();
    void* Data();
};
```

Each SafeList represents an entire list, not just a single node. Most operations, such as InsertFirst, are list-as-a-whole operations, not operations on a single node. For operations that are inherently concerned with a single node, a new paradigm is needed: the cursor. To iterate over the list, ask the list for a cursor. To advance to the next in list, supply a reference to a pointer to the cursor, which is updated by the SafeList object. If you want to operate on a position in the list, supply a cursor to indicate the position. Note that clients need know nothing about UnsafeNode except that it exists — the forward declaration is sufficient. The concept of a cursor will be discussed at length in later chapters; the point here is that the typesafe wrapper is more than just a few parameters and <>'s thrown around — the semantics of the data structure have been redefined. This is typical of unsafe, recursive data structures and is common in other contexts as well.

CHAPTER 4 — *Taking Exception*

If your programs always execute flawlessly, perhaps you can afford to skip this chapter. For the rest of you, let's talk about exception handling, both according to the book and in real life.

The basic idea of exception handling is to restore state, then take alternate action when an error occurs. Suppose you have some block of code lying around and you aren't sure whether it will run to completion. The program might run out of memory while that block is executing, or perhaps there might be a communications problem, or maybe one of those annoying little client objects might have passed a bad parameter. Wouldn't it be nice if you could write a program like this?

```
if (block_of_code will work) {
    block_of_code;
    }
else {
    do_something_else;
    }
```

That is to say, peer into a crystal ball, and if it shows your block of code crashing and burning, change the future by bypassing the block. I wouldn't hold your breath waiting for someone to create a language that allows you to do this, but exception handling is the next best thing. Using exception handling, you can try the suspect block of code, and if an error occurs, the compiler helps you unwind things back to where they were before the block so that you can go on about your business.

ANSI Standard Exception Handling

The good news is that there is an ANSI standard for exception handling — or, as is always the case with C++, a proposed standard. I've looked into the matter, and the reason we have years of proposed standards and no real ones is that our economy couldn't absorb all the members of the standards committee if they had to find other work. Better to give them a fulfilling, lifelong hobby while the rest of us snap up the real jobs. But I digress.

The bad news is that many C++ compilers still don't support standard exception handling. The good news is that more and more compilers are coming up to speed on this. The bad news is there's still a lot of legacy code out there based on the old compilers. Sigh. Let's start by talking about the way things *should* be done, then we'll worry about variations you are likely to encounter in the real world.

Syntax for Throwing Exceptions

Here is a function that may want to smack the wrist of its caller if a parameter is bad. The ruler it uses is the `throw` expression. There are two errors that can occur in this function, represented by instances of the enum Gotcha.

```
enum Gotcha { kTooLow, kTooHigh };
void fn(int x) throw(Gotcha) {
    if (x < 0)
        throw kTooLow; // Function terminates here
    if (x > 1000)
        throw kTooHigh; // Or here
    // Do something meaningful
}
```

The first line defines a type of exception. Exceptions can be of any type: integers, enums, structs, even classes. The second line declares the function's interface, including a new appendage, called the *exception specification* that declares what sorts of exceptions the function might throw at a caller. In this case, the only type of exception it might throw is one of type Gotcha. The fourth and sixth lines show how to throw an exception, which must be an instance of one of the types in the exception specification for the function. Following are the rules governing exception specifications.

Declarations and Definitions. Function declarations must have exactly the same exception specification as the function definition.

```
void Fn() throw(int); // A declaration
// In a .cpp file somewhere
void Fn() throw(int) {
    // Implementation
}
```

If the definition had been different from the declaration, the compiler would have crossed its arms over its chest and refused to compile the definition.

Functions with No Exception Specification. If a function does not have an exception specification, it may throw any kind of exception it wants. The following function can throw anything, anytime.

```
void fn(); // Can throw any type of exception
```

Functions That Don't Throw Exceptions. If the list of exception types in the exception specification is empty, the function is not allowed to throw any exceptions. It is obviously good coding practice to use this form whenever you can assure a caller that no exceptions will be thrown.

```
void fn() throw(); // Will not throw exceptions
```

Functions That Throw Multiple Types of Exception. Inside the parentheses you can list as many exception types as you want, separated by commas.

```
void fn() throw(int, Exception_Struct, char*);
```

Functions That Rethrow Exceptions. If you don't list any exception types following the function signature, the function won't generate any new exceptions but might propagate any exceptions it receives from functions it calls.

```
void fn() throw;
```

Exceptions and Function Signatures. The exception specification is not considered to be part of a function's signature. That is, it is not legal to have two functions whose interface is identical except (no pun intended) for their exception specifications. The following two functions cannot coexist in a program.

```
void f1(int) throw();
void f1(int) throw(Exception); // Duplicate signature!
```

Exception Specifications for Virtual Functions. In Chapter 2, we talked — well, I talked, you listened — about the fact that overloading and overriding don't mix. If you list a virtual function in a derived class with a new signature, not present in the base class, that function shadows all other functions of the same name in the base class. (See that section if you aren't clear about that; it's important to understand.) The same sort of principle applies to exception specifications.

```
class Foo {
public:
    virtual Fn() throw(int);
};
class Bar : public Foo {
public:
    virtual Fn() throw(char*); // Oops!
};
```

The compiler may look at you funny, but it will compile this. As a result, someone staring at a Foo* may only be prepared for an int to be thrown back, not knowing that the object is really a Bar that may throw something altogether different.

The implication is clear: Don't change the exception specification of a virtual function in derived classes. This is the only way to preserve the contract between clients and a base class providing that only certain sorts of exceptions will be thrown.

What if I Throw the Wrong Kind of Exception? If you throw a type of exception not listed in the exception specification of the enclosing function, the program reformats your hard disk. No, just kidding. It calls a function called unexpected(). The default behavior is to then call terminate(), which is discussed later, but you can modify this to instead call your own function. Here are the relevant interfaces from the except.h header file.

```
typedef void (*unexpected_function)();
unexpected_function
    set_unexpected(unexpected_function unexpected_func);
```

The typedef declares the interface to your function. The function set_unexpected() takes a function of that type and makes it the function to call in place of the default. The return value of set_unexpected() is the current unexpected exception handler. This allows you to temporarily set the unexpected exception handler, then later restore whatever used to be in its place. The following code fragment illustrates the technique.

```
unexpected_function my_handler(void) {
    // Handle the unexpected exception
}
{ // About to do something bizarre, so install handler
    unexpected_function old_handler =
        set_unexpected(my_handler);
    // Do the weird stuff
    set_unexpected(old_handler);
}
```

Your handler function cannot return to the calling program. If you put a return statement into the function or if your function exits scope, the results are undefined. It is legal, however, to throw an exception from within the function. This has the effect of continuing the search for a catch that matches the new exception.

Syntax for Catching Exceptions

To catch an exception, precede the block that might fail with the keyword try, then follow that block with one or more catch statements, called handlers.

```
try {
    // stuff that might throw exceptions
}
catch (Exception_Type t) {
    // recover from exception of type Exception_Type
}
// An arbitrary list of catchers, optionally followed by
catch (...) {
    // recover from any other exception types
}
```

Each handler, with the exception (still no pun intended) of the one with the three dots, corresponds to one specific type of failure. If an exception is thrown from code called by the try block, the compiler searches the list of handlers in the order in which they appear, looking for one expecting the type of the exception thrown. The three dots match any kind of exception; if such a handler is present, it must be the last one in the list.

Within a handler, you can do anything you want to recover from the situation. The exception itself is available as the argument to the catch, except (still no pun intended) for the handler with the three dots, which has no idea what the exception was.

Program Flow After an Exception. If no exception occurs during the try block, the program blithely ignores all those handlers and resumes with the first expression following the last handler. If a handler is invoked, it will be the only one invoked from the list and when it is done the program continues after the last handler in the list. There are two exceptions (no pun intended) to this: a goto (shudder) is legal from within a handler, or the handler may choose to throw an exception itself. If a handler throws an exception, it may propagate the same exception or it may create a new one.

```
catch(int exception) {
    // Do something, then
    throw("Help!"); // Throws a char*
    }
```

As with any throw, a throw from within a handler immediately terminates the enclosing function or block.

What if My Exception Isn't Caught? If an exception doesn't match any handler, the default behavior is to call a global function called terminate(). Any guesses what it does? If left to its own devices, eventually terminate() calls the library routine abort(), which abnormally terminates the whole program. You can change this by installing your own termination function using the library routine set_terminate(). Here are the relevant lines from except.h.

```
typedef void (*terminate_function)();
terminate_function
    set_terminate(terminate_function t_func);
```

The typedef declares the interface to your termination function. set_terminate() allows you to install your termination function to be called by terminate() instead of calling abort(). The return value is the old termination function, which you can later restore by calling set_terminate() again.

Your termination function *must* terminate the program and must not throw another exception. It can clean things up first, but it can never return to the calling program.

Nested Exception Handling. Yes, it is legal to nest try/catch blocks, although I wouldn't do it very often if you want to remain friends with the people who maintain your code.

```
{
    try {
        try {
            try {
                // something that might fail
                }
            catch(...) {
                }
            }
        catch(...) {
            }
        }
    catch(...) {
        }
}
```

It isn't often that you want to create such spaghetti code, but occasionally it is important to separate the stack-based objects into separate scopes.

External Exceptions Can't Be Caught! It is possible to catch any exception initiated by a throw. However, there are other exceptions that can't be caught in a portable way. For example, if the user uses the right control-key combination to abort a running program, there is no guarantee that the operating system will turn that into an exception that can be caught by your handlers. In general, exception handling applies to exceptions generated by your code; anything beyond that is nonportable.

Constructors and Destructors

One of the principle benefits of standard exception handling is called *unwinding the stack*. When an exception is thrown, destructors of all stack-based objects in between the throw and the catch are automatically called.

```
void fn() throw(int) {
    Foo aFoo;
    // Something went wrong!
    throw(bad_news);
}
```

When the throw occurs, before popping the stack up to whatever handler handles the exception, the destructor of aFoo is called. The same logic is applied in the caller's try block.

```
{
    try {
        Bar b;
        fn(); // Causes an exception
        }
    catch(int exception) {
        // destructor of b was called before we got here
        }
}
```

More generally, it is guaranteed that destructors will be called for all stack-based objects constructed since the beginning of the try block. This can be important to close open files, prevent memory leaks, or for any number of other reasons. Some subtleties arise, however.

What Gets Destroyed. It is guaranteed that destructors will be called for all stack-based objects constructed since the beginning of the try block, but for no others. For example, suppose an array is being constructed when the exception occurs. Destructors will be called for those objects in the array that were constructed before the exception occured.

Heap-based objects, that is, those created using operator new, are another matter. You're on your own keeping track of them. If you allocate objects on the heap that should be destroyed in the event of an exception, it is a common practice to wrap the heap-based object in a stack-based baby-sitter object.

```
class TempFoo {
private:
    Foo* f;
public:
    TempFoo(Foo* aFoo): f(aFoo) {}
    ~TempFoo() { delete f; }
};
try {
    TempFoo tf(new Foo);
    // etc.
}
catch(...) {
    // The Foo was destroyed by tf's destructor
}
```

Later chapters discuss this and more sophisticated strategies for managing heap-based objects in the face of exceptions.

Exceptions During Construction. Consider this construction sequence.

```
class Foo {...}
class Bar : public Foo {
private:
    A a;
    B b;
public:
    Bar();
};
Bar::Bar()
{
    X x;
    throw(bad_news);
    Y y;
}
```

If an exception occurs while an object is being constructed, destructors are called for those components — base classes and data members — whose constructors finished before the exception occured. The construction of Bar is incomplete at the time of the throw. The constructors of the base classes (Foo) and data members (a and b) have finished, however, so their destructors will be called before the exception is tossed up to a handler. Similarly, the destructor of x, a local variable, will be called. The destructor of y will not be called because it has not yet been constructed. The destructor of Bar will not be called because its construction was not complete before the exception was thrown.

Suppose the constructor of b had thrown an exception. The destructors of Foo and a would be called, but not the destructors of b, Bar, x, or y.

The same principles apply whether the object being constructed is stack- or heap-based. If an exception occurs during construction of a heap-based object, exactly the same destructors will be called as if it had been stack-based.

Order of Destruction. It is guaranteed that destructors will be called in the reverse order that constructors were called. This applies to local variables as well as to data members and base classes of those objects.

Nonstandard Exception Handling

Many libraries and a few compilers handle exceptions in a nonstandard way. Most use macros to simulate a try/catch paradigm, but fail to unwind the stack properly by calling destructors of things that have been constructed. Most are very machine- and operating-system-specific.

There are also, unfortunately, a lot of compilers that claim standard exception handling but don't do things entirely according to Hoyle.

I have learned from bitter experience to test the compiler's exception handling if I do anything out of the mainstream, even if it is supposed to be standard. If you find yourself in this situation, do us all a favor: Hire the compiler-writer for some supposedly hot project at your company, then make her write and debug exception-handling code with her own compiler for the next five years. Better yet, make her port code that works perfectly well on some other compiler to hers.

If, for whatever reason, you find yourself with nonstandard exception handling, the biggest headache will be reclaiming memory from heap-based objects that were allocated before the exception occurred, but are no longer reachable from any variable. This is 99 percent of what exception handling gets used for in real life, with an occasional need to close files thrown in. You can either design very elaborate data structures that thread new heap-based objects to something high up on the stack and, therefore, keep them reachable, or you can use the scavenging techniques described in the last section of the book. Both approaches are about equally grubby, so take your pick.

Conventions in This Book

In this book, I will not use throw and catch, but will instead stick in a generic comment where an exception should be signaled. This should make it easier to follow the code if you do not have standard exception handling. If you see something like the following code fragment, and you have standard exception handling, mentally turn the comment into a throw.

```
f()
{
    if(pool->Allocate(size) == NULL)
        // exception - out of memory
}
```

SECTION 2 — *Indirectly Speaking*

When is a pointer not really a pointer? When it is a smart pointer and the language is C++. One of the most powerful — and most underused — ideas in advanced C++ usage is the idea that an object can masquerade as a pointer. This section discusses in gory detail all the different ways an object can do that and interweaves practical applications of the idioms. This is not so much a "how-to" section as a collection of new tools for your workbench — you still have to provide the craftsmanship, but having the right tools sure makes the job easier.

CHAPTER 5

Smart Pointers

Forget for a moment everything you ever knew about C and the lowly -> and take a fresh look at the subject. Consider this code fragment.

```
class Foo {
public:
    void MemberOfFoo();
};
Foo* aFoo = new Foo;
aFoo->MemberOfFoo();
```

Think of this as the built-in "operator->" being applied to a built-in pointer "class," the address held in aFoo. C++ supplies such an operator for use with any object whose type is pointer-to-struct, pointer-to-class, or pointer-to-union. Those built-in operator->'s access the member named by the right-hand side, in this case MemberOfFoo(). In effect, you are referring to a member of one object, the Foo, using another object and that object's operator->. That the other object is a pointer is a special case; it could also have been one of your own classes with a custom operator-> designed by you.

This is the correct way to think about operator-> in C++, because like all other operators except ., -> can be overloaded. The raw syntax was discussed in Chapter 2, but the design implications are huge and will occupy this and several more chapters.

Dumb Pointers

C++ provides a bunch of built-in data types such as ints, doubles, and pointers. It is relatively simple to wrap most built-in types inside classes of your own design. For example, if ints aren't good enough for you, you can create a plug-compatible Integer class like this.

```
class Integer {
private:
    int value;
public:
    Integer() : value(0) {}
    Integer(int v) : value(v) {}
    operator int() { return value; }
    Integer operator+(Integer i)
        { return Integer(value+i.value); }
    Integer operator+=(Integer i)
        { value += i.value; return *this; }
    // etc. for other arithmetic operators
};
int f(int);
f(Integer(17)); // Works because of operator int()
```

The constructors allow you to create Integers from nothing, from ints, or from other Integers. You might also add constructors taking char* (doing an atoi() conversion) or other numeric types as well. Because you might want to use an Integer somewhere where a true int is expected, such as when calling a function expecting an int argument, we provide an operator int() to do the conversion automatically. All of the semantics of integer arithmetic are replicated through the various and tedious operators. Voilá! Anywhere you can use an int, you can now use an Integer. You have managed to create a new class that is plug-compatible with the lowly int. Go have a milkshake.

Back already? In all the fervor of abstract data types in C++ (the underlying politically correct term to use for these wrapper classes), suppose you've now decided that *-style pointers just aren't for you and you want to hide them inside your own classes. (Don't ask me why you might want to do that; I said it was your idea, didn't I?) Let's do a thought experiment and see what would be required. Here is a first attempt.

```
class PFoo {
private:
    Foo* foo;
public:
    PFoo() : foo(NULL) {}
    PFoo(Foo* f) : foo(f) {}
    operator Foo*() { return foo; }
    PFoo operator+(ptr_diff offset)
        { return PFoo(foo+offset); }
    PFoo operator+=(ptr_diff offset)
        { foo+=offset; return *this; }
    ptr_diff operator-(PFoo pf)
        { return foo-pf.foo; }
    // etc. for all other pointer arithmetic operators
};
```

Voilá! You now have a class that is plug-compatible with Foo*! The arithmetic operators are a little more complicated than they were for ints; for example, I bet you had to run to a reference manual to find out that ptr_diff is the portable way to describe the difference between two memory addresses, didn't you? This is tedious, since it is specific to Foo, but at least you can claim to be able to use a PFoo in place of all uses of Foo*... or can you? Wait a minute; put down that second milkshake. This doesn't work.

```
PFoo pf(new Foo*);
pf->MemberOfFoo(); // Wrong
((Foo*)pf)->MemberOfFoo(); // Works, but YUCK!
```

operator Foo*() will allow you to pass a PFoo as an argument to functions that expect Foo*'s and all the pointer arithmetic is replicated, but the full semantics of pointerism aren't maintained because ->'s just don't work the same way. I call this a dumb pointer because it is very naive and doesn't always behave as a real pointer would.

Let's sum up what is more complex about pointers than other basic types:

1. The compiler actually creates one pointer type for each struct, class, or union type. If you want to wrap all pointers, you have to figure out how to do so for all possible pointer types. The PFoo class just described only works for Foo's and derived classes of Foo.

2. There are other, related types such as size_t and ptr_diff. If we wanted to completely wrap pointers up inside our own classes, we would have to create equivalents to those types as well.

3. The whole idea of a built-in pointer is to eventually access members of the thing pointed to using ->. A conversion operator isn't adequate to replicate those semantics.

The Smart Pointer Idiom

Let's fix one problem at a time. I'm going to ignore pointer arithmetic for a while, so hold on to those ptr_diffs.

Operator->

Now you know why -> was made an overloadable operator. From the syntax presented in Chapter 2, PFoo now gets its own bouncing baby operator->(). A conversion operator suffices to call non-member functions. The call to f() below works because the compiler is smart enough to look for a conversion operator in order to match a function signature, and in this case operator Foo*() fits the bill nicely.

```
class PFoo {
private:
    Foo* foo;
public:
    PFoo() : foo(NULL) {}
    PFoo(Foo* f) : foo(f) {}
    operator Foo*() { return foo; }
    Foo* operator->() { return foo; }
};
void f(Foo*);
PFoo pf(new Foo);
f(pf); // Works because of operator Foo*()
pf->MemberOfFoo(); // Works because of operator->()
```

The reason that pf->MemberOfFoo() works is less obvious. The left-hand side of operator-> is a user-defined type, so the compiler looks for an overload of operator->. It finds one, evaluates it, and replaces pf with the return value of operator-> as the new left-hand side of operator->. This logic continues recursively until the left-hand side becomes a basic type. If that basic type is pointer-to-struct, pointer-to-class, or pointer-to-union, the compiler accesses the named member. If the basic type is something else, say an int, the compiler laughs an evil laugh and spits out an error message listing all sorts of inferences it has drawn about your intelligence and future job prospects from the fact that you tried to access a member of something that doesn't have members. In either case, the search is over as soon as a basic type is reached. For the morbidly curious, most compilers I have used don't trap a true recursion, such as

```
PFoo operator->() { return *this; }
```

Here a user-defined type's operator-> returns an instance of that type as the value. C++ compilers generally prefer to stretch you out on the rack of a run-time infinite loop.

Now we have a pointer class that can be used wherever a Foo* could be used: as an argument to functions expecting Foo*, as the left-hand side of an ->, or, if pointer arithmetic semantics are added, anywhere you can add or subtract Foo*'s.

Parameterized Smart Pointers

One obvious way to create general-purpose smart pointers is to use templates.

```
template <class Type>
class SP {
private:
    Type* pointee;
public:
    SP() : pointee(NULL) {}
    SP(Type* p) : pointee(p) {}
    operator Type*() { return pointee; }
    Type* operator->() { return pointee; }
};
void f(Foo*);
Ptr<Foo> pf(new Foo);
f(pf); // Works because of operator Type*()
pf->MemberOfFoo(); // Works because of operator->()
```

This template can be used with any class, not just Foo. This is one of the basic smart pointer forms. It is broadly useful and even handles typecasting pointer-to-derived to pointer-to-base, assuming that you have a decent compiler.

```
class Bar : public Foo {...};
Ptr<Bar> pf1(new Bar);
Ptr<Foo> pf2 = pf1; // Works but why is not obvious!
```

A good C++ compiler will handle this properly using the following logic:

1. Is there a constructor of P<Foo> that accepts a P<Bar>? No. Look further.

2. Is there an operator P<Foo>() in P<Bar>? No. Bummer. Keep looking.

3. Is there a user-defined conversion from P<Bar> to a type that matches a signature of some constructor of P<Foo>? Yes! operator Bar*() turns a P<Bar> into a Bar*, which can be promoted by the compiler to Foo*. Evaluate this as if it were Ptr<Foo> pf2(Foo*(pb.operator Bar*())), where the cast from Bar* to Foo* is done as for any other built-in pointer.

As I said, this is *supposed* to be how it works, but be aware that some compilers don't handle this properly. Even on the good ones, the net result of nesting the inlined operator Bar*() inside the inlined P<Foo>(Foo*) may not be what you had in mind; many compilers create out-of-line (read: less efficient) copies of inlined member functions rather than generate nested inlined code. The bottom line: This template *should* do what you want, but your compiler may have other thoughts.

Hierarchies of Smart Pointers

An alternative approach to templates is to maintain parallel hierarchies of pointers and pointees. You would only do this if you didn't have templates or had a poorly implemented compiler.

```
class PVoid { // Replaces void*
protected:
    void* addr;
public:
    PVoid() : addr(NULL) {}
    PVoid(void* a) : addr(a) {}
    operator void*() { return addr; }
};
class PFoo : public PVoid {
public:
    PFoo() : PVoid() {}
    PFoo(Foo* p) : PVoid(p) {}
    operator Foo*() { return (Foo*)addr; }
    Foo* operator->() { return (Foo*)addr; }
};
class PBar : public PFoo {
public:
    PBar() : PFoo() {}
    PBar(Bar* b) : PFoo(b) {}
    operator Bar*() { return (Bar*)addr; }
    Bar* operator->() { return (Bar*)addr; }
};
PBar pb (new Bar);
```

```
PFoo pf (pb); // Works because PBar derives from PFoo
pf->MemberOfFoo(); // Works because of PFoo::operator->
```

This works as long as you don't mind lots of copy/paste and, depending on your compiler, perhaps a few warnings about PBar::operator->() shadowing PFoo::operator->(). It is clearly not as elegant as the built-in pointer types or the Ptr template.

Pointer Arithmetic

Following is a sample of arithmetic operators needed to replicate pointer arithmetic for smart pointers. For a full, plug-compatible implementation, you would want to add ++ and -- as well.

```
template <class Type>
class Ptr {
private:
    Type* pointee;
public:
    Ptr() : pointee(NULL) {}
    Ptr(Type* p) : pointee(p) {}
    operator Type*() { return pointee; }
    Type* operator->() { return pointee; }

    ptr_diff operator-(Ptr<Type> p)
        { return pointee-p.pointee; }
    ptr_diff operator-(void* v)
        { return ((void*)pointee) - v; }
    Ptr<Type> operator-(long index)
        { return Ptr<Type>(pointee-index); }
    Ptr<Type> operator-=(long index)
        { pointee-=index; return *this; }
    Ptr<Type> operator+(long index)
        { return Ptr<Type>(pointee+index); }
    Ptr<Type> operator+=(long index)
        { pointee+=index; return *this; }
};
```

The difference between ptr_diff and an integer index is important. When you subtract one address from another, the result is an offset, presumably in bytes. When you add an integer to a pointer, the actual change in the address is the integer times the size of whatever the thing is that is being pointed to. Remember that in C++, as in C, a pointer points not just to a single object, but to a theoretical array of them. The indices in the overloads described earlier are indexes into this theoretical array, not byte counts.

Having said all this, I don't recommend going to all this trouble for smart pointers — not because I'm lazy, but because if you do so, you lock in a class of designs you may not always intend. As soon as you allow the user to add and subtract pointers, you are locked into supporting the idea that a pointer always indexes this hypothetical array. As you will see in coming chapters, many uses of smart pointers do not require or even work properly with this array paradigm.

How Much Does a Smart Pointer Cost?

For a class with no virtual member functions, each object is as large as is needed to fit all its data members. In the case of the smart pointers we have discussed so far, there is only one data member, a *-style pointer; that is, the smart pointer is exactly the same size as a built-in pointer. A good C++ compiler should provide special treatment for trivial inline member functions, including those in the smart pointer template.

```
template <class Type>
class Ptr {
private:
    Type* pointee;
public:
    Ptr() : pointee(NULL) {}
    Ptr(Type* p) : pointee(p) {}
    operator Type*() { return pointee; }
    Type* operator->() { return pointee; }
};
```

There should be no difference in computational cost, for example, between using operator-> from this template and using a built-in pointer with operator->. Notice all the qualifications here, all the uses of words like *good* and *should*. Assuming a good implementation, there is, therefore, no performance overhead for the smart pointers we have discussed so far. At the least, we have done no harm so far.

Applications

Smart pointers are amazingly useful little creatures, and we will spend quite some time putting them to use. For the simple smart pointers discussed in this chapter, there are some equally simple but powerful applications.

Dereferencing Nil

Here is a variation on the smart pointer theme:

```
template <class Type>
class SPN {
private:
    Type* pointee;
public:
    SPN() : pointee(NULL) {}
    SPN(Type* p) : pointee(p) {}
    operator Type*() { return pointee; }
    Type* operator->()
        {
            if (pointee == NULL) {
                cerr << "Dereferencing NULL!" << endl;
                pointee = new Type;
                }
            return pointee;
        }
};
```

If an attempt is made to use operator-> at a time when pointee is NULL, an error message pops up on stderr, then a dummy object is created and pointed to by the smart pointer to allow the program to limp along.

There are as many variations on this theme as there are programmers silly enough to dereference nil. Here are a few of them.

Using #ifdef. If the computational cost of this logic has you seeing red, it is a simple matter to surround the if block with #ifdefs to compile in the error-trapping code only for debugging releases of the software. When you compile for production use, the over-loaded operator-> collapses back to performance equivalent to a built-in pointer.

Throwing Exceptions. Rather than spitting out error messages, which can be problematic in some graphical programs, you could instead throw an exception.

```
template <class Type>
class Ptr {
private:
    Type* pointee;
public:
    enum ErrorType {DereferenceNil};

    Ptr() : pointee(NULL) {}
    Ptr(Type* p) : pointee(p) {}
    operator Type*() { return pointee; }
    Type* operator->() throw(ErrorType)
        {
            if (pointee == NULL) throw DereferenceNil;
            return pointee;
        }
};
```

(In practice, ErrorType would have been a global type used for lots of different kinds of errors; the code fragment above is a generic treatment.) This can be combined with other variations. For example, you might want the program to use a dummy object in debug mode but throw an exception in a released product.

Screamers. Another variation is to keep an object I call a *screamer* sitting in a static data member, waiting for someone to attempt to dereference nil.

```
template <class Type>
class AHHH {
private:
    Type* pointee;
    static Type* screamer;
public:
    AHHH() : pointee(NULL) {}
    AHHH(Type* p) : pointee(p) {}
    operator Type*() { return pointee; }
    Type* operator->()
        {
            if (pointee == NULL) return screamer;
            return pointee;
        }
};
```

What's the big deal, you may ask? Suppose screamer isn't really of type Type*, but is instead from a derived class all of whose (presumably virtual) member functions spit out error messages to cerr before calling their base class counterparts. Now you can not only keep the program limping along, but also keep separate track of when an attempt is made to access member functions of the dummy object.

Debugging and Tracing

Another way to use smart pointers is to watch the use of the pointee very carefully. Because all accesses must go through operator Type*() or operator->(), you have two convenient bottlenecks in which to watch the proceedings as the program runs. The debugging applications are endless, but here is a sample.

Setting Breakpoints. The simplest way to take advantage of the bottlenecks is to make these functions out-of-line when they are in debugging mode, then set breakpoints on their implementation.

```
template <class Type>
class PTracer {
private:
    Type* pointee;
public:
    PTracer() : pointee(NULL) {}
    PTracer(Type* p) : pointee(p) {}
    operator Type*();
    Type* operator->();
};
template <class Type>
#ifndef DEBUGGING
inline
#endif
PTracer<Type>::operator Type*()
{
    return pointee; // Set breakpoint here
}
template <class Type>
#ifndef DEBUGGING
inline
#endif
Type* PTracer<Type>::operator->()
{
    return pointee; // Set breakpoint here
}
```

This is sometimes easier to do with the nonparameterized versions of the pointers, since not all development environments support setting breakpoints on lines of parameterized functions.

Tracing. It is a simple matter to have the conversion operator and operator-> spit out diagnostic information to cout or cerr as appropriate.

Class Statistics. It is also a simple matter to store statistics about the use of operator Type*() and operator->() in static data members of the parameterized class.

```
template <class Type>
class SPCS {
private:
    Type* pointee;
    static int conversions;
    static int members;
public:
    SPCS() : pointee(NULL) {}
    SPCS(Type* p) : pointee(p) {}
    operator Type*()
        {   conversions++; return pointee; }
    Type* operator->()
        {   members++; return pointee; }
    int Conversions() { return conversions; }
    int Members() { return members; }
};
```

This requires that the global variables be defined somewhere. Typically, this would be in Foo.cpp.

```
// In Foo.cpp
int Ptr<Foo>::conversions=0;
int Ptr<Foo>::members=0;
```

Of course, you can #ifdef these to only apply to debug releases.

Object Statistics. This is a little dicier and perhaps should wait until we have a chance to discuss master pointers, but it is also possible to use a smart pointer to keep individual statistics by object, rather than by class. It will not do to simply make the data members just shown nonstatic — that is, one per pointer — because we have no way (yet) of assuring that there is a one-to-one correspondence between pointers and objects. Instead, the statistics must be stored in the objects themselves. Here is a useful mixin class from which you can multiply inherit from the pointee class, along with a smart pointer class that knows about its properties. By declaring the pointer to be a friend, you give it access to the protected members derived from Counter.

```
class Counter {
protected:
```

```
    Counter() : conversions(0), members(0) {}
    Counter(const Counter&)
        : conversions(0), members(0) {}
    Counter& operator=(const Counter&) { return *this; }
public:
    int conversions;
    int members;
    int Conversions() { return conversions; }
    int Members() { return members; }
};
template <class Type>
class SPOS {
private:
    Type* pointee;
public:
    SPOS() : pointee(NULL) {}
    SPOS(Type* f) : pointee(f) {}
    operator Type*()
        {   pointee->conversions++; return pointee; }
    Type* operator->()
        {   pointee->members++; return pointee; }
};
```

There are variations on this theme, some of which will surface when we talk about master pointers.

Caching

A hint of things to come occurs when you no longer even insist that the pointee be physically in memory at all times, just when it needs to be accessed. In the following sample, presumably ReadObject() knows how to use the on-disk address information to instantiate the object and point to it from pointee. When either operator is accessed, if the object isn't already in memory it is read in automatically.

```
typedef unsigned long DiskAddress; // Change this to
            whatever applies
template <class Type>
class CP {
```

```
private:
    DiskAddress record_number;
    Type* pointee;
    void ReadObject(); // Reads object from disk
public:
    CP(DiskAddress da) : pointee(NULL),
    record_number(da) {}
    CP(Type* f) : pointee(f),
record_number(f->RecordNumber()) {}
    operator Type*()
        {   if (pointee == NULL) this->ReadObject();
            return pointee;
        }
    Type* operator->()
        {   if (pointee == NULL) this->ReadObject();
            return pointee;
        }
};
```

It is probably a little ahead of the game to discuss caching this early because there are a lot of issues to deal with that we aren't ready for yet. If you want to make sure that only one copy of the object is read in regardless of how many objects point to it, or if you want to trash the object as soon as possible after these operators are through, you'll have to wait until later chapters on master pointers and still later on memory management. However, in simple read-only cases in which you can live with multiple copies of an object, this technique works fine with simple smart pointers.

A common trick with these caching pointers is to steal a few bits by combining the disk address and memory address into a single data member. These are the two simplifying assumptions needed:

1. The disk address is no larger than one bit less than a memory address.

2. The memory management facilities used by operator new never return an odd address.

If both of these are true, you can use the same data member to store both addresses. When the low-order bit is set — that is, the "address" is odd — the other 31 bits are the disk address. When the low-order bit is clear, the entire 32 bits are the memory address. If you need to write the object back out as well as reading it in, the object had better know its own on-disk address, because the one stored in the pointer got trashed when the reading occurred.

Behind the smoke and mirrors of this caching pointer lies an interesting concept: smart pointers can become a general means to access objects, *regardless of whether or where the objects actually live.* As we move deeper into the jungles of C++, we'll turn this concept over and over in our hands until it starts to gel into one of those Zen concepts I talked about in the opening chapter.

CHAPTER 6

Master Pointers and Handles

It doesn't take much mucking about with smart pointers before one runs across some fundamental problems. Many of them revolve around the fact that there may be any number of smart pointers pointing to a single object. If that might be the case, how do you know when to delete the object? Who keeps track of statistics about the object and access to it (assuming you want to do such things)? Who creates the object? What does it mean to assign one smart pointer to another? Are the Cleveland Indians for real this season, or will they just break our hearts once again? For the answers to these and other daunting questions, read on.

Master Pointer Semantics

A special case of smart pointers occurs when no two smart pointers are allowed to point to the same object at once. Except for the special case of a smart pointer pointing to nil, the pointers and the pointees are in one-to-one correspondence. When this design constraint exists, the pointers are said to implement *master pointer* semantics.

You could simply announce in an ad in the local newspaper that the pointers should be used in that way and that way only, or you could choose to protect your users from themselves automatically by enforcing the rules of master pointer semantics using language features of C++. If you wisely choose the latter course, here is what you have to do:

1. The pointees should be created by the pointers in their constructors.
2. The destructor of the pointer should delete the pointee.
3. The copy constructor should make a carbon copy of the pointee.
4. The assignment operator, operator=, should delete the current pointee of the left-hand side and replace it with a copy of the pointee of the right-hand side.

In addition, there are two more things it is *wise* to do:

5. Take away the keys to the constructors of the pointee class.
6. Use *factory functions* to create the pointees.

Each of these will be explained fully in the sections that follow. The prototypical master pointer we are going to flesh out looks like this.

```
template <class Type>
class MP {
private:
    Type* t;
public:
    MP(); // Creates a pointee to point to
    MP(const MP<Type>&); // Copies the pointee
    ~MP(); // Deletes the pointee
    MP<Type>& operator=(const MP<Type>&);
            // Deletes lhs, copies rhs
    Type* operator->() const;
};
```

Construction

Suppose you allow users to create their own pointee objects, then hand them in to the master pointers during construction.

```
template <class Type>
class MP {
private:
    Type* t;
public:
    MP() : t(NULL) {}
    MP(Type* pointee) : t(pointee) {}
    ~MP() { delete t; }
    // etc.
};
Foo* foo = new Foo;
MP<Foo> mp1(foo);
MP<Foo> mp2(foo); // Oops!
```

Wouldn't life be much simpler if we didn't have to deal with users like these? When mp1 gets deleted, foo goes bye-bye. That leaves mp2 pointing off into space. Why would anyone want to do something like this? As they say in the beer commercial, "Why ask why?" The fact is that if you leave an opening like this, someone, somewhere will hatch a diabolical plot to exploit it and blame the resulting problems on your code.

A user like this is crying out, "Stop me before I kill," and there is an airtight way to do that: take away the keys to the constructors of the pointee class.

```
class Foo {
friend class MP<Foo>;
protected:
    Foo(); // Only MP<Foo> can get at this now
public:
    // The rest of the interface
};
template <class Type>
class MP {
```

```
private:
    Type* t;
public:
    MP() : t(new Type) {}
    // etc.
};
```

Ah, much better. When the pointer is created, its constructor builds the pointee as well. By declaring the pointer to be a friend, we can make the constructor(s) of Foo private or protected, yet still get at them from the pointer's constructors. Now, there is no way for clients to get at the Foos without going through MP<Foo>s. We'll come back to this issue of how, when, and where to create pointees several times as the book wears on, but for now let's leave it at this treatment.

If the constructors of Foo require arguments, there are two alternatives:

1. Create a custom master pointer class MPFoo for Foo, rather than using the generic master pointer template. For each constructor of Foo, add a constructor of MPFoo with exactly the same signature, and pass its arguments along to the constructor of Foo.

2. Use a no-argument constructor to create the object; then provide a separate initialization function that a client can call after construction.

This is the second approach.

```
class Foo {
friend class MP<Foo>;
protected:
    Foo(); // The one and only constructor
public:
    Initialize(int, char*);
    // The rest of the interface
};
MP<Foo> mpf;
mpf->Initialize(17, "Hello"); // Finish construction
```

This is a little clumsy, but it allows the use of a generic master pointer template. There are other reasons to use initialization functions, discussed in later chapters. Either approach is perfectly acceptable for our immediate purposes.

Destruction

This is too easy: In the destructor of the master pointer, delete the pointee.

```
template <class Type>
class MP {
private:
    Type* t;
public:
    ~MP() { delete t; }
};
```

Copying

Oops! There go those darned users again.

```
MP<Foo> mpf1; // Creates a Foo to point to
MP<Foo> mpf2 = mpf1; // Oops!
```

Don't be fooled by the equal sign; this is construction, and it is the same as MP<Foo> mpf2(mpf1). If we don't overload the copy constructor and allow the C++ compiler to throw in its two bits instead, this results in two master pointers that point to the same Foo. By default, the compiler-supplied copy constructor will merrily copy the address in the data member t from the old pointer to the new one. Fixing this is relatively easy.

```
template <class Type>
class MP {
private:
    Type* t;
public:
    MP(); // The normal constructor
```

```
MP(const MP<Type>& mp) // The copy constructor
    : t(*(mp.t)) {}
};
```

The copy constructor here is making a duplicate of the pointee by using the pointee's copy constructor. Lazy, but it works. In some situations that we'll stumble over later, it is better just to not allow copying. A simple way to do that is to make the copy constructor private and have it do nothing.

```
template <class Type>
class MP {
private:
    Type* t;
    MP(const MP<Type>&) // Will never be called
        : t(NULL) {}
public:
    MP(); // The normal constructor
};
```

This will prevent inadvertent copying in situations like this.

```
void f(MP<Foo>);
MP<Foo> mpf;
f(mpf); // Results in a temporary copy
```

An alternative to taking away the keys to copying is to use handles, as described later in this chapter.

Assignment

Aaaah! Don't those users ever rest?!

```
MP<Foo> mpf1;
MP<Foo> mpf2;
mpf2 = mpf1; // Groan
```

There are two problems here. First, the pointee created by the constructor of mpf2 is never deleted. It becomes a Flying Dutchman, doomed to sail forever through the ocean of RAM. Second, the default operator= used by the compiler copies the address contained in t from one pointer to another, resulting in two master pointers pointing to the same pointee. The correct code overloads operator= to delete whatever the left-hand side currently points to and replaces it with a copy of whatever the right-hand side points to.

```
template <class Type>
class MP {
private:
    Type* t;
public:
    MP(); // The normal constructor
    MP<Type>& operator=(const MP<Type>& mp)
        {   if (&mp != this) {
                delete t;
                t = new Type(*(mp.t));
                }
            return *this;
        }
};
```

Of course, if you don't want to support assignment at all, you can simply make operator= private, and that's that.

The Prototypical Master Pointer Template

Here is the end result, with inlines moved to their accustomed position following the class declaration. These are the requirements of the parameter, the pointee class:

1. It must have a no-argument constructor.
2. Either it must overload the copy constructor, or the compiler-supplied default copy constructor must be appropriate for use by the master pointer template.

If either of these is not the case, modifications will have to be made to the pointee, the master pointer, or both. Remember: The copy constructor of the pointee — that is, the parameter to the template — will be used to implement both the copy constructor and assignment operator of the master pointer.

```
// Master pointer template
template <class Type>
class MP {
private:
    Type* t;
public:
    MP(); // Creates a pointee to point to
    MP(const MP<Type>&); // Copies the pointee
    ~MP(); // Deletes the pointee
    MP<Type>& operator=(const MP<Type>&);
    Type* operator->() const;
};
template <class Type>
inline MP<Type>::MP() : t(new Type)
{}
template <class Type>
inline MP<Type>::MP(const MP<Type>& mp)
    : t(new Type((*mp.t)))
{}
template <class Type>
inline MP<Type>::~MP()
{
    delete t;
}
template <class Type>
inline
MP<Type>& MP<Type>::operator=(const MP<Type>& mp)
{
    if (this != &mp) {
        delete t;
        t = new Type(*(mp.t));
        }
    return *this;
}
template <class Type>
inline Type* MP<Type>::operator->() const
{
    return t;
}
```

C++ Handles

Now that we've turned up the heat on smart pointers by turning them into master pointers, let's add one more ingredient to the stew: the C++ handle. Don't confuse this with the term *handle* as used in the Macintosh or Windows operating systems. There are analogies to those terms, but the C++ handle idiom carries its own unique set of semantics and rules.

The basic idea is to use smart pointers to point to the master pointers. The pointers-once-removed are the handles. Here is a first attempt that we build on later.

```
template <class Type>
class H {
private:
    MP<Type>& ptr; // A reference to the master pointer
public:
    H() : ptr(*(new MP<Type>)) {} // See below
    H(MP<Type>& mp) : ptr(mp) {}
    MP<Type>& operator->() const { return ptr; }
};
```

The no-argument constructor of H creates a new master pointer to point to. The master pointer, in turn, creates an object to point to. There is a second constructor taking a master pointer and initializing ptr to it. The default copy constructor and operator= are acceptable, since multiple handles are allowed to any given master pointer. operator-> relies on the recursive algorithm used by the compiler: The handle's operator-> returns a master pointer; then the master pointer's operator-> returns a Type*, which is one of the compiler's basic types.

I said that this is rough because the nested templates are messy and the question of when and how to delete the master pointer looms large. Also, should a user be allowed to directly create and destroy master pointers, or must they be encased inside handles in the same way we encased pointees inside master pointers? Have we gone to all the trouble of solving these problems for pointees, only to shift them over to master pointers? Patience; these questions and more will all be dealt with in good time.

What Good Is It?

Let's start with a simple application of master pointers, then build up to uses that will please the more sophisticated palate. Applications of handles are harder to come by at this stage but will become very important in later chapters.

Counting the Objects

Suppose you want to keep track of how many objects of a given class have been created, or how many are currently in memory. One solution is to put the information into static data members of the class itself.

```
class CountedStuff {
private:
    static int current;
public:
    CountedStuff() { current++; }
    CountedStuff(const CountedStuff&) { current++; }
    CountedStuff& operator=(const CountedStuff&)
        { } // Don't change the count due to assignment
    ~CountedStuff() { current--; }
};
```

You can play around with this a little to improve it, but no matter how much you twist and squirm, you'll end up having to change the code in the target class itself, if only by having it inherit from this class. Now suppose the pointee is an off-the-shelf class that you don't want to change. Bummer. You don't want to — in fact, probably cannot — make any change. Enter the counting master pointer class.

```
template <class Type>
class CMP {
```

```
private:
    static int current;
    Type* ptr;
public:
    CMP() : ptr(new Type) { current++; }
    CMP(const CMP<Type>& cmp) : ptr(new Type(*(cmp.ptr)))
        { current++; }
    CMP<Type>& operator=(const CMP<Type>& cmp)
        {   if (this != &cmp) {
                delete ptr;
                ptr = new Type(*(cmp.ptr));
                }
            return *this;
        }
    ~CMP() { delete ptr; current--; }
    Type* operator->() const { return ptr; }
    static int Current() { return current; }
};
```

Now the master pointer does all the counting for you. This can be used without modifying the pointee class. For that matter, this one template can be used with *any* class, as long as you can arrange to slip the master pointers between clients and the pointees. Even if you didn't care about modifying the original pointee class, this level of modularity would be extremely difficult to achieve without master pointers. (For example, if you tried to make this a base class, you would end up with one static data member current shared by all derived classes.)

This is a trivial example, but even so it illustrates an important principle of C++ design that will grow with time: Using smart pointers pays, even if you're not quite sure why at the beginning. If your program had been written in terms of smart pointers, this change would be transparent and quick to make. If you have to go back and change all those *'s to smart pointers in midstream, prepare to burn some midnight oil.

In Chapter 14, we will use a minor variation on this counting theme to easily implement a simple yet powerful memory management strategy: reference-counted garbage collection.

Read-Only Pointers

Suppose you want to make sure that a given object is never updated, at least not by the common rabble of clients. This is easy to guarantee with master pointers: Make operator-> a const member function.

```
template <class Type>
class ROMP {
private:
    Type* t;
public:
    ROMP(); // Creates a pointee to point to
    ROMP(const ROMP<Type>&); // Copies the pointee
    ~ROMP(); // Deletes the pointee
    ROMP<Type>& operator=(const ROMP<Type>&);
    const Type* operator->() const;
};
```

Now you have locked up the pointee so tight the CIA couldn't get through. This can also be done with simpler smart pointers, but master pointers make it airtight, because the client never gets direct access to the pointee.

Read-Write Pointers

Yet another variation on the same theme is what I call the "read-write" pointer. In many applications, there is an optimal way to represent an object as long as it is accessed in a read-only manner. When a client wants to access it for update, the form of the object must be changed.

It would be easy to do this if one could have two overloads of operator->, one returning a Foo* and the other returning a const Foo*. Unfortunately, different return types do not make the signatures unique, so if you try to declare two operator->'s the compiler will laugh long and hard. This throws the burden back on the programmer to call a member function ahead of time that performs the switch from a read-only to a read-write version of the pointee.

One application of this is in distributed objects. It is easy to throw copies of an object all over the place in a network, as long as they won't be updated by the local client. It is another matter to coordinate updates across multiple surrogates. We might impose the rule that any number of read-only copies are allowed but only one master; in order to update the object, one must first obtain the master from whoever currently owns it. There are obviously a lot of details to attend to, such as how a master copy gets relinquished, but the basic idea is amazingly simple to implement and is completely transparent to clients if master pointers are used properly.

CHAPTER 7

Facets and Other Smarter Pointers

If this chapter were put to music it would be called "Variations on a Theme of Smart Pointers." In the last two chapters, I introduced the basic concept of a smart pointer, a class that is designed to take the place of *-style built-in pointers, and the master pointer, a pointer that is in one-to-one correspondence with the pointee. This chapter continues that theme and introduces several more harmonic voices.

Interface Pointers

You may have thought that the interface to a class is fully spelled out in its class declaration, but in fact any given class may have a number of different interfaces, depending on the client:

- A class and its friends see one interface, including all members of the class and all protected and public members of its base classes.

- Derived classes see only the protected and public members of the class and its base classes.

- All other clients see only the public members of the class and its base classes.

- If you cast a pointer to the object to be a pointer to one of its base classes, the interface is limited further to public members of the base class.

Public, private, and protected members; public and private derivation; polymorphism; and friendship are all really just crude, syntactic approximations to a more general design idea: One object can have lots of specialized interfaces.

Replicating the Interface

Let's see if we can generalize this concept using "smarter" pointers. To do so, we must start by dropping our old friend operator-> for a while. One of the limitations of operator-> is that, in order for a client to use the pointer, it must also know all about the interface to the pointee.

```
class Foo {
// Interface stuff you'd just as soon be hidden
};
Ptr<Foo> pf(new Foo);
```

Hmm. In order to allow a client to use the pointer, you have to reveal everything there is to know about the pointee, Foo. Here is an alternative approach. Be patient; it isn't quite as outrageous as it seems at first glance.

```
class Foo {
friend class PFoo;
protected:
    Foo();
public:
    void DoSomething();
    void DoSomethingElse();
};
class PFoo {
private:
    Foo* foo;
```

```
public:
    PFoo() : foo(new Foo) {}
    PFoo(const PFoo& pf) : foo(new Foo(*(pf.foo))) {}
    ~PFoo() { delete foo; }
    PFoo& operator=(const PFoo& pf)
        {   if (this != &pf) {
                delete foo;
                foo = new Foo(*(pf.foo));
                }
            return *this;
        }
    void DoSomething() { foo->DoSomething(); }
    void DoSomethingElse() { foo->DoSomethingElse(); }
};
```

What we have done is to exercise those nifty copy/paste features of your development environment, duplicating the interface of the pointee in the pointer. Instead of lazily using operator-> to do all the hard work of delegation, we boldly reimplement each member function so that each delegates directly to some counterpart in the pointee. Pointers that reimplement the interface of the pointee are called *interface pointers*.

Hiding the Pointee

It may seem at first glance that we really haven't solved anything. In order for these inlines to work, the interface of Foo still has to be in the .h file ahead of the class declaration of PFoo. However, if we are now willing to pay a small computational cost for our pointers, we reap an immediate and sizable benefit.

```
class Foo1; // All that the client sees or knows of Foo
class PFoo1 {
private:
    Foo1* foo;
public:
    PFoo1();
    PFoo1(const PFoo1& pf);
    ~PFoo1();
```

```
    PFoo1& operator=(const PFoo1& pf);
    void DoSomething();
    void DoSomethingElse();

};
class Foo1 {
friend class PFoo1;
protected:
    Foo1();
public:
    void DoSomething();
    void DoSomethingElse();
};
PFoo1::PFoo1() : foo(new Foo1)
{}
PFoo1::PFoo1(const PFoo1& pf) : foo(new Foo1(*(pf.foo)))
{}
PFoo1::~PFoo1()
{
    delete foo;
}
PFoo1& PFoo1::operator=(const PFoo1& pf)
{
    if (this != &pf) {
        delete foo;
        foo = new Foo1(*(pf.foo));
        }
    return *this;
}
void PFoo1::DoSomething()
{
    foo->DoSomething();
}
void PFoo1::DoSomethingElse()
{
    foo->DoSomethingElse();
}
Foo1::Foo1()
{
}
```

```
void Foo1::DoSomething()
{
    cout << "Foo::DoSomething()" << endl;
}
void Foo1::DoSomethingElse()
{
    cout << "Foo::DoSomethingElse()" << endl;
}
```

See what has happened here? Foo no longer exists as far as clients are concerned. For all practical purposes, the pointer has *become the object*. In fact, we might well want to rename things at this point, dropping the P in front of the pointer and changing the name of Foo to something suitably private and mysterious. The only hint that a second class exists is the forward declaration class Foo;.

The cost of this is the noninline function call in each of the pointer's member functions. In a small number of applications and for a small subset of classes, even this small cost will be unacceptable. In those cases, there are two alternatives to boost speed: use operator->-based smart pointers, or use interface pointers but put the class declaration of the pointee into the .h file, bypassing the benefits of encapsulation. As you will see in the remainder of this chapter, this latter alternative may still have some benefits.

Changing the Interface

One of the benefits of interface pointers is that they allow you in effect to change the interface of the pointee without having to modify the pointee class. The interface presented by the interface pointer is completely under your control; you can omit some member functions of the pointee, change their signatures, add additional member functions of your own, and generally have a jolly good time reinventing the pointee.

Facets

Many class libraries, particularly those dealing with graphical user interfaces, contain massive classes of dozens to over a hundred member functions. A visual portion of screen real estate is variously called a *view,* a *window,* or a *pane.* The following might be a typical outline of a class representing such a drawable whatever-you-call-it.

```
class View { // In practice will derive from something
protected:
    // Stuff intended for derived view classes only
public:
    // Construction and initialization stuff
    // Destruction and deactivation stuff
    // General "I'm an object" stuff
    // Event handling stuff
    // Drawing stuff
    // Geometry, such as "what did the mouse hit?"
    // View hierarchy management
};
```

Each of these subsections might contain from a few to a dozen member functions. Understanding these classes can be like stepping into a house of mirrors: Everywhere you turn you see a different reflection of the same class. One could argue that this could have been better factored if each set of interfaces had been set up in its own base class and had been brought together through the miracle of modern multiple inheritance, or if complexes of objects that work together by delegating to each other had been built. There are problems with each of these suggestions:

- Do you really want your users to have to remember to bring all these pieces together for each concrete class?

- Alternatively, if you bring them together into a generic class from which users then derive, you have re-created the problem at some level of the class hierarchy, no matter how clean it was at some higher level.

- It can be a daunting design problem to make one base class work properly with another when the two aren't combined until some concrete class brings them together.
- Designing large complexes of interoperating objects is also not for the faint of heart.

Is there a way to factor such a class without resorting to complicated derivation or delegation? Using smarter pointer technology, the answer is "Of course." Just create multiple pointers to the same object, each of which deals with some aspect of the overall object.

```
class ViewEvents {
private:
    View* view;
public:
    // Member functions having to do with event handling
};
class ViewDrawing {
private:
    View* view;
public:
    // Member functions having to do with drawing
};
// etc.
```

Each of these smarter pointers replicates the interface to a subset of the member functions of the View class, delegating to the counterpart member function of the view object itself. The object itself can be composed in any way you like — single or multiple inheritance, delegation among complexes of objects, or one gigantic blob — and clients need not be concerned about the choice. I call these interface pointers, which limit a client to a subset of the full interface, *facets*.

This basic idea has taken root in at least one commercial technology, the Component Object Model used by Microsoft, which calls these pointers *interfaces*. A small Smalltalk vendor, Quasar Knowledge Systems, has proposed this same idea for Smalltalk objects, and calls them *suites*. Whatever they are called, the idea is bound to become one of the most important design idioms of object-oriented programming in the future, because it is more flexible and modular than simply relying on derivation and delegation to factor programs.

Although the concept is simple, there are lots of details to attend to in order to get it right. It is well worth spending the time to go through them one by one.

Converting a Pointee to a Facet

Given a pointee, you will want to be able to get facets. There are many ways to do this, but the most straightforward C++ style is to use conversion operators.

```
class View {
public:
    operator ViewEvents()
        { return new ViewEvents(this); }
    operator ViewDrawing()
        { return new ViewDrawing(this); }
};
```

An alternative is to allow the user to use the constructors of the facet classes directly.

```
ViewEvents ve(aView);
```

One could make a case for either treatment, but I tend to prefer the former for reasons that will be discussed in a moment. One additional treatment that deserves mention is to assign each facet type a unique identifier, then provide a single, general-purpose facet-generating member function of all classes that accepts a facet type identifier as an argument and returns a facet if it is supported by the object or NULL if it isn't. Those of you who use Microsoft's Component Object Model and OLE recognize this as the QueryInterface facility supported by all objects.

Gemstones

If you instead have one facet and want to obtain another for the same object, the most straightforward approach is to put the conversion operators into the facets as well. Here is a simplistic approach.

```
class ViewEvents {
private:
    View* view;
public:
    operator ViewDrawing()
        { return ViewDrawing(*view); }
    // etc. for the other facets
};
```

This is a little C++-ism that delegates the work to the target view's operator ViewDrawing(). If the number of facets is small, this is a practical solution. As the number of facets grows, the number of conversion operators grows with the square of the number of facets, because each one has to be able to convert to every other one. A modification is in order then to reduce it back to an order n problem, where n is the number of facets. Continuing with an admittedly weak metaphor, I call an object that collects and displays facets a *gemstone*.

```
class View;
class ViewEvents;
class ViewDrawing;
class ViewGemstone {
private:
    View* view;
public:
    ViewGemstone(View* v) : vicw(v) {}
    bool operator!() { return view == NULL; }
    operator ViewEvents();
    operator ViewDrawing();
    // etc.
};
class ViewEvents {
friend class ViewGemstone;
```

```
private:
    View* view;
    ViewEvents(View* v) : view(v) {}
public:
    bool operator!() { return view == NULL; }
    operator ViewGemstone();
};
class ViewDrawing {
friend class ViewGemstone;
private:
    View* view;
    ViewDrawing(View* v) : view(v) {}
public:
    bool operator!() { return view == NULL; }
    operator ViewGemstone();
};
```

In sum, there is one object, the gemstone, that knows how to generate all the facets; each facet, in turn, knows how to find a gemstone. That gemstone is the only object that can create facets, due to their private constructors and friendship with the gemstone. The gemstone concept is flexible — the gemstone may be the entire, original object, an abstract base class of the object, or it may itself be a facet.

It seems at first glance that this is needlessly clumsy for the user, who must do two successive typecasts. One could argue that ViewGemstone should be a base class for all the others. This could be done, but takes away some of the important benefits we will talk about soon. The above model is completely flat; that is, there is no derivation among the facets. This yields a tremendous amount of freedom to the implementer to use derivation, delegation, and aggregation (embedded data members) to support these interfaces. The cost of the extra typecast is well worth those benefits.

Variations on a Theme of Facets

You can use several techniques to implement facets. Together they form a superset of what C++ supports through derivation and data members.

Subsets of Members as Facets. The simplest form of facet is one that provides an interface to a subset of the members of the pointee.

```
// In Pointee.h
class Pointee;
class Facet {
friend class PointeeGemstone;
private:
    Pointee* pointee;
    Facet(Pointee* p) : pointee(p) {}
public:
    void Fn1();
    int Fn2();
    void Fn17();
};
class PointeeGemstone {
private:
    Pointee* pointee;
public:
    PointeeGemstone(Pointee* p) : pointee(p) {}
    operator Facet();
};
// In Pointee.cpp
class Pointee {
public:
    void Fn1();
    int Fn2();
    void Fn3();
    char* Fn4();
    // etc.
    void Fn17();
};
```

Here the facet simply lops off all the member functions it doesn't care about. To the client of the facet, the "object" it is dealing with is of much lighter weight than the full pointee, but behind the scenes the full object is still there.

Data Members as Facets. A facet may be an interface pointer to a data member. This may allow reuse of a facet in different gemstones or to interface to a stand-alone instance. If the pointee has a data member of class Bar, one facet may be a simple interface pointer to Bar.

```
// In Pointee.h
class BarFacet {
private:
    Bar* bar;
public:
    BarFacet(Bar* b) : bar(b) {}
    // Interfaces to member functions of Bar
};
class PointeeGemstone {
private:
    Pointee* p;
public:
    operator BarFacet();
    // etc.
};
// In Pointee.cpp
class Pointee {
friend class PointeeGemstone;
private:
    Bar bar; // An embedded data member of Pointee
public:
    // etc.
};
PointeeGemstone::operator BarFacet()
{
    return BarFacet(&p->bar); // Facet of data member
}
```

This works fine if C++'s relatively shallow consistency rules are sufficient. In the more general case you will probably want to do better using some of the techniques described later under "Enforcing Consistency." One problem with this simplistic treatment, for example, is that you can "cast" from a gemstone to BarFacet, but cannot then cast back given the information available in the facet.

Base Classes as Facets. In the same way, you can use facets to provide the equivalent to a built-in cast from a derived class to its base class.

```
// In Pointee.h
class FooFacet {
private:
    Foo* foo;
public:
    FooFacet(Foo* f) : foo(f) {}
    // Interfaces to member functions of Foo
};
class PointeeGemstone {
private:
    Pointee* p;
public:
    operator FooFacet();
    // etc.
};
// In Pointee.cpp
class Pointee : public Foo {
friend class PointeeGemstone;
public:
    // etc.
};
PointeeGemstone::operator FooFacet()
{
    return FooFacet(p); // Compiler casts p to Foo*
}
```

As with data member facets, this may allow you to reuse the same facets for Foos as base classes, as data members, or as stand-alone objects, although once again more specialization is needed to enforce the more rigorous consistency rules discussed later. For example, in this treatment you can cast from the gemstone to Foo-Facet, but cannot then cast back to the gemstone.

Delegates as Facets. The first three alternatives — subsets of interfaces, data members as facets, and base classes as facets — all involved glomming several objects into one. Another alternative is to use a network of cooperative objects and have one facet for each object in the network. This is very similar to the data-member-as-facet approach, except that the address pointed to by the facet is not physically embedded as a data member in the pointee.

```cpp
// In Pointee.h
class BarFacet {
private:
    Bar* bar;
public:
    BarFacet(Bar* b) : bar(b) {}
    // Interfaces to member functions of Bar
};
class PointeeGemstone {
private:
    Pointee* p;
public:
    operator BarFacet();
    // etc.
};
// In Pointee.cpp
class Pointee {
friend class PointeeGemstone;
private:
    Bar* bar; // No longer an embedded data member
public:
    // etc.
};
PointeeGemstone::operator BarFacet()
{
    return BarFacet(p->bar);
}
```

This suffers from the same consistency problems as the data-member-as-facet style.

Combinations and Variations. If you are in a particularly creative mood, you can also create facets that use combinations of these four techniques. A single facet could, for example, include a subset of the interface of the pointee, an interface function that delegates to a data member, another that delegates to a base class, and yet another that delegates to a delegate of the pointee. On Capitol Hill, this has been introduced as the Full Employment For C++ Idiomites Act of 1995.

Encapsulating the Pointee

If the underlying View object is at the hub of all this activity, how can we keep it out of the public eye? After all, that was supposed to be one of the benefits of using interface pointers, wasn't it? Look again at the view gemstone. If that strategy is used, does the user really need to ever see the pointee? All that is really needed is to create gemstones that can in turn be used to obtain the needed facets. If this is done, the facets and gemstone can be placed in the .h file and the pointee hidden in a .cpp file.

This works particularly well when you add in some of the other idioms discussed elsewhere. Malleable types allow pointee objects to be swapped at run time. Homomorphic class hierarchies allow one set of facets to serve as the interface to family trees of derived or recomposed pointee classes. Master pointers can be used to help enforce some of the consistency rules discussed later.

Validating Facets

Let's stretch this idiom a bit further by suggesting that an object may or may not support a desired facet. We will talk about why and how that might happen when we discuss malleable types later in this chapter, but for the moment let's answer this question: How does a client know whether or not a given object supports a given facet? One solution involves another C++-ism, overloading operator!

```
class ViewEvents {
private:
    View* view;
public:
    ViewEvents(View* v) : view(v) {}
    bool operator!() { return view == NULL; }
```

```
    // etc.
};
// In client code
ViewEvents ve(aViewGemstone);
if (!ve) {
    cerr << "View is not an event handler!" << endl;
    throw interface_error;
    }
```

aViewGemstone is presumably the sort of view gemstone we talked about earlier, including an operator ViewEvents(). The key line View-Events ve(aViewGemstone); works in two steps: first the view gemstone's operator ViewEvents() is invoked to do the conversion, then ViewEvents' copy constructor is used to construct ve. If the view gemstone decides that the view does not handle events, it can construct a ViewEvents instance with view equal to NULL. operator!() then tests to see whether or not the facet returned is valid. Member functions of the facet can also check to make sure the object is there before they attempt to delegate.

```
void ViewEvents::DoSomething()
{
    if (!*this) // that is, if(view == NULL)
        // bomb or throw an exception here
    view->DoSomething();
}
```

Enforcing Consistency

C++ is airtight in most ways and like a sieve in others. One of the loopholes in C++ is its inconsistent treatment of typecasting. You can take the address of a data member, but then given that address, you can't safely get back the enclosing object. The compiler is friendly enough to automatically cast from derived* to base*, but then won't cast backward to derived* again; you have to do a notoriously unsafe explicit cast yourself to get back to square 1. Most C++ programmers and designers just heave one of those big sighs normally reserved for arguments with spouses, then live with the inconsistencies. The facet idiom provides a golden opportunity to "fix" this aspect of C++. There are three properties that together provide the consistency C++ lacks. In the following, a=>b means that facets of type A have a conversion operator producing a facet of type B; a and b are the specific instances of types A and B, respectively. Although these rules are generic to C++ and facets, they are also part of the standard design discipline used with the Component Object Model from Microsoft:

1. *Symmetry.* If a=>b then b=>a. Implications: a data-member-as-facet must be able to reconstruct the enclosing object from which it came and a base class-as-facet must be able to "cast" back to the correct derived class safely.

2. *Transitivity.* If a=>b and a=>c and b=>c2, then c and c2 must be equivalent; that is, they must be facets of the same object providing identical functionality on that object. They need not be physically the same facet.

3. *Facet persistence.* As long as a facet exists, it functions properly. Put another way, if you delete the pointee, all facets to it should gracefully start returning false in response to operator! and should throw exceptions when member functions are called. Some would argue that this should be worded more strongly: The pointee cannot go away as long as any facet on it exists; that is the rule in the Component Object Model, for example.

It is easy to enforce the first two rules, though frequently there is some space and performance cost involved. If you stay up late thinking about the problem, especially gorged out on greasy pizza, you'll come up with ways to enforce these twin rules, but following are some suggestions. Facet persistence is another matter; we'll take up the subject here but defer solutions until later chapters.

Symmetry. The simplest way to proceed is to simply keep two data members in the facet: One is the address of the component object used by that facet, and the other is the address of the gemstone or the original pointee.

```
class BarFacet {
private:
```

```
    Bar* bar;
    PointeeGemstone* gemstone;
public:
    BarFacet(Bar* b, PointeeGemstone* agg)
        : bar(b), gemstone(agg) {}
    operator PointeeGemstone() { return *gemstone; }
    // Interfaces to member functions of Bar
};
```

This backpointer supports symmetry; given a gemstone we can get the facet, and given the facet we can get the gemstone. The biggest problem with this is that BarFacet isn't reusable when Bar is used as a component of different gemstones; there must be a different facet for each embedded use.

Transitivity. This is really a matter of design discipline. Transitivity is broken under circumstances like these.

```
class Foo {
private:
    Blob* blob;
    Bar* bar;
};
class Bar {
private:
    Blob* another_blob;
};
```

If you ask Foo for its Blob, it will give you the one pointed to by its own data member. If you ask Foo for its Bar, then ask the Bar for its Blob, you get a different object, the one pointed to by the Bar.

This is more common when you use multiple inheritance and derive from the same base class more than once, albeit indirectly. Reworking the previous fragment, it is easy to create the same problem using derivation.

```
class Blob {...};
class Foo : public Blob {...};
class Bar : public Foo, public Blob {...};
```

There is ambiguity built into this, since it isn't clear what you really mean when you typecast a Bar* to a Blob*; is that the immediate base class or the one from which Foo derived? Assuming you can resolve the ambiguity, you are still left with broken transitivity, a condition like unto the heartbreak of psoriasis.

How do you avoid these problems? I could go into all sorts of fancy explanations, but they all amount to the same thing: control yourself. Don't derive *publicly* from the same class more than once in a given class's ancestry (private derivation is generally OK since you can't typecast to a private base class). Don't embed instances of the same class in more than one component as a data member or, if you do, don't provide interfaces to more than one of them.

Facet Persistence. In pure C++, this arises when, for example, you take the address of a data member or base class, then delete the enclosing object. The pointer to the data member or base class is now garbage. Maintaining consistency in the face of this sort of conundrum is not a problem you solve over lunch one day. The stronger form — pointees must continue to exist as long as there are facets on them — will have to wait until the chapters on memory management. The weaker form is easy to solve using master pointers. If a facet accesses the object through a master pointer, the master pointer can be asked, "Do you currently point to a valid pointee?" If the answer is no, operator! returns true, and member functions start throwing exceptions all over the place. That leaves the problem of deciding how and when to delete the master pointers, a subject also best dealt with after discussing memory management strategies.

Facets and Master Pointers

The ideas of facets and gemstones mesh well with the idea of a master pointer. There are two basic approaches.

Stick a Master Pointer in the Middle. Insert a conventional master pointer, perhaps using operator->, between the pointee and the facets. The facets then become a form of handle, reaching the members of the pointee indirectly through the master pointer. The master pointer has the responsibility to generate at least a gemstone, which clients can then use to generate the other facets. If all access to the object is to come through facets, consider making operator-> in the master pointer private and the facets friends.

Turn a Gemstone into a Master Pointer. Designate a gemstone to act as the master pointer. The gemstone then both generates other facets and also maintains the master pointer semantics for construction and destruction. The facets obtain their access to the pointee *through the gemstone.* This can be facilitated by providing a private operator-> in the gemstone and making the facets friends of the gemstone. The facets in effect become handles, getting access to the pointee indirectly through the gemstone.

Malleable Types

The basic idea of a malleable type is a class whose instances can appear to change their type at run time. This being C++, that isn't literally what happens, of course — if that really happened you'd get really chummy with your debugger. However, through the miracle of modern pointer technology, you can accomplish much the same thing.

Polymorphic Pointees

In the basic master pointer, there is a data member whose type is Pointee*. Who's to say that the object it points to has to be a real Pointee, as opposed to some class derived from Pointee?

```
// In Foo.h
class Foo {
protected:
    Foo();
public:
```

```
    // Members of Foo
};
class PFoo { // A master pointer
private:
    Foo* foo;
public:
    PFoo();
    Foo* operator->() const { return foo; }
    // and all the usual cabal of master pointer stuff
};
// In Foo.cpp
class DerivedFromFoo : public Foo {
private:
    // Stuff private to this derived class
public:
    DerivedFromFoo(); // Public, but hidden in .cpp file
    // Overrides of Foo's member functions
};
PFoo::PFoo() : foo(new DerivedFromFoo)
{
}
```

A little sleight of hand and presto, chango, the master pointer has managed to slip in something other than a Foo, and clients are none the wiser. Aha! Now you see why that constructor of Foo was declared to be protected all along, rather than private! It isn't necessary to declare PFoo to be a friend anymore; it is only the constructor of DerivedFromFoo that needs access to constructors of Foo.

In Section 3, we will talk about the sorts of derivation needed to make this scheme work, namely that derived classes of Foo all share the same public interface as Foo itself. For now, let's stick to implications for pointers.

Selecting the Pointee Type During Construction

If our master pointer is now smart enough to pick one derived class during construction, why not allow it free rein to pick from among several derived classes?

```
// In Foo.cpp
class DerivedFromFoo : public Foo {...};
class AlsoDerivedFromFoo : public Foo {...};
PFoo::PFoo(bool x)
    : foo(x?new DerivedFromFoo:new AlsoDerivedFromFoo)
{
}
```

In general, the interface pointer is free to pick the derived class it feels like instantiating based on any information available at construction time. The client is none the wiser, since this is all hidden behind the interface pointer.

Changing the Pointee at Run Time

The interface pointer can also choose to swap pointees in midstream if it so desires.

```
class Foo;
class PFoo {
private:
    Foo* foo;
public:
    PFoo();
    void DoSomething(bool x);
    // Other member functions
};
void PFoo::DoSomething(bool x)
{
    if (x) {
        delete foo;
        foo = new DerivedFromFoo;
        }
    foo->DoSomething();
}
```

We already saw an example of this in the last chapter: a pointer that changes the form of the pointee when an attempt is made to access it in a non-const fashion. In general, this works fine as long as no one has done something foolish like taking the address of a member of the pointee.

Proxies

Another use of interface pointers is to hide the fact that the pointee is somewhere off in cyberspace, not sitting next door in memory. This happens all the time in distributed object systems. One design objective is to keep client objects fat, dumb, and happy; they shouldn't know or care whether the pointee is a stone's throw away or in some PC in Myanmar. An object that stands in for another, remote object is called a *proxy*. There are many variations on this theme, but the simplest one is to use an interface object or facet locally. The local proxy can then use remote procedure calls or whatever message-sending mechanism is handy to communicate back and forth with the original.

This concept can be extended to cover situations in which the remote "object" isn't an object at all. It could be an entire existing application wrapped up inside an object-oriented shell by the proxy, or perhaps data in a database together with library "member" functions.

There is nothing new or unique about the idea of wrapping non-object-oriented code inside C++ objects. What is relevant here is the encapsulation. Just what does a client have to know about the real situation? operator->-based smart pointers aren't a good choice. The client must know about the interface to the pointee; therefore, the client must know whether the pointee exists, what its interface looks like, and so on. Interface pointers, including facets, are better. The interface shown to the client is entirely declared in the pointer class. If your code is written in terms of interface pointers, it is much easier to slip in new code that implements some of those pointers as proxies. Easier, but not totally transparent — yet. Remember the basic form of an interface pointer? There is a forward declaration needed.

```
class Pointee; // Forward declaration
class Interface {
private:
    Pointee* pointee;
```

```
public:
    // Member functions here
};
```

The problem is the pointee data member. The client has to be aware that *something* is being pointed to by the pointer, even if it is ignorant of what. In Section 3, we will try to remove even that restriction, but for now it is a minor inconvenience.

What we end up with is a classic tradeoff: the performance price of interface pointers (no inline member functions) for the ability to slip in dramatically different implementations without altering client code. In most projects and for most classes, the cost of entry is more than paid back in lower lifecycle costs.

Functors

Let's close this chapter with a C++ curiosity called a *functor*, which is to functions what an interface pointer is to objects. One problem that has always dogged C programmers is that functions all live in a global space; that is, when a function is called, it has access only to data contained in its arguments and in global variables. If you pass a function's address to someone else and that someone calls the function, the function has no memory of what the world was like when its address was taken.

Languages like Pascal solve this problem neatly by taking a *closure* at the time that a function's address is taken.

```
procedure p(n : integer)
var
    procedure fn
    begin
        do_something(n);
    end
begin
    callbackfn(@fn);
end
```

The procedure callbackfn takes as its argument the address of some procedure. In this case, it gets the address of fn. When and if call-backfn calls fn, fn *has access to variables that were on the stack at the time its address was taken.* In this example, fn has access to the variable n's value at the time that callbackfn was called.

Closures are very valuable ways to handle callback situations because the callback function knows something about why it is being called. In C, there are no nested functions and therefore no closures. Enter the functor.

```
class Fn {
private:
    int number;
public:
    f(int n) : number(n) {}
    void operator() () { do_something(number); }
};
void callbackfn(Fn);
void p(int n)
{
    callbackfn(Fn(n));
}
void callbackfn(Fn fn)
{
    // Doodle about for a while
    fn(); // Call the "function" fn using operator()
}
```

The whole secret lies in two expressions. callbackfn(Fn(n)) passes an anonymous instance of the class Fn to the function. The argument to its constructor is the information to be included in the almost-a-closure maintained in Fn's data members. The expression fn(); may look like an ordinary function call, but it is really invoking the member function operator() of the class Fn. That, in turn, calls the global function do_something() using the closure information. Who needs Pascal, anyway?

operator() can take any arguments. To add arguments, insert them in the second set of parentheses in the class declaration. It is also legal to overload operator() more than once with different signatures. Here is the same example reworked to give one version of operator() an argument.

```
class Fn {
private:
    int number;
public:
    f(int n) : number(n) {}
    void operator() () { do_something(number); }
    void operator() (char* s)
        {   do_something(number);
            cout << "I'm doing something to " << s << endl;
        }
};
void callbackfn(Fn);
void p(int n)
{
    callbackfn(Fn(n));
}
void callbackfn(Fn fn)
{
    // Doodle about for a while
    fn("callbackfn");
}
```

This is a neat little idiom that would be even neater if it weren't for the fact that you can do the same thing without operator().

```
class Fn {
private:
    int number;
public:
    f(int n) : number(n) {}
    void do_something() { ::do_something(number); }
    void do_something() (char* s)
        {   do_something(number);
            cout << "I'm doing something to " << s << endl;
        }
};
void callbackfn(Fn);
```

```
void p(int n)
{
    callbackfn(Fn(n));
}
void callbackfn(Fn fn)
{
    // Doodle about for a while
    fn.do_something("callbackfn");
}
```

Any member function name will do as well. The only reason to use operator() is to clearly express your design intent. If the only reason a class exists is to service this sort of callback, use operator(); otherwise, use normal member functions.

CHAPTER 8

Collections, Cursors, and Iterators

Designing and implementing collection classes — bunches of objects held together by some other object — present as old a design problem as object-oriented programming itself. There is no sense in repeating here all the design tips you could read elsewhere about teenage mutable serializable indexed ninja collections. If you want information about the data structures and transformations involved, an excellent place to start would be to study Smalltalk collection classes, then to proceed through some of the commercial C++-based class libraries that you see advertised in all the software trade mags these days. I am going to focus here on the C++-isms that make collections fit into the Zen of C++ design and usage, regardless of what data structures and class hierarchies you use.

The first part of the chapter deals with indexed collections, that is, collections in which you use some object as an index to retrieve some other object hidden deep in the bowels of the collection. We'll use operator[] to make these look like abstract arrays, not just because that often makes for the most readable code, but also because it points out many of the idioms used with collections, such as cursors and iterators. We'll then plunge into the pool of cursors and their brethren, iterators, then take a vigorous swim through the choppier aspects of collections that are modified as they are enumerated.

Arrays and operator[]

operator[] is amazingly versatile in ways most C++ programmers never consider.

Bounds Checking and Assignment to Slots

Here is a simple application of overloading operator[]: an array that checks its bounds when its elements are accessed and behaves somewhat sensibly — or at least, safely — under all conditions.

```
class ArrayOfFoo {
private:
    int entries;
    Foo** contents; // A vector of Foo*
    static Foo* dummy; // For out-of-bounds indices
public:
    ArrayOfFoo() : entries(0), contents(NULL) {}
    ArrayOfFoo(int size)
        : entries(size), contents(new Foo*[size]) {}
    ~ArrayOfFoo() { delete contents; }
    Foo*& operator[](int index)
        {   return (index<0 || index >= entries)?
                dummy : contents[index];
        }
};
// Somewhere deep in a .cpp file
Foo* ArrayOfFoo::dummy = NULL;
```

The return value from operator[] is a Foo*&, a reference to the address of a Foo. This peculiar idiom is common in collections because it allows the value returned to be used as either the left- or right-hand side of an assignment expression, among other reasons.

```
Foo* foo = array[17];
array[29] = foo; // Works - you can assign to an index
```

If the return value of operator[] had been a simple Foo*, the contents of a slot in the array would have been copied and the copy returned to the caller. By returning a Foo*&, we provide the caller with the means to alter the original slot, not just access the value stored there. The value returned for an out-of-bounds index is the address of a fixed data member whose value we don't really care about. This allows a program to keep limping along, perhaps only when it is surrounded by the right #ifdefs in debug mode, rather than trashing your aunt's phone number or some other random spot in memory.

If you are hyperventilating over the computational cost of this treatment compared to straight C/C++ arrays, simply surround all the extra logic and data members with #ifdefs, and you will be left with an array that compiled one way is completely safe and compiled another way is the same size and performance as a normal array.

Nonintegral Arguments to operator[]

operator[] can be overloaded to take any argument, not just integers. This allows operator[] to be used to represent any dictionary, a collection in which one object uniquely identifies another. Here is the outline of an association class that maintains a set of pairs of Strings, where the first string in each pair acts as an index used to retrieve the second.

```
class Association {
// Private implementation details spared here
public:
    const String& operator[](const String& key);
};
// In client code
String str = association[another_string];
```

This is much more elegant and expressive of the designer's intent than is a purely member-function-based interface like the following.

```
String str = association.Lookup(another_string);
```

Simulating Multidimensional Arrays

operator[] can be overloaded to accept any single argument type. The following attempt at a multidimensional array would be laughed at by your compiler because it uses more than one argument to operator[].

```
class WontWork {
public:
    Foo& operator[] (int x, int y); // Ha, ha, ha, ha
};
```

Compilers love this sort of thing, something that seems to make perfect sense to you and me but somehow got left out of the language specification. It gives them a chance to stretch out and use all those obscure error messages they've been saving for a rainy day. But when the error messages stop spewing out, you can still have the last laugh, because there is an easy workaround.

```
struct Index {
    int x;
    int y;
    Index(int ex, int why) : x(ex), y(why) {}
    bool operator==(const Index& i)
        { return x == i.x && y == i.y; }
};
class WorksFine {
public:
    Foo& operator[](Index i);
};
array[Index(17,29)].MemberOfFoo(); // Works
```

Index is a struct with a trivial constructor. The reason for the overloaded operator== will be seen later. The phrase Index(17,29) is an anonymous instance used to stuff two dimensions into a single argument. Neat, huh? Take that, compiler!

Multiple Overloads of operator[]

It is also legal to overload operator[] more than once in a given class, as long as the signatures remain unique. You might, for example, want to provide one version that accepts an int and another that accepts a char* and does a conversion to int using atoi(). More likely, you have a collection that can be indexed more than one way.

```
class StringArray {
public:
    const String& operator[] (int index);
    int operator[] (const String&);
};
String str = array[17]; // Uses first form
int index = array[String("Hello")]; // Second form
```

The first operator[] implements the semantics of an array: Given an integral index, return the value at that index. The second provides an inverse mapping: Given a value, find the index at which that value occurs in the array. There are a couple of assumptions behind this, including a unique integer to return as the index for a value that doesn't exist, but the idea is straightforward.

Virtual operator[]

As with any operator or function, operator[] can be declared virtual and overridden in derived classes. This allows you to define an abstract interface in some base class, then provide all the implementation details in the derived classes. This combines nicely with the techniques of homomorphic class hierarchies discussed in Section 3.

Cursors

The previous section glossed over the subject of assignment to a slot in an array. It worked fine for an array of Foo*s, but the string association would not have worked had you tried to assign to a "location."

```
association[String("Hello")] = String("Good lookin");
```

The reason is that the left-hand side is neither an lvalue nor a class that overloads operator=. In this case, you could construct an argument that a function-based interface for insertion into the collection should be used because, after all, it isn't *really* an array, just something we've dressed up to look like one using operator[]. That's a cop-out, if for no other reason than that many classes that overload operator[] really *are* semantically arrays but use fancy data structures to optimize the implementation. Let's look at the specific problem of sparse arrays, then return to more general collections, such as associations.

A Simple Sparse Array Class

One of the most basic data structures is the sparse array. This is a matrix in which most of the cells are expected to be empty at any one time. Maybe you're one of those people with 256 gigabytes of RAM in your machine, but most of the rest of us don't have enough memory to preallocate room for all cells of a 1000x1000x1000 matrix, nor would we want to if only 1000 of those billion cells were in use at any one time. Your brain is no doubt already blowing mental cobwebs off the various data structures you studied in your Introduction to Data Structures 101 course in college: linked lists, binary trees, hash tables, and just about anything else out of Knuth. It isn't important here what data structures are used for the low-level implementation; the immediate concern is how do we use all this grubby, low-level stuff while allowing client objects to think that what they have is a dyed-in-the-wool, ordinary array?

The following is one brute-force implementation using linked lists to store the data. The Index struct is the same one used previously.

```
class SparseArray {
private:
    struct Node {
```

```
        Index index; // The index into the array
        Foo* content; // The content of that index
        Node* next; // Next entry in the list
        };
    Node* cells; // A linked list of entries
public:
    SparseArray() : cells(NULL) {}
    Foo* operator[](Index i);
};
inline Foo* SparseArray::operator[](Index i)
{
    SparseArray::Node* n = cells;
    while (n != NULL) {
        if (n->index == i) // Uses overloaded operator==
            return n->content;
        n = n->next;
        }
    return NULL;
}
Foo* foo = array[Index(17,29)]; // Works
```

This is fine for accessing cells of the array. If an index exists, the content at that index is returned. If the index is not in the array, a value of NULL is perfectly consistent with the idea that an array should be preinitialized to all NULLs. But wait a minute: How do we add new cells or reassign existing ones? The value returned by operator[] is neither a lvalue nor a class that overloads operator=, so you can't assign to it.

```
array[Index(31,37)] = foo; // Won't work
```

Your compiler lies awake nights waiting for opportunities such as this to dump all over cerr. We could create some functional interface, but that would mean breaking the illusion for the client that this is a normal, honest-to-goodness array. Is there a way to use operator[] as the left-hand side of an assignment for indices that don't yet exist? It turns out that the answer is yes, but we have to introduce a new idiom for the purpose: the cursor.

Cursors and Sparse Arrays

Let's try again. The basic objective is to return something from operator[] with the following properties:

1. It can be cast to the type of the contents of the array.
2. It can be used as the left-hand side of an assignment to change the content of the corresponding cell.

That something is a class known as a *cursor*. Here is the same sparse array using a cursor with operator[]:

```
class ArrayCursor;
class SparseArray {
friend class ArrayCursor;
private:
    struct Node {
        Index index;
        Foo* content;
        Node* next;
        Node(Index i, Foo* c, Node* n)
            : index(i), content(c), next(n) {}
        };
    Node* cells;
public:
    SparseArray() : cells(NULL) {}
    ArrayCursor operator[](Index i);
};
class ArrayCursor {
friend class SparseArray;
private:
    SparseArray& array; // Backpointer to owning array
    Index index; // Slot this cursor represents
    SparseArray::Node* node; // If non-nil index exists
    // Constructors are private so only SparseArray
    // can use them. First constructor is used for
    // an index that doesn't exist yet, the second
    // when the index is already in the array.
    ArrayCursor(SparseArray& arr, Index i)
        : array(arr), index(i), node(NULL) {}
    ArrayCursor(SparseArray& arr, SparseArray::Node* n)
```

```
                 : array(arr), node(n), index(n->index) {}
public:
    // The following operator= allows assignment to
    // a cursor to be translated into assignment to
    // the corresponding slot in the array.
    ArrayCursor& operator=(Foo* foo);
};
ArrayCursor& ArrayCursor::operator=(Foo* foo) {
    if (node == NULL) { // Index does not exist
        node = new SparseArray::Node
                        (index, foo, array.cells);
        array.cells = node;
        }
    else
        // Index already exists, change its value
        node->content = foo;
    return *this;
}
ArrayCursor SparseArray::operator[](Index i)
{
    SparseArray::Node* n = cells;
    while (n != NULL)
        if (n->index == i)
            return ArrayCursor(*this, n); // Exists
        else
            n = n->next;
    return ArrayCursor(*this, i); // Does not exist yet
}
```

Whoa! What's going on in all this convoluted code? The magic is all in the two member operators, SparseArray::operator()() and ArrayCursor::operator=(). SparseArray::operator()() returns an ArrayCursor, regardless of whether or not the index already exists (that knowledge is passed along to the ArrayCursor in the choice of constructor). ArrayCursor::operator=(Foo*) does one of two things: If the index already exists it is changed, and *if does not exist it is dynamically added to the array.* This is the essence of cursordom (cursidity?): an overloaded operator= that assigns not to the cursor itself, but to the data structure from which the cursor sprang. Now assignment works regardless of whether the index currently exists or not.

```
array[Index(17,29)] = new Foo; // Adds the index
array[Index(17,29)] = new Foo; // Reassigns same index
```

Not bad for an hour's work, is it? It walks, talks, and quacks like a normal array. Almost.

Conversion Operators and operator->

There are a couple more details to add. For one thing, operator[] will no longer work as the right-hand side as written since it returns an ArrayCursor, not a Foo* or Foo*&. Not to worry, because operator Foo*() will automatically convert an ArrayCursor to a Foo* when the need arises. Another problem is that operator[] cannot be used as the left-hand side of operator->; an operator->() rides to the rescue!

```
class ArrayCursor {
friend class SparseArray;
private:
    SparseArray& array;
    Index index;
    SparseArray::Node* node;
    ArrayCursor(SparseArray& arr, Index i)
        : array(arr), index(i), node(NULL) {}
    ArrayCursor(SparseArray& arr, SparseArray::Node* n)
        : array(arr), node(n), index(n->index) {}
public:
    ArrayCursor& operator=(Foo* foo);
    operator Foo*()
        { return node!=NULL ? node->content : NULL; }
    Foo* operator->()
        {   if (node == NULL)
                // bomb or throw an exception
            else return node->content;
        }
};
Foo* foo = array[Index(17,29)]; // Works
array[Index(17,29)]->MemberOfFoo(); // Also works
```

Ah, now we can relax. To a client object, this is just like any other array. This means that you can program to the simpler semantics of arrays and separately decide how to internally implement the actual data structures, even at late stages of a project.

Haven't I Seen This Somewhere Before?

Take another look at the ArrayCursor class. It is an object that indirectly refers to a Foo, has an operator Foo*(), and has an overloaded operator-> allowing access to members of Foo through the cursor. Does all this sound familiar? It should. Cursors are really just a next generation of smart pointer. Everything said about smart pointers in the last three chapters can be easily extended to apply to cursors as well. By the same token, we can extend some of our concepts of smart pointers by studying cursorology. Overloading operator= for a smart pointer can often solve some thorny problems. For example, recall the idea of a caching pointer, one that reads the object in at the last second in operator->. Overloading the assignment operator to do the same thing can often clean up code that would otherwise get messy in a hurry. Another generally useful technique is tying a smart pointer to some other data structure, in the same way that ArrayCursor is tied specifically to the SparseArray class. This sort of harmonic convergence of design ideas is a good indication that we are closing in on that elusive Zen of C++. The more advanced the idioms you use in C++, the more everything tends to look the same.

Iterators

Now that you can access one element of your collection at a time, how about enumerating all the elements in it? The brute force for loop just won't cut it.

```
for(int i=0; i<...what?
```

The way the sparse array has been implemented, there is no upper bound on the size of any dimension of the array. Even if there were, do you really want to iterate over all 1,000,000,000 indices looking for the thousand or so that are in use? I know, I know, your RISC workstation can complete an infinite loop in seven seconds, but let's get real. If the collection has an optimal way to access only cells actually in use, a client ought to take advantage of that. But remember that we want our clients totally ignorant of the internal details of our collections; that is, after all, why we went to all the trouble of inventing cursors. Welcome to the wonderful, wacky world of iterators, classes used to, well, iterate over collections. Wonderful, because they solve so many design problems so simply. Wacky, because no two C++ designers seem to be able to agree on the idioms to use in implementing them.

Active Iterators

An active iterator is one that advances itself to the next position.

```
class Collection {
public:
    class Iterator {
    public:
        bool More();
        Foo* Next();
    };
    Collection::Iterator* Iterate(); // Makes an iterator
};
Collection::Iterator* iter = collection->Iterator();
while (iter.More())
    f(iter.Next());
```

Iterators tend to be specific to the collections they enumerate; therefore, it is common to declare them as nested classes. The More() member function returns true if there is another element to retrieve and false if not. The Next() member function returns the next element and advances the iterator's position.

If you are willing to indulge in the cost of virtual member functions, this can also be implemented as a generic template usable with any and all collections.

```
template <class Type>
class Iterator { // Serves all collections and types
public:
    virtual bool More()=0;
    virtual Type* Next()=0;
};
```

Each collection can reimplement this in a derived class, and clients are none the wiser about how the iteration takes place or even what sort of collection is on the other side of the fence. Unfortunately, some collections will want to provide capabilities not supportable from all types of collections, such as that of constraining the range of iteration, so this is not as universally useful as it may seem at first glance.

I call these *active iterators* because their member functions are called to do the heavy lifting. It is almost as if one broke off a piece of the collection and put it into a portable little object; that object itself knows how to proceed once it is constructed.

Passive Iterators

On the other side we have iterators that don't really do anything. They store state information put there by the collection, but the collection itself does the advancing and other work. The same member functions are needed — we just throw them from the iterator back into the collection, which uses the iterator to store the state information needed by those member functions. The basic iterator and iteration loop now looks like this.

```
class Iterator;
class Collection {
public:
    Iterator* Iterate(); // Returns a passive iterator
    bool More(Iterator*);
    Foo* Next(Iterator*);
};
Iterator* iter = collection->Iterate();
while (collection->More(iter))
    f(collection->Next(iter));
```

These are *passive iterators* because the iterators themselves don't do anything — they serve only to store information for the member functions of the collection.

Which Is Better?

The choice between active and passive iterators is mostly a matter of style, but I prefer the active sort for several reasons:

- You will more likely be able to reuse a complete iterator class rather than a couple of member functions in a larger class.

- Sooner or later, you will want to provide several different ways to enumerate the contents of the collection. The same generic interface to the Iterator class will service all purposes, while the member function form will require your creating pairs of member functions for each new type of enumeration.

- Passive iterators have no public interface, yet they are visible to client objects through their addresses. This is an odd bird indeed.

- All other things being equal, I generally prefer active to passive objects because they provide better encapsulation.

That said, there are good examples of both forms in commercial class libraries. Arguments over active versus passive iterators mirror general arguments over active versus passive objects, so perhaps consistency with your overall design tendencies is the most important thing to consider.

Doubtful but Common Variations

You are unlikely to see exactly either form of iterator in commercial class libraries. Everyone has a personal twist on one theme or the other. Here are some variations you are likely to encounter in your C++ travels, along with some irreverent comments on their benefits and drawbacks.

Unscoped, Monomorphic Active Iterators. Sorry to use a ten-dollar word for such a simple concept. These are unscoped because they aren't declared nested snugly inside the collection, and are monomorphic because they don't use virtual member functions.

```
class Collection {...};
class CollectionIterator {
private:
    Collection* coll;
public:
    CollectionIterator(Collection* coll);
    bool More();
    Foo* Next();
};
CollectionIterator iter(collection); // Create iterator
while (iter.More())
    f(iter.Next());
```

There are so many problems with this, it's amazing that they all spring from so few lines of code:

- If you use a derived class of Collection, each client must know which new class of iterator to use in place of the old Collection-Iterator.

- The data members of the iterator are visible to the public at large. Even if they aren't national secrets, it is annoying to have to recompile all your client code every time you change your mind about how to implement the iterator.

- Putting the iterators on the stack interferes with some of the multithreading strategies discussed in the next chapter.

- Code reuse is lousy.

For all these reasons, it is much, much better to ask the collection class to "Please, Sir, make me an iterator," rather than create it yourself on the stack. Despite these problems, this is a very common form of iteration in commercial class libraries.

Void* Passive Iterators. The most common variation on the theme of passive iterators is to not bother with a forward declaration of the iterator class, instead fooling your clients into thinking they really have a void*. This is often dressed up as some fancy name using a typedef, but you can't hide an ugly void* quite so easily.

```
typedef void* AprilInParis;
class Collection {
public:
    AprilInParis Iterate(); // Return a perfumed void*
    bool More(AprilInParis&);
    Foo* Next(AprilInParis&);
};
```

Internally, this is, of course, something much more sensible than a void*, so the implementation code in Collection must constantly cast the void* back to reality. I don't know about you, but trusting my client code not to mess with a void* before I can cast it back gives me the shivers. It is also devilish to debug this sort of code, since the debugger has no more idea than your client what that thing really is. Putting a fancy name on the iterator doesn't change the basic ugliness of this approach.

Untyped Next(). Many iterator classes are written generically in terms either of void*s or of some abstract base class. You, as client, must cast the return value from Next() back to the correct type, and woe be unto you if you screw it up. This is what templates were invented for, so there is really no justification anymore for this sort of nonsense.

Better Variations

I will stick to active iterators from here on, but everything said in that context transfers to passive iterators as well. Some variations on the theme of iterators depend greatly on the characteristics of the collection, but others are more generic. Here they are, in no particular order.

Rewinding. Some iterator classes provide a member function that restarts the iteration from the beginning. I call this the Rewind() function. Not all collections can support this — for example, a data stream coming from a communications port.

Range Constraints. If the set represented by the collection is ordered, the iterator should provide some way to constrain the enumeration to a specific range of values.

```
class Collection {
public:
    class Iterator {
    public:
        Iterator(Key* low, Key* high);
        // etc.
    };
    // etc.
};
```

In this fragment, low and high are the lowest key value to consider and the highest, respectively. More() and Next() will discard any elements not between those inclusive boundaries. Variations on this variation include "everything greater than X," "everything less than X," and exclusive boundaries (< rather than <=).

Backing Up. If the collection supports it, iterators may also support a Previous() member function to back up one notch. This is often coupled with a Current() member function that returns whatever Next() returned the last time it was called.

Cursors. It is very useful to combine the concepts of this chapter by returning from Next(), not a *-style pointer, but a cursor that knows where the element came from. This allows the user to delete, replace, or insert before or after the current object. This can be implemented in one of two ways: return a cursor from Next(), or add those cursorlike operations as member functions of the iterator itself, operating on the last-retrieved position. The first approach involves an iterator collaborating with a cursor; the second combines the two into a single class.

An Abstract Array Iterator

Now for a simple example, using our sparse array. The array class and cursor are lifted verbatim from the earlier discussion, except that now the array class also returns an iterator over only those cells containing non-nil entries. The generic iterator template is not used because the Next() member function is friendly enough to return both the index and the object at that index, which requires a nonstandard interface to Next(). The cursor and sparse array classes are as just described. (I make no claim that this is a *good* sparse array, just one whose design is simple enough to stay out of the way while I make my points about iterators.)

```
// SparseArray.h
class ArrayCursor;
class SparseArray {
friend class ArrayCursor;
private:
    struct Node {
        Index index;
        Foo* content;
        Node* next;
        Node(Index i, Foo* c, Node* n)
            : index(i), content(c), next(n) {}
        };
    Node* cells;
public:
    class Iterator {
    private:
        Node* next;
    public:
        Iterator(Node* first) : next(first) {}
        bool More() { return next != NULL; }
        Foo* Next(Index& index)
            {
                Foo* object = next->content;
```

```
                index = next->index;
                next = next->next;
                return object;
            }
        };
    Iterator* NonEmpty()
        { return new SparseArray::Iterator(cells); }
    SparseArray() : cells(NULL) {}
    ArrayCursor operator[](Index i);
};
class ArrayCursor {
friend class SparseArray;
private:
    SparseArray& array;
    Index index;
    SparseArray::Node* node;
    ArrayCursor(SparseArray& arr, Index i)
        : array(arr), index(i), node(NULL) {}
    ArrayCursor(SparseArray& arr, SparseArray::Node* n)
        : array(arr), node(n), index(n->index) {}
public:
    ArrayCursor& operator=(Foo* foo);
    operator Foo*()
        { return node!=NULL ? node->content : NULL; }
    Foo* operator->()
        {   if (node == NULL)
                throw nil_error;
            else return node->content;
        }
};
```

This is probably not the sort of thing you'd want to show a potential employer as evidence of your C++ prowess, but it is simple and fast, and it gets the job done. Here are some variations you might want to consider in commercial-grade code:

- Encapsulate SparseArray::Iterator by turning it into an abstract base class, then return a derived class from within the hidden implementation of NonEmpty(). (That's a good idea for the array and cursor classes as well, an idea we'll develop further in Section 3.)

- Provide additional iterators that include both empty and non-empty cells.

- Guarantee the order in which cells are visited.

- Return a cursor from Next() rather than a pointer so that clients can alter the contents of a cell during iteration. If this is done, the cursor can hold the index, so it needn't be returned as a separate reference argument of Next().

Collection Operators

Lots of collections are indexed in one or more ways and map well onto operator[], but nothing in the discussions of cursors or iterators requires that operator[] be used or that the collection be indexed. Cursors merely indicate an internal position in the collection; that position needn't be something users understand or care about. If you take away the Index& argument to Next(), the iterator just described could just as well be used with something other than an array.

Most collections have some operations in common. As with operator[], it is common to see C++ operators overloaded to make the use of the collection more intuitive and readable. While there is no univerally agreed-upon set of collection operators, the following should get you started in your own designs. These are all faithful to the semantics of the corresponding operations on numbers.

```
template <class Element>
class Set {
public:
    Set(); // An empty set
    Set(const Set<Element>&); // Duplicate the set
    Set(Element*); // A set with one initial element

    // Binary operations and relations on (Set,Set)
    // (also |=, &=, -=, <, <= variants)
```

```
Set<Element> operator|(const Set<Element>&) const;
// Union of sets
Set<Element> operator&(const Set<Element>&) const;
// Intersection
Set<Element> operator-(const Set<Element>&) const;
// Set difference
bool operator>(const Set<Element>&) const; // True if
    // this is a proper superset of the argument
bool operator>=(const Set<Element>&) const; // True if
    // this is a superset of the argument
bool operator==(const Set<Element>&) const; // True if
    // the sets have the same content

// Binary operations, relations on (Set,Element*)
// (also |=, -= variants)
Set<Element> operator|(Element*);
// Add element to this
Set<Element> operator-(Element*);
// this minus the element
bool operator>(const Element*) const; // True if
    // element is in the set but not the only element
bool operator>=(const Element*) const; // True if
    // element is in the set
bool operator==(const Element*) const; // True if
    // element is the only element in the set
};
```

There is one additional operator overload that I reluctantly list here. I have never quite gotten used to the use of << and >> to "bit shift" to and from streams, but they are now so ingrained into the C++ culture that one has to use that stream idiom, not just bit shifting, as the basis for further extensions. This leads to additional usages of << and >> in the context of collections and iterators:

- Operator<< may be used as a synonym for the Next() member function in iterators.

- Operator>> may be used as a synonym for the more verbose Set& operator|=(Element*) as a way to "bit shift" new elements into a collection.

In both idioms, the operator must be overloaded as a non-member function, since the Element*, not the Set, is the left-hand side of the operator. The >> idiom is most natural with collections that maintain the original order of insertion, such as lists.

We will revisit these subjects in Section 3 when we talk about homomorphic class hierarchies.

Smarter Cursors and Threaded Iterators

A cursor can be used to implicitly insert into a collection at a specified location, whether or not that location is currently reflected in the internal data structures of the collection. That was the idea behind overloading operator= for cursors. This can be generalized to include other cursor operations. Here are some typical extended cursor operations, expressed as member functions of the cursor class.

```
void InsertBefore(Foo* f); // Insert f before cursor
void InsertAfter(Foo* f); // Insert f after cursor
void RemoveAt(); // Remove object at cursor
```

These apply to a broad class of collections, those that maintain a well-defined serial order to the elements. These operations can also be provided by iterators that do not return a cursor as the value of their Next() member function, but rather hide the current location inside the iterator.

These operations can make it difficult to maintain consistent semantics of iteration or, in a worst case, they lead to serious design problems that can cause programs to bomb. These problems exist even without the extended operations if changes to the collection are permitted while cursors and iterators are active against it. What happens when some piece of code deletes the object pointed to by a currently active cursor? Special care must be taken to keep everything orderly. The general problem here is to make cursors *threadsafe;*

that is, they continue to operate gracefully as the underlying collection is updated.

Let's take a linked list collection and its iterator as an example.

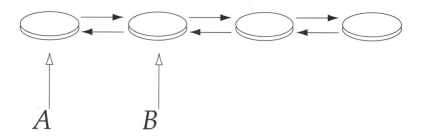

Cursors A and B are used to keep track of the current location of two iterators over the same list. This works fine as long as the list is left unchanged, but if the client of one iterator or the other starts using the cursor to update the list, the trouble begins:

- If the client does an "insert after" operation on cursor B, both iterators will "see" the newly inserted object when iteration resumes.

- If the client does an "insert before" on B or an "insert after" on A, the iterator owning A will see the newly inserted object, but the iterator owning B will not.

- If the client deletes the object at B, A will never see that object, even though it was there when A's iterator started walking through the list.

- If the client deletes the object at A, B will have already seen it before the deletion takes place.

- Some insertion algorithms will infinitely recurse if an insertion is done after either cursor, because each newly inserted object may generate another object to insert.

- If A and B happen to point to the same list node and one of them does a deletion, it's "Hello, debugger."

The semantics of enumeration get tossed like a salad any time changes to a collection are performed during iteration; when there are two or more iterators operating at once it's more like a Dice-A-Matic.

Lists are actually a reasonably simple case. Consider instead what happens if the collection is stored as an array (whether or not the client sees it that way) and the cursors have an integral index into the array.

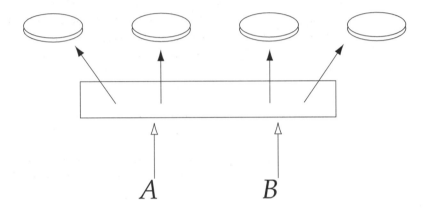

To support "insert before/after" and "remove at," you must shove elements of the array above the point of insertion or remove one slot higher or lower in the array. In the diagram, if you delete at A and shove everything above that spot down one slot, B ends up skipping a slot. If you insert at A, B will see the same object twice.

The semantics of enumeration should be much cleaner and more predictable than this. For most applications, the enumeration should be fixed at the time it begins and should not be affected by subsequent insertions and deletions. For most applications, two rules should be designed into iterator and cursor idioms:

1. An iterator should enumerate those objects in the collection at the time that the iterator was constructed.

2. A cursor should remain valid from the time it is constructed to the time it is destroyed. That is, there should be no operation performed elsewhere in the program that can result in a currently active cursor becoming unusable. This is not to say that the value stored in the cursor must remain the same, only that the cursor remains usable.

These rules bring some order to what otherwise would be utter chaos. The first of these can be called *shadowing*, since changes to a collection after an iterator is constructed are hidden, or shadowed, from that iterator. This is a major design issue in its own right, and one could easily devote a book just to that subject, but fortunately our objective is more mundane: to illustrate the C++ idioms that encapsulate the actual solutions.

Private Copies of Collections

If an iterator and its cursor do not allow modifications to the collection, there is a simple way to avoid trouble: make a copy of the collection in the iterator's constructor. In pseudocode,

```
class Iterator {
private:
    Collection collection;
    Cursor location; // Current location in copy
public:
    Iterator(Collection& c)
        : collection(c), location(collection.First()) {}
    bool More();
    Foo* Next();
};
```

The constructor of the iterator uses the copy constructor of the Collection class to make a private copy of the collection. This is one of those rare occasions when you really do care about the fact that data members are constructed in the order in which they are listed; collection must be constructed before location, or the First() member function will likely get you up close and personal with your debugger.

Collections of Objects or Collections of Pointers? This scheme is usually used when the collection consists of pointers or references to objects that are otherwise independent of the collection. Other collections contain embedded objects, not pointers or references to them.

```
template <class Type, int Size>
class Array {
private:
    int size; // Number of Type's
    Type elements[Size]; // The (embedded) objects
// and so on
};
```

Here the objects are literally embedded into the collection. To duplicate the collection, you must duplicate not just pointers, but the objects as well, which may be too expensive. On the other hand, the iterator may need to return a pointer or reference to the original object from the original collection, not a copy. In either case, forget the private collection technique.

The same principle applies whenever the collection acts as a set of master pointers to its contents. Yes, it contains pointers, not objects, but the collection is free to delete those objects, so a private collection of them is fragile. (There are memory management — specifically, garbage collection — issues here that will be dealt with in Section 4 of the book.)

Simplifying the Private Collection. Suppose the original collection is a btree or some similarly complex data structure. Is it really necessary to reproduce all that overhead of trees of blocks, given that you won't be doing any indexed access? A common variation is to create the simplest, serializable type of collection as the private "copy." This is easier if each collection class has a conversion operator generating an instance of this lowest common denominator.

Instead of using the collection's copy constructor, this iterator uses the collection's conversion operator.

```
class SimpleCollection; // A bare bones form
class ComplexCollection {
public:
    operator SimpleCollection*();
};
```

A closely related alternative is to give SimpleCollection a constructor for each other kind of collection, but this is poor design practice — every time you invent some spiffy new sort of collection, you'll have to modify the SimpleCollection class to convert it. This is the sort of situation for which conversion operators were made.

If this variation is used, the iterator becomes reusable across all the types of collections. The iterator need not know anything about the original collection. The address of the serializable collection is passed to the iterator's constructor in place of the original collection, leaving the modified interface looking like this.

```
class Iterator {
private:
    SimpleCollection* collection;
    Cursor location; // Current location in copy
public:
    Iterator(SimpleCollection* c)
        : collection(c), location(collection->First()) {}
    bool More();
    Foo* Next();
};
```

Internal and External Iterators

Let's move on to iterators that operate over the original collection. There are two cases: those that are purely internal implementation details of the collection — for example, SimpleCollection, just shown — and those published to the outside world. These are internal and external iterators, respectively.

An internal iterator is usually a dumb, unthreaded iterator that enumerates the collection in its then-current state. If an insertion or removal takes place, the internal iterator will exhibit the sorts of bizarre inconsistencies we talked about at the start of this section. For that reason, they are carefully hidden away from prying client eyes. The internal iterator is usually closely matched to the actual data structures used to implement the collection. As with any other iterator, it may return either a *-style pointer or a cursor, depending on your needs.

External iterators superimpose the logic of shadowing on top of the internal iterator. There are many ways to do this, some of which are discussed later in this chapter and in Chapter 9. The key, as always, lies not in the particular algorithms or data structures, but in how you hide them from the public.

Temporary Internal Iterators. If your external iterator creates a private collection as in the preceding section, and no conversion operator or constructor is appropriate for turning the existing collection into a private one, an internal iterator can be used in the external iterator's constructor. Here is a code fragment that illustrates two internal iterators combined to implement a single external one.

```
class ExternalIterator {
private:
    SimpleCollection collection;
    SimpleIterator* my_iter; // Returned by collection
public:
    ExternalIterator(ComplexCollection* c)
        {   InternalIterator* iter = c->Iterator();
            while (c->More())
                collection += *(c->Next());
            delete iter;
            my_iter = collection->Iterator();
        }
    bool More() { return my_iter->More(); }
    Foo* Next() { return my_iter->Next(); }
};
```

ComplexCollection provides an internal iterator that lives only as long as it is needed to make the copy. SimpleCollection returns one that is used to implement the More() and Next() member functions of the external iterator. It would be much cleaner, of course, if either Simple-Collection had a constructor whose argument was a ComplexCollection, or if ComplexCollection had a conversion operator SimpleCollection(), but even in the absence of both of these the iterator class just shown will provide all the encapsulation a client could want.

Persistent Internal Iterators. I use the term *persistent* here to mean that the internal iterator lives as long as the external one, as with my_iter in the last example. The internal iterator can be a data member of the external one as shown, or if you are careful you can privately derive the one from the other. Here is an example of the use of private derivation.

```
// In the .h file
class Collection {
public:
    class ExternalIterator {
    public:
        virtual bool More()=0;
        virtual Foo* Next()=0;
    };
    ExternalIterator* Iterator();
};
// In the .cpp file
// The actual class returned to clients
class RealExternalIterator
    : public ExternalIterator, private InternalIterator
{...};
Collection::ExternalIterator* Collection::Iterator()
{
    return new RealExternalIterator(this);
}
```

The locally scoped ExternalIterator provides the abstract interface presented to the client. The actual class returned, RealExternalIterator, publicly derives from Collection::ExternalIterator and also — unbeknownst to the client — privately derives from SimpleIterator. As in most C++ design problems, private derivation is simpler, delegation to a data member more general. For example, you can swap a data member in midstream to chain together several internal iterators within a single external one.

Filtered Iterators. One problem that arises with this idiom is the implementation of the More() member function. Presumably, the external iterator's Next() may choose to skip over something that the internal Next() returns. For example, if the internal iterator returns something inserted after the external iterator was constructed, the external iterator might want to skip it. The internal iterator's More() member function may say there is another element there, only to have it turn out to be a reject when you retrieve it using Next(). One way to solve this problem is to add a Peek() member function to the internal iterator. Peek() returns the same thing Next() returns, but does not advance the cursor to the next location. With that addition, here is a boilerplate way to embed an internal iterator into an external one.

```
class RealExternalIterator : public ExternalIterator {
private:
    InternalIterator* iter;
    bool Accept(Foo*); // The filter function
public:
    RealExternalIterator(Collection* c)
        : iter(c->Iterator()) {}
    virtual bool More()
        {   while (iter.More()) {
                if (Accept(iter->Peek()))
                    return true;
                (void)iter->Next(); // Discard and advance
                }
            return false;
        }
    virtual Foo* Next() { return iter->Next(); }
};
```

Every time the client calls More(), including at the beginning of the loop, the internal iterator moves forward until it hits something that will pass the external iterator's filter function Accept().

If you have an especially obnoxious collection, you may have to store a copy of the last-seen object in order to implement Peek(), but for most collections you can easily do a nondestructive read of the current position.

This technique is obviously not limited just to iterator shadowing; it can be applied to any situation in which an outer iterator needs to strip off objects returned by an inner one. Accept(), for example, could apply constraints of a database query.

Timestamping

One of the simplest tricks for sorting out insertions is to timestamp the insertions in the collection and also timestamp iterators. If the timestamp on an iterator is earlier than that of a slot, it skips the object at that slot. The timestamp can either be taken literally as some number of clock ticks, or it can be a serial number stored in a static data member somewhere, or a serial number stored as a data member of the collection object.

Removal can be handled in a similar vein. If someone tries to remove an object from a collection, behind the scenes it really stays around until all the old iterators are gone. Current clients and newer iterators ignore it, while iterators constructed before the removal continue to act as if no one bothered to inform them of the object's demise. The object is actually removed when it can be proven that no one needs it. That is a garbage collection issue that will be covered in Section 4; the collection is easily compacted either when it is written to storage or at any time that there are no active iterators or cursors.

It is possible that an object can be in both an inserted and a removed state at once — inserted after some iterator was constructed and removed before that iterator is destroyed. In fact, it is possible to have a whole history of inserting and removing the same object if an iterator is long-lived enough to span all that activity. One could use many different data structures to keep track of this history. That is an interesting side discussion, but there isn't any particular relevance to C++ idioms in that choice. Let's leave it with a nice encapsulation, a modification to the internal iterator idea of the preceding section.

A Timestamping Class. The following class encapsulates the notion of time. You can modify it to use the system clock rather than the progressive counter, and clients are none the wiser. Notice that the copy constructor and operator= are *not* overloaded. Passing a Timestamp by value will create a temporary Timestamp with the same time as the original, and assignment of one Timestamp to another changes the left-hand side's time to be the same as that of the right-hand side.

```
class Timestamp {
private:
    static int last_time; // Used to assign a number
    int stamp;
public:
    Timestamp() : stamp(++last_time) {}
    bool operator>(Timestamp ts)
        { return stamp > ts.stamp; }
    bool operator>=(Timestamp ts)
        { return stamp >= ts.stamp; }
    bool operator<(Timestamp ts)
        { return stamp < ts.stamp; }
    bool operator<=(Timestamp ts)
        { return stamp <= ts.stamp; }
    bool operator==(Timestamp ts)
        { return stamp == ts.stamp; }
    bool operator!=(Timestamp ts)
        { return stamp != ts.stamp; }
};
```

A Timestamped Internal Iterator. The internal iterator must also be modified to take the time into account. Following are the relevant portions of the interface. Implementation details will depend heavily on the collection's data structures.

```
class InternalIterator {
public:
    bool More(Timestamp as_of);
    Foo* Next(Timestamp as_of);
    bool Peek(Timestamp as_of);
};
```

The internal iterator will skip over any objects that were not present in the collection as of the indicated time.

Internal Implementation Techniques. One possible way to implement this is to have each slot in the collection maintain a vector of timestamps, with the oldest entry the original time of insertion and each subsequent entry alternating between insertion and deletion. If the vector has an odd number of entries, the object is currently in the collection, and the head of the vector is the time it was most recently inserted. If the number is even, the object is currently not in the collection, and the head of the vector is the time most recently removed. When the collection is compacted, the history is also compacted to only the most recent time of insertion. There are other ways to implement this, such as exception lists, but this timestamped history technique serves at least as a proof of concept.

A Timestamped External Iterator. The external iterator is a trivial wrapper around the internal iterator just described.

```
class RealExternalIterator : public ExternalIterator {
private:
    InternalIterator* iter;
    Timestamp my_time; // Time of construction of 'this'
    bool Accept(Foo*); // The filter function
public:
    RealExternalIterator(Collection* c)
        : iter(c->Iterator()) {}
    virtual bool More()
        {  while (iter.More(my_time)) {
```

```
                    if (Accept(iter->Peek(my_time)))
                        return true;
                    (void)iter->Next(my_time);
                    }
            return false;
        }
    virtual Foo* Next() { return iter->Next(my_time); }
};
```

The no-argument constructor of Timestamp will fill in the current time. In many cases, the Accept() member function will always return true and can be omitted.

An Example

Let's close out this drawn-out chapter with an example: a template that implements a set of objects whose type is the parameter to the template. In a set, each object occurs exactly once; an attempt to insert an object already in the set leaves the set unchanged. We will use the timestamping technique of implementing threaded iterators, rather than making a private copy of the set each time an iterator is made. This shows the sort of hoop you will have to jump through when you try to make reasonable use of unreasonable off-the-shelf collection classes.

An Off-the-Shelf, Unthreaded Dictionary. In the real world, you seldom have to start completely from scratch. There are usually some collection classes lying around. Even if they aren't exactly what you want, they can save you the tedium of reimplementing your favorite chapters of Knuth just to get the basic data structures. In the real world, these classes usually don't pay much attention to the problem of threaded iteration, so this example isn't too far-fetched. Keeping it realistic, we'll presume that the collection is a dictionary, indexed by a void* and returning a void* as the value of the key. The iterator is passive, a type called Slot whose actual structure is hidden inside the bowels of the dictionary class. Here is the public interface.

```
class Dictionary {
public:
    Dictionary(); // Creates an empty dictionary
    Dictionary(const Dictionary&); // Copy constructor
    ~Dictionary();
    Dictionary& operator=(const Dictionary&);

    void AddEntry(void* key, void* value);
    bool At(void* key, void*& value);
    void RemoveEntry(void* key);

    class Slot; // Actual declaration is buried
    Slot* First(); // Returns Slot for iteration
    // Equivalent to our "Peek"
    bool GetCurrent
        (Slot* slot, void*& key, void*& value);
    // Equivalent to our "Next"
    bool GetNext
        (Slot*& slot, void*& key, void*& value);
};
```

AddEntry() is used to stick a new value into the dictionary for the given key. If the key already exists with a different value, the value of that key is changed to the new one. At() returns a bool indicating whether or not the key is in the dictionary; if so, it returns true and value is the returned value of that key. RemoveEntry() removes a key and whatever value is currently associated with it. First() returns a passive iterator aimed so that the first call to GetNext() will retrieve the first entry in the dictionary. GetCurrent() returns the pair at the location of the current Slot. GetNext() returns the key-value pair and advances the iterator to the next entry. The only difference is whether or not the logical position is advanced after the object is retrieved.

We will use the dictionary as follows: The key is the object stored in our set, and the value of that key is the insertion/removal history of the object.

A History Class. The following is the public interface to a class that keeps track of the insertion/removal history of an object. It uses the Timestamp class just discussed. This is the "value" side of the key-value pairs stored in the dictionary. The implementation isn't particularly interesting and is omitted here.

```
class History {
public:
    History(); // An empty history
    void Insert(Timestamp); // An insertion at given time
    void Remove(Timestamp); // Removal at given time
    bool Exists(Timestamp); // As of given time
    bool Exists(); // As of now
};
```

The Exists(Timestamp) member function returns true if at the given time the most recent operation was insertion, false if there were no earlier operations before that time or if the most recent one was removal. Exists() with no argument is a synonym for Exists(Timestamp) with a very large value for the time — in other words, as of now.

Abstract Base Class. The set class will be divided into two pieces: an abstract base class that trades in void*'s and a derived parameterized class that adds type safety. Here is the abstract base class.

```
// In Set.h
class SetBase : private Dictionary {
friend class InternalIterator;
protected:
    SetBase(); // To make it abstract
public:
    class Iterator { // Base of external iterator class
    public:
        virtual bool More()=0;
        virtual Type* Next()=0;
    };
Iterator* SetBase::ProvideIterator()
{
    return new InternalIterator(this);
}
void SetBase::AddObject(void* entry)
{
```

```
        void* v;
        History* h;
        if (At(entry, v)) { // Already there - check time
            h = (History*)v;
            if (!h->Exists()) // Must do an "insertion"
                h->Insert(Timestamp());
            }
        else { // Not there yet
            h = new History;
            h->Insert(Timestamp());
            AddEntry(entry, h);
            }
    }
void SetBase::RemoveObject(void* entry)
{
    void* v;
    History* h;
    if (At(entry, v)) { // Already there - check time
        h = (History*)v;
        if (h->Exists()) // Must do a deletion
            h->Remove(Timestamp());
        }
    }
bool SetBase::Exists(void* entry, Timestamp ts)
{
    void* v;
    return At(entry, v) && ((History*)v)->Exists(ts);
}
bool SetBase::Exists(void* entry)
{
    void* v;
    return At(entry, v) && ((History*)v)->Exists();
}
```

There are other things you might want to add, but this will do to illustrate the techniques of this chapter.

The Internal Iterator. To implement the ProvideIterator() member function, we set up both an untyped internal iterator, private to the .cpp file and derived from SetBase::Iterator, and an external one in the parameterized, typesafe wrapper. Following is the internal iterator, declared static, that is, local to the .cpp file and not derived from anything. The timestamp logic is buried in the implementation of this class.

```
// In Set.cpp
class InternalIterator: public SetBase::Iterator{
private:
    Dictionary* dictionary;
    Dictionary::Slot* slot; // Current position
    Timestamp my_time; // Time this iterator was born
public:
    InternalIterator(Dictionary* d)
        : dictionary(d), slot(d->First()), my_time() {}
    virtual bool More();
    virtual void* Next();
};
bool InternalIterator::More()
{
bool InternalIterator::More()
{
    void* key;
    void* h;
    if (!dictionary->GetCurrent(slot, key, h))
        return false; // slot already beyond bounds

    do if (((History*)h)->Exists(my_time))
            return true;
        while (dictionary->GetNext(slot, key, h));
    return false;
}
void* InternalIterator::Next()
{
    void* key;
    void* key1;
    void* h;
    // We assume the client called More() first, so
    // the object at GetNext is current
    dictionary->GetCurrent(slot, key, h);
    dictionary->GetNext(slot, key1, h);
```

```
        return key;
}
```

Typesafe Parameterized Wrapper. Finally, all this becomes type-safe and eye-pleasing in the following parameterized class. The external iterator is a parameterized wrapper around the internal iterator provided by SetBase.

```
template <class Type>
class Set : private SetBase {
public:
    // Default no-argument and copy constructors are OK
    // Default operator= is OK
    Set<Type>& operator+=(Type* object)
        { AddObject(object); return *this; }
    Set<Type>& operator-=(Type* object)
        { RemoveObject(object); return *this; }
    bool operator>=(Type* object)
        { return Exists(object); }
    class Iterator {
    private:
        SetBase::Iterator* iter;
    public:
        Iterator(Set& s)
            : iter(s.ProvideIterator()) {}
        bool More() { return iter.More(); }
        Type* Next() { return (Type*)(iter.Next()); }
    };
    Iterator* ProvideIterator()
        { return new Set::Iterator(*this); }
};
```

There is more that one might want to add to the parameterized class, but you get the idea. One rarely derives further from a parameterized class like this, so the nested iterator class is set up with inlines. In fact, this iterator could simply be declared on the stack.

```
Set::Iterator iter(aSet);
```

This works fine, but is inconsistent with the normal idiom of returning the iterator from the collection. One more alternative is worth considering: making SetBase a data member rather than a private base class, which allows you to stuff SetBase into a .cpp file that the client never sees. This requires constructors and an operator= for the Set template, but it is otherwise a very straightforward adaption of this template.

CHAPTER 9

Transactions and Brilliant Pointers

This is the final chapter on indirection — though definitely not the last word on the subject — so let's see how far we can push the envelope with smart pointers. So far, the idioms and examples of smart pointers, smarter pointers, cursors, and iterators have all been localized, mostly to a single encapsulated object. It is time to stop dilly-dallying around and talk about entire architectures enabled if we apply these idioms on a grander scale. The sorts of pointers we'll be talking about here are so smart it's scary. In fact, *smart* isn't good enough to describe them. *Astoundingly, blazingly, unbelievably intellectually gifted* is a little wordy, so I'll lump them all under the category *brilliant*.

Warning: This chapter is a test of your imagination as well as your C++ skills. The problems and idioms that follow are the software equivalent of a twisty mountain road open only to bicycles. Wear your helmet, and stop frequently for water breaks.

Some Gnarly Design Problems

In most of this book, applications of idioms are discussed after the idioms themselves. Allow me to deviate from that form for this chapter by discussing some design problems that establish the need for the tricks we'll be discussing as the chapter unfolds.

Transactions

In database and client/server applications, often there are multiple remote users requesting updates against a single database or data structure. A single unit of change or *transaction* as perceived by the client may involve many individual changes to the database or data structure. Several rules of consistency stolen from the world of database management systems guide designers in these situations:

1. Transactions should be atomic. Either all of the updates needed to carry out the transaction are recorded against the data, or none are.

2. During one client's transaction, the data should appear as it was at the start of all other clients' uncompleted transactions. A transaction does not become visible to other clients until it has completed; until then, it is as if the transaction had not yet begun.

3. If more than one client attempts to change a given object as part of their transactions, at most one of the transactions will be allowed to complete.

The last rule assures that at most one client at a time will update a given object. There are two strategies for this:

1. Before it begins to perform updates, each transaction locks for update all objects it intends to change. If a transaction cannot obtain a needed lock, it never begins.

2. Locks are not requested at the beginning, but rather during each transaction as updates are performed. If a needed object is already locked by some other client, either the transaction waits for it to be freed, or the transaction fails.

The second strategy can result in deadlocks; transaction A has a lock on object X and needs a lock on object Y, while transaction B has a lock on object Y and needs a lock on object X.

There is a tremendous body of literature on all these points in the ivory tower world of database management system internals, so there is no point in going further with the technology here. The relevant things here are the C++ idioms and features that facilitate solutions to this general class of problem.

Undo

Most graphical user interface applications are kind enough to allow users to undo the last operation. This may seem simple, but in practice it is not always so easy. There are few design problems in the object-oriented world that generate more stomach acid than supporting undo in a complex application. Most programmers hard-code operation-specific data structures to support undo, but these are error-prone and fragile during the maintenance lifecycle of the program.

In some languages, such as Lisp, you can literally take a snapshot of memory at various points in time. Rolling back to an earlier version of the application is then very simple. Sigh. In C++, we have to work with a much cruder set of tools; but then, *our* programs will work in less than 3 gigabytes of RAM and will generally finish before dinnertime, so this isn't so much a criticism of C++ as an observation that there's a design problem to solve.

There are two variations on the theme to keep track of as we proceed. In some environments, the standard is to provide only a single level of undo, while in others, the user can keep selecting the "Undo" menu item and each time the state of the data rolls back one more operation. There are ultimately some limits, but they are pretty generous. This is called multilevel undo, a problem we'll address after solving the single-level undo problem. The second variation is context-sensitive undo. If a user performs an operation in one window on the screen, then an operation in a second window, then returns to the first and chooses "Undo," generally what should get undone is the last operation in that first window, not the last operation performed in the entire application. That is, undo is sensitive to the context of the application at the time it is invoked.

Enough Motivation?

There are other problems that fall into the same class as these, but this should serve as sufficient motivation for our C++ meanderings. Most programmers approach these as isolated, application-specific design problems, but as you'll see, there are some design ideas supported by specific — some would say, peculiar — C++ syntax that go a long way toward general solutions. Remember that our purpose here is to explore C++ and its idioms, not rehash data structures and software design practices; other architectures and variations are not listed here and their absence is not a negative reflection on them.

Images and Pointers

We couldn't go far into a new chapter without talking about a new breed of pointer, now could we? There are two different ways to restore the state of an object: store before and after images, or store enough information to perform the inverse of whatever change has been made. Images are easy and general, while trying to invert an operation tends to be very specific to the object and application; therefore, I'll stick to the idea of keeping around multiple copies of the same object. The key concept to enable this in C++ is the image pointer, a pointer that, invisibly to clients, keeps more than one copy of the pointee. There are lots of variations and combinations possible, depending on your mood at the moment.

A Simple Image Pointer

This is the simplest treatment of the problem, one that we will build on for some number of pages to come. For the moment, this is a master pointer that deletes objects to which it points.

```
template <class Type>
class ImagePtr {
private:
    Type* current; // Current image presented to client
    Type* undo; // Previous image
public:
    ImagePtr() : undo(NULL), current(new Type) {}
    ImagePtr(const ImagePtr<Type>& ip)
        :   current(new Type(*(ip.current))),
            undo(NULL) {}
    ~ImagePtr() { delete current; delete undo; }
    ImagePtr<Type>& operator=(const ImagePtr<Type>& ip)
        {   if (this != &ip) {
                delete current;
                current = new Type(*(ip.current));
                }
            return *this;
        }
    void Snapshot()
        {   delete undo; // In case there was an old one
            undo = current;
            current = new Type(*undo);
        }
    void Commit() { delete undo; }
    void Rollback()
        {   if (undo != NULL) {
                delete current;
                current = undo;
                undo = NULL;
                }
        }
    Type* operator->() const { return current; }
};
```

The pointer always returns the "current" image as the value of operator->, but behind the scenes it may have an earlier version of the pointee stuffed away. The Snapshot() member function creates that image, using the pointee's own copy constructor. To change its mind and trash the changes, the client can call Rollback(); if the client is happy when the changes are done, it calls Commit().

The copy constructor and operator= maintain master pointer semantics, but do not take a snapshot on construction or immediately after assignment. Remember, it is states of the point*ee* that we are keeping track of here, not states of the point*er*. When a new copy of an object is created to maintain master pointer semantics, there are as yet no prior images of that copy to keep track of.

The destructor makes the assumption that if the client has not explicitly called Commit(), something is wrong, and it trashes the copy before exiting. This is the database specialist's skeptical view of the world: If anything unusual happens, assume the worst. In many applications it may be more appropriate to simply Commit() when the pointer is destroyed rather than Rollback(), assuming that whatever has happened up to that point was sensible.

Image Stacks

For multilevel undo, you may need to keep track of a stack of previous images. One way to do that is to store a stack in each image pointer. The following code assumes that you have access to a parameterized Stack class with member functions Empty(), Push(), Pop(), and DeleteAll(). Pop returns the top of the stack or NULL if the stack is empty. DeleteAll() empties the stack, deleting all the objects in it as they are popped. Each pointer keeps a stack of prior images. If the stack is empty, there have been no images taken. If the stack is non-empty, the bottom of the stack is the original object, which Rollback() finds and restores. The copy constructor and operator= work as for the simpler image pointer just described.

```
template <class Type>
class ImageStackPtr {
private:
    Type* current; // Current image presented to client
    Stack<Type> history; // Previous images
public:
    ImageStackPtr() : current(new Type) {}
    ImageStackPtr(const ImageStackPtr<Type>& ip)
        :   current(new Type(*(ip.current))) {}
    ~ImageStackPtr() { Rollback(); delete current; }
    ImageStackPtr<Type>&
        operator=(const ImageStackPtr<Type>& ip)
        {   if (this != &ip) {
                history.DeleteAll();
                delete current;
                current = new Type(*(ip.current));
                }
            return *this;
        }
    void PushImage()
        {   history.Push(current);
            current = new Type(*current);
        }
    void Commit() { history.DeleteAll(); }
    void PopImage() // Roll back one level
        {   if (!history.Empty()) {
                delete current;
                current = history.Pop();
                }
        }
    void Rollback() // Roll back to oldest image
        {   Type* old = history.Pop();
            Type* older = NULL;
            if (old != NULL) { // At least one
                while ((older = history.Pop()) != NULL) {
                    delete old;
                    old = older;
                    }
                delete current;
                current = old;
```

```
                    }
                }
        Type* operator->() const { return current; }
};
```

Having each pointer keep its own stack is reasonable for small numbers of objects per transaction, but if a single transaction has oodles of updated objects to keep track of, it is better to combine all these oodles of tiny stacks into one big one. This will be done later when we talk about transactions.

Images of Automatic Objects

The idea of an image can be generalized a bit to include not just objects pointed to by *'s and allocated using operator new, but automatic objects as well. Automatic objects include stack-based objects as well as data members and base class components of enclosing objects, whether or not the enclosing object is allocated on the heap.

```
template <class Type>
class AutoImage {
private:
    Type current;
    Type image;
    bool have_image; // True if there is an image
public:
    AutoImage() : have_image(false) {}
    AutoImage(const AutoImage<Type>& ai)
        : current(ai.current), image()
        , have_image(false) {}
    AutoImage<Type>& operator=(const AutoImage<Type>& ip)
        {   if (this != &ip) {
                current = ip.current;
                have_image = false;
                }
            return *this;
        }
    AutoImage<Type>& operator=(const Type& t)
        {   current = t;
            return *this;
```

```
        }
    operator Type&() { return current; }
    void Snapshot()
        {   image = current;
            have_image = true;
        }
    void Commit() { have_image = false; }
    void Rollback()
        {   current = image;
            have_image = false;
        }
    bool HaveImage() { return have_image; }
};
```

This template works with all classes that meet both of the following conditions:

1. The type used as the parameter has a no-argument constructor. This is used by the constructor of AutoImage for both current and image.

2. The type used as the parameter can be assigned correctly, using either the compiler-supplied default operator= or a type-specific overload. This is used by Snapshot() and Rollback().

All basic types such as ints and doubles meet these conditions. Other classes that have no-argument constructors and a workable operator= will also pass muster. (The longer I deal with C++, the stronger I feel that not meeting these conditions should be considered professional malpractice, the punishment for which should be two years at hard labor breaking rocks with BASIC. I would also throw copy constructors that work the way they should into the legal requirements.)

The copy constructor of AutoImage follows in the footsteps of ImagePtr and ImageStackPtr, using the no-argument constructor to create a dummy image and setting have_image to false. operator= does the same, except that there is no convenient way to destroy the object in the image data member. As a lesser of two evils, it is left unchanged and is subsequently ignored, since have_image is set to false. If that is a problem, if you really need to leave image uninitialized until it contains an actual snapshot and it really has to be destroyed as soon as have_image is set to false, two variations on this template will make it so:

1. Change image from a Type into a Type* and allocate it, using operator new. This requires more overhead than allowing it to be automatic, but it gives you control over the timing of construction and destruction.

2. Use the "virtual constructor" idiom of Chapter 13. Without going into details, that would allow you to declare image to be something bland like unsigned char image(sizeof Type), then to manually decide when to invoke Type's constructor and destructor on that space. C++ compilers don't like having you muck about like this, so put on your hip waders and carefully read the material in Chapter 13 before you attempt this.

As a final variation when AutoImage will only be used with structs or classes, add an operator->.

```
Type* operator->() { return &current; }
```

Note that unlike earlier operator->'s, this cannot be a const member function, because current is embedded inside *this, and there is no way to guarantee that the -> isn't being used to access a non-const member function of current.

The following class illustrates the use of this template. The enclosing Foo object needn't take its own image, as in the earlier image pointers, because all of its data members are capable of keeping their prior images separately.

```
class Foo {
private:
    AutoImage<int> some_integer;
    AutoImage<Bar> bar;
public:
    void Rollback()
        {   some_integer.Rollback();
            bar.Rollback();
        }
    void Commit()
        {   some_integer.Commit();
```

```
                bar.Commit();
        }
    void Snapshot()
        {   some_integer.Snapshot();
            bar.Snapshot();
        }
    int ProvideInt() const { return some_integer; }
    void ChangeInt(int new_value)
        {   if (!some_integer.HaveImage())
                some_integer.Snapshot();
            int&(some_integer) = new_value;
        }
    const Bar& ProvideBar() const { return bar; }
    Bar& UpdateBar()
        {   if (!bar.HaveImage())
                bar.Snapshot();
            return Bar&(bar);
        }
};
```

This assumes that Bar meets the necessary conditions. The last four member functions take spontaneous snapshots before allowing an update of a data member. For the int, providing a copy of the value is by definition const with respect to the data member being copied. When a member function that changes the value of the data member gets called, it's time to take a picture. The other data member, bar, is handled by the provision of both const and non-const member functions. It would be nice to simply overload the same function name ProvideBar(), with one overload returning a const Bar& and the other a non-const Bar&, but then the signatures would be identical. Remember that two functions cannot match in name and arguments yet have different return types. I have never understood this limitation in C++, which also prevents the creation of separate const and non-const versions of operator->.

```
const Type* operator->() const; // No snapshot taken
Type* operator->() const; // Takes a snapshot
```

This would have simplified life a lot, but arcane rules like this give the C++ nerds something to show off at those C++ cocktail parties.

While I'm complaining about limitations of C++, here's another one. Look at the code in Foo, just shown. Several member functions do nothing more than call the same member function of all data members and, in a more general case, base classes. Foo::Commit() just calls Commit() for all its members. You have to write such repetitive code manually; this cries out for a macro capability in the language so you can say, "For all members, call their Commit() member functions." The compiler already knows how to do that enumeration — it is used for constructors — but refuses to share it with you.

Images of Pointers (Pointer Images)

An interesting application of the AutoImage template is its use to keep track of a *-style pointer. There are times when you don't want to take extra images of the pointee, just to keep track of what the pointer pointed to in a previous life. This would be the case any time the pointer is not a master pointer. It also helps keep track of objects that were created or destroyed during a transaction.

```
AutoImage<Foo*> f;
```

f can now be restored to point to whatever it was pointing to when the transaction began, including nil. However, there is good reason to create a custom template for use with pointers: the need to overload operator-> so that the image pointer can be used as the left-hand side of something like ptr->MemberOfPointee();. Used with pointers, AutoImage is like the dumb pointers we dumped early on in Chapter 5. This template is more like the simpler smart (but not master) pointers.

```
template <class Type>
class PtrImage {
private:
    Type* current;
    Type* image;
    bool have_image; // True if there is an image
public:
    PtrImage() : current(NULL), image(NULL),
```

```
                       have_image(false) {}
         PtrImage(const PtrImage<Type>& pi)
             : current(pi.current), image(NULL)
             , have_image(false) {}
         PtrImage<Type>& operator=(const PtrImage<Type>& pi)
             {   if (this != &pi)
                     current = pi.current;
                 return *this;
             }
         PtrImage<Type>& operator=(Type* t)
             {   current = t; return *this; }
         operator Type*() { return current; }
         Type* operator->() const { return current; }
         void Snapshot()
             {   image = current;
                 have_image = true;
             }
         void Commit() { image = NULL; have_image = false; }
         void Rollback()
             {   if (have_image) {
                     current = image;
                     have_image = false;
                     }
             }
         bool HaveImage() { return have_image; }
};
// An example of its use
PtrImage<Foo> f;
f = new Foo; // Uses operator=(Foo*)
f.Snapshot();
f->MemberOfFoo(); // Uses operator->
```

If you want to automate things a little further, you can add a call to Snapshot() to both operator='s.

With so many variations wandering about this terrain, terminology gets to be a bother. I use the term *image pointer* to refer to pointers that maintain multiple images, almost always as master pointers, while *pointer images* describes to the sort of class shown here that keeps multiple images of a pointer's value.

Combinations and Variations

Once you have this much in your collection of building blocks, the combinations are endless. If you pick one from each column, you've got a special-purpose way to manage images:

- simple vs. master pointers
- automatic vs. operator new–allocated images
- one vs. stacks of images
- images of objects vs. images of pointer values
- spontaneous image-taking vs. manually calling Snapshot()

The specific combinations shown in this section are absolutely not an all-inclusive list, but rather a representative sample of ideas, all of which revolve around the same theme of image management and all of which are very peculiar to C++ and its unique syntax and semantics, such as constructors and operators. Let your mind stretch out and use these ideas to suit the problem at hand. That's what we'll do in the remainder of the chapter.

Transactions and Undo

Solving the problems of transactions goes a long way toward solving the problems of undo and multithreaded iterators, so let's bend our minds toward transactions first. To do that, we have to have a way to prevent more than one transaction at a time from updating a given object. Assuming that an image pointer of some sort will help, let's take a fresh look at the generic image pointer from earlier in the chapter.

```
template <class Type>
class ImagePtr {
private:
    Type* current; // Current image presented to client
    Type* undo; // Previous image
public:
```

```
    ImagePtr();
    ImagePtr(const ImagePtr<Type>& ip);
    ~ImagePtr();
    ImagePtr<Type>& operator=(const ImagePtr<Type>& ip);
    void Snapshot();
    void Commit();
    void Rollback();
    Type* operator->() const;
};
```

In a world of transactions, a few changes are needed:

- An object can be locked by at most one transaction at a time.
- If it is unlocked, it cannot be changed by anyone.
- If it is locked, it can only be updated by an object that is part of the owning transaction.

This means we have to have some representation of a transaction and will also need to flex our C++ muscles to build in these semantics. For a transaction, we'll use a class of that name. For a lock, we'll use an updating pointer; that is, normal clients will use a smart pointer that does not allow updating, while clients within the owning transaction will have access to a different pointer that does allow updating. What follows is a straightforward implementation of this architecture, though not necessarily a very efficient one. Later we will lift these simplifying assumptions through extensions to the architecture:

1. We are concerned only with undoing changes to existing objects, not with undoing creation and destruction of objects as part of a transaction.
2. The logic that chooses when to lock an object is outside the realm of the basic architecture that follows.

Transactions and Locks

A transaction is really nothing more than a collection of image pointers, together with a few member functions that iterate over the collection. One annoyance is that a single transaction may update objects of any number of different types. The transaction class itself, therefore, must be written in terms of something that will work with all types — sounds like an abstract base class to me.

```
// In Transaction.h
class Lock {
friend class Transaction;
protected:
    Transaction* transaction; // Trans this is owned by
    Lock() : transaction(NULL) {}
    void RegisterLock(Transaction* t) {
        if (transaction != NULL)
            // exception - already owned by someone else
            cerr << "Lock::RegisterLock - already locked"
            << endl;
            }
        else {
            t->AddLock(this);
            transaction = t;
            }
        }
    virtual ~Lock() {}
    virtual void Rollback()=0;
    virtual void Commit()=0;
};
class Transaction {
friend class Lock; // To give it access to AddLock()
private:
    Collection<Lock> locks;
    void AddLock(Lock*); // Add a lock to the transaction
public:
    ~Transaction();
    void Commit(); // Commit all images
    void Rollback(); // Rollback all images
    bool OwnsLock(Lock*); // true if lock is in 'locks'
};
```

Transaction maintains a collection of locks using a hypothetical Collection template. The RegisterLock() member function is put into the base class Lock so that it can get at the private AddLock() member function of Transaction. Friendship is not inherited, so declaring Lock to be a friend does not make its derived classes friends. The implementations are straightforward.

```
// In Transaction.cpp
void Transaction::AddLock(Lock* lock)
{
    locks += lock; // Uses overloaded += for collection
}
Transaction::~Transaction()
{
    Rollback();
    locks.DeleteAll();
}
void Transaction::Commit()
{
    Collection<Lock>::Iterator* iter
        = locks->Iterator();
    while (iter->More())
        iter->Next()->Commit();
    delete iter;
}
void Transaction::Rollback()
{
    Collection<Lock>::Iterator* iter
        = locks->Iterator();
    while (iter->More())
        iter->Next()->Rollback();
    delete iter;
}
bool Transaction::OwnsLock(Lock* lock)
{   return locks >= lock; }
```

The assumptions here are that the Collection template has a DeleteAll() member function that deletes all objects pointed to by the collection, that an overloaded operator+=(Type*) adds an element to the collection, that an overloaded operator>= indicates membership, and that a nested iterator class is returned by an iterator() member function. These are generic; use whatever you have.

Const Pointers

Derived classes of Lock will need to point to something akin to the
read-only pointers discussed earlier in the book.

```
template <class Type>
class LockPtr; // Fwd reference - derived from Lock

template <class Type>
class ConstPtr {
friend class LockPtr<Type>;
private:
    Type* old_image; // Pre-transaction image
    LockPtr<Type>* lock; // Current lock, if any
    ~ConstPtr() { delete old_image; }
    ConstPtr<Type>& operator=(const ConstPtr<Type>& cp)
        {   return *this; } // No assignment allowed
public:
    ConstPtr() : old_image(new Type), lock(NULL) {}
    ConstPtr(const ConstPtr<Type>& cp)
        : old_image(new Type(*(cp.old_image)))
        , lock(NULL) {}
    const Type* operator->() const { return old_image; }
    LockPtr<Type>& Lock(Transaction* t);
};
template <class Type>
LockPtr<Type>& ConstPtr<Type>::Lock(Transaction* t)
{
    if (lock != NULL && !t->OwnsLock(lock))
        // exception - already locked by someone else
    else {
        lock = new LockPtr<Type>(t, this);
        return *lock;
        }
}
```

It is OK to construct a new ConstPtr from an old one — the new one
starts out unlocked — but assignment implies a change, which is
only permitted from LockPtrs, not ConstPtrs. You enforce this by
defining a dummy operator= and making it private, so no one can get
at it. Because this is a master pointer, deleting the pointer also deletes

the pointee, which is about as drastic a change as you can imagine. Therefore, the destructor is also made private to prevent anyone from attempting to delete a ConstPtr.

You can handle the exception in the Lock() member function by throwing an exception; by changing the interface to return a boolean as well as the lock, the former indicating whether the lock succeeded; by returning a LockPtr<Type>* with NULL indicating that the lock failed; by returning a dummy lock with an overloaded operator! that can test whether the lock is valid; or by providing a separate CanLock(Transaction*) member function returning a boolean. The choice is a matter of style. It is not obvious that a throw is appropriate here; failure to lock is a reasonable outcome.

Lock Pointers

Aha! Now we come to the center of the whole design, the pointers that permit updates of the pointee. The pretransaction (undo) image is kept in the associated ConstPtr; the current, updated image is accessible only through the LockPtr. LockPtr has the member functions you've already come to cherish: Rollback() and Commit(). There is no need for a Snapshot() member function, since LockPtr takes spontaneous images in operator-> whenever this is needed.

```
template <class Type>
class LockPtr : public Lock {
friend class ConstPtr<Type>;
private:
    ConstPtr<Type>* master_ptr;
    Type* new_image;
    Transaction* transaction;
    LockPtr(Transaction* t, ConstPtr<Type>* cp);
    virtual ~LockPtr();
    virtual void Rollback();
    virtual void Commit();
public:
    Type* operator->() const { return new_image; }
};
```

```
template <class Type>
LockPtr<Type>::LockPtr(Transaction* t,
                       ConstPtr<Type>* cp)
    : transaction(t), master_ptr(cp)
    , new_image(new Type(*(cp->old_image)))
{
}
template <class Type>
LockPtr<Type>::~LockPtr()
{
    // This is, in effect, a rollback
    delete new_image; // Get rid of changes
    master_ptr->lock = NULL; // Leave ConstPtr in place
}
template <class Type>
void LockPtr<Type>::Rollback()
{
    delete new_image;
    new_image = new Type(*(master_ptr->old_image));
}
template <class Type>
void LockPtr<Type>::Commit()
{
    delete master_ptr->old_image;
    master_ptr->old_image = new_image; // Move to master
    new_image = new Type(*new_image); // Need a new copy
}
```

The destructor is made private so that no one can directly delete a
LockPtr; instead, the owning Transaction must do so through the base
class Lock. Rollback() and Commit() are virtual so that they can do
type-specific things like creating and destroying images. Both leave
the ConstPtr locked after finishing their work.

Creation and Destruction of Objects

Time for a little backfilling. Not many transactions are complicated
enough to need all this claptrap, yet simple enough that they don't
create or destroy objects. Those should be undoable; if an object is

created, undo should destroy it, and if an object was destroyed, undo should bring it back from the dead. This requires changes in both ConstPtr and LockPtr. We got a leg up on this by making ConstPtr's destructor private, so that only a friend or a ConstPtr can use the destructor. Now let's clean up the rest.

Changes to ConstPtr. Creation of a pointee is certainly a change and, therefore, should go through a LockPtr. But in order to have a LockPtr, you first have to have a ConstPtr and its Lock() member function. That means the constructor of ConstPtr just described won't work; it creates the pointee before Lock gets called. ConstPtr must start out in a NULL state until such time as a LockPtr allocates an object and commits that change. The changes needed to ConstPtr are these:

- Have its no-argument constructor set old_image to NULL.
- Add an operator! that tests for a NULL address.
- Throw an exception in operator-> if the address is NULL.
- Either disallow copying or set the copy's old_image to NULL.

The problem with allowing a normal copy constructor for ConstPtr is that it might create a new copy of the pointee, but not allow the creation to be rolled back. Here is the revised ConstPtr. Member function definitions that are unchanged from the simpler version above are not shown.

```
private:
    ConstPtr(const ConstPtr&)
        : old_image(NULL), lock(NULL) {}
public:
    ConstPtr() : old_image(NULL), lock(NULL) {}
    bool operator!() { return old_image == NULL; }
    const Type* operator->() const
        {   if (old_image == NULL)
                // exception
            return old_image;
        }
```

Changes to LockPtr. LockPtr is going to be a lot busier now:

- It has to create pointees on demand. A new function, Make(), will be added for that.

- We have to throw an exception in operator-> if the address is NULL.

In this code, only definitions of member functions that have changed are listed.

```
// In the declaration of LockPtr
public:
    void Make(); // Create a new pointee
    void Destroy(); // Destroy the pointee
// Definitions that have changed
template <class Type>
LockPtr<Type>::LockPtr(Transaction* t,
                          ConstPtr<Type>* cp)
    : transaction(t), master_ptr(cp)
    , new_image(cp->old_image != NULL ?
                   new Type(*(cp->old_image)) : NULL)
{
}
template <class Type>
void LockPtr<Type>::Commit()
{
    delete master_ptr->old_image;
    master_ptr->old_image = new_image;
    if (new_image != NULL)
        new_image = new Type(*new_image);
}
template <class Type>
Type* LockPtr<Type>::operator->() const
{
    if (new_image == NULL)
        // exception
    return new_image;
}
template <class Type>
void LockPtr<Type>::Make()
{
```

```
    delete new_image; // In case it is non-nil currently
    new_image = new Type; // A blank new object
}
template <class Type>
void LockPtr<Type>::Destroy()
{
    delete new_image;
    new_image = NULL;
}
```

Make() follows the semantics of assignment, allowing one to Make() over an existing pointee by deleting whatever the LockPtr currently points to and replacing it with a new, blank object.

Simplifying Object Creation

Creating an object is now a three-step process: Create a ConstPtr that points to NULL, ask it for a Lock, then ask the lock to Make() an object. While this may strike your colleagues as an impressive feat of engineering prowess, they'll probably give you a funny look as they bypass it all and go back to using operator new, which is, only one step, and they are, after all, very busy people. There are several ways to reduce creation to a single step, but the best is to add another constructor to ConstPtr.

```
template <class Type>
ConstPtr<Type>::ConstPtr(Transaction* t)
    : old_image(NULL), lock(NULL)
{
    LockPtr<Type>& lp = Lock(t);
    lp.Make();
}
```

A later call to Lock() will return the already allocated LockPtr.

Undo

This is too easy. If you've been singing along with the transaction songbook, all you need to implement undo in a safe, generic way is to add in a base line from your favorite graphical user interface class library. This will have a *command* or *event* class that is the perfect place to create and manipulate the transaction data structures. An event object is created to carry out some command or make a change. For example, the user chose Delete from the Edit menu, or perhaps hit the Delete key on the keyboard. An object is created from a class that is positively brilliant about Deleting whatever was selected. That object subsequently not only carries out the change, but also supports the Undo command in the Edit menu. In its constructor, create a Transaction, use that Transaction to store all changes, then use it to support Undo.

Variations

There isn't much sense in throwing out more code relating to transactions. If you haven't gotten the general idea by now, throwing more wood on the fire won't help, but if you have followed to this point, the details of implementing the following variations won't present any trouble. Therefore, I'll just spend a brief moment or two outlining a few important variations on the theme.

Nested Locking

If this approach is to make any sense, we have to take away the keys to the pointees and make everyone go through ConstPtrs and LockPtrs. This includes not only changes made to pointees directly by clients, but also changes one pointee makes to another. This means that in general the pointees have to refer to one another through ConstPtrs and LockPtrs, just as clients do.

```
class A {
private:
    ConstPtr<B>& b; // ConstPtr as above
    // etc.
};
```

If an instance of A in this example wants to call a non-const member function of b, it must first obtain a LockPtr on b. This means that A must know what transaction it is carrying out when it tries to change b, and that information must come from the client. For the sake of discussion, let's call objects directly accessed by clients *primary* and objects indirectly updated by a pointee *secondary* to the pointee. (A single object may be both primary and secondary.)

If a primary object encapsulates a secondary one — that is, the secondary one is invisible to the rest of the world — it may be possible to bypass this rule. The primary object's copy constructor must duplicate the secondary object, and the primary object's operator= must duplicate the right-hand side's secondary object. If these hold, the image-taking logic of ConstPtrs and LockPtrs will work properly with the encapsulated objects. This is automatically the case if the secondary object is embedded in the primary one; that is, rather than store a pointer to b, each A simply embeds a B as a data member.

```
class A {
private:
    B b; // Embedded member
    // etc.
};
```

The compiler will automatically invoke B's copy constructor whenever an A is copied and will invoke B's operator= whenever an A is assigned.

Assuming A does need to lock b, where does the Transaction* come from? Ultimately from outside A — that is, from the client. However, there are three options for accomplishing that. As every moviegoer knows, that tense music you hear in the background signals that this is but a foreshadow of an issue that will reach a climax in later chapters: Who describes an object? Briefly, these are the options:

- Pass the Transaction* to each member function of A that might need to call a non-const member function of B.
- Pass the Transaction* to A once when it is locked and store it there in a data member.

- Make A's ConstPtr even more brilliant: Give it the ability to lock the secondary objects on behalf of A.

The last of these should come with a warning label saying "Professional stunt driver; don't try this at home." However, there are times when it is the best option for implementing transactions with off-the-shelf pointee classes. It may even be possible to use this strategy to allow A to continue to store its beloved B*'s and not know anything about ConstPtrs and LockPtrs; A's increasingly ingenious ConstPtr and/or LockPtr can swap addresses around inside A without A's knowledge, as images are taken and committed. We will roll into, around, and over this idea of objects that describe and/or manipulate other objects as the book unfolds, and we will come back to this problem of interobject references toward the end.

Deadlocks and Queuing

If all this transaction artillery is turned loose on a situation in which there can't be more than one transaction at a time, you can relax. If more than one transaction at a time may be messing around with your objects, we have a little more hill to climb. This might be because your application serves more than one user, or because it is a graphical application that provides context-sensitive undo, in which you might have an undoable command pending on more than one window at once. The last hill is designing how your software should behave if it tries to lock something that is already locked.

Conservative Locking. Under conservative locking, a transaction locks all objects it might need before making any changes. If it can't lock them all, either it waits for them to become available before beginning, or it throws up its hands and tells the user it respectfully declines to honor her request. One way to implement conservative locking is to subclass Transaction and attempt to lock everything in sight in the derived class's constructor, assuming you have standard exception handling, or in a separate initialization function of the derived Transaction if not.

Aggressive Locking. Under aggressive locking, a transaction can begin whenever it has a mind to, locking objects as it goes. I like to call this "just in time" locking, because only objects that are, in fact, updated get locked, and they get locked just before being updated for the first time.

Queuing and Deadlocks. Whether or not to support queuing of lock requests is a separate design decision. If queuing is not supported and a transaction tries to lock something already locked by some other transaction, basically the transaction fails. If conservative locking is used, the transaction never starts, and if aggressive locking is used, the transaction rolls itself back, crosses its hands over its binary chest, and gives the user a hard stare. This is fine for some applications, but for most it is the sort of thing a customer support hot line person might dream up to ensure job security. Rather than trash the second transaction, it is usually better to make it wait until the thing it wants to lock becomes available, when the transaction currently holding the lock releases it.

If queuing is not permitted, you never have to worry about deadlock situations in which A waits for B while B waits for A; the transaction that first requests a lock it can't have gets killed first. If queuing is permitted, when a transaction is told it can't have a lock, the locking code should scan to see if that transaction owns any locks for which others are queued up. If so, one of the transactions needs to be put out of its misery.

This is getting dangerously close to the point at which you should either split your one application into several collaborative ones and let the operating system do its scheduling thing, or use one of the commercially available threading libraries. In any case, there aren't any additional C++-isms or C++-specific implications here, so we'll rest at having raised the issue. There are lots of good books on queuing, locks, and multithreading available from the database section of your bookstore.

Multilevel Rollback

Extending transaction semantics to cover multilevel rollbacks is pretty simple, given the StackPtr ideas we discussed earlier. There are two major flavors.

LockPtrs with Image Stacks. The most straightforward way to implement multilevel rollback on the scale of transactions is to put a stack of old images into each LockPtr. This borrows from the StackPtr code discussed earlier. However, this is only practical for conservative locking; under aggressive locking, an object can lock for the first time after others have already been changed. This makes it difficult to roll back the transaction one set of changes at a time, since the stacks in the various LockPtrs aren't in sync.

Stacks of LockPtr/Image Pairs. It is also possible to slice the problem the other way: give each Transaction a stack, each level of which is a collection of old image/LockPtr pairs. Each level contains only LockPtrs that existed at the time that level was committed. This works better in the general case. It is also slightly more efficient to use one big stack rather than lots of little ones.

Optimizing Space

Another variation is the rearrangement of the data structures to reduce the overhead for unlocked ConstPtrs, although at the cost of some speed. Only two things separate the ConstPtrs in this chapter from the read-only pointers discussed in Chapter 6 that didn't know a transaction from a hole in the ground: They have a reference to a ConstPtr stuffed in a data member and a Lock() member function. We can get rid of the former and make a slight change to the latter.

Imagine a global data structure, perhaps stored as a static data member of the Transaction class, that maintains a table showing which Transactions have locks on which ConstPtrs. For each such pair, the table contains a corresponding LockPtr. Whenever any ConstPtr's Lock() member function is called, it looks to see whether 'this' appears already in the table; if so, it matches the transaction passed as argument to the one stored in the table, and, if everything checks out, it returns the LockPtr it finds lurking in the table. If the ConstPtr doesn't find itself in the table, it adds a new triplet (ConstPtr, Transaction, LockPtr). If it finds itself under a different transaction, it signals an exception.

This is slightly more space-efficient than the scheme presented earlier; it does not waste space on NULL data members for all those objects that aren't locked at any one time. It is obviously more complicated and slower; a single indirection through a data member zips by while a data structure is just getting its search engine warmed up.

You might wonder why the Lock() member function needs to stay with the ConstPtr, as opposed to becoming a member of some other class or even a global function. If we get rid of the LockPtr* data member and the Lock() member function, ConstPtr reduces to a common, everyday read-only pointer that when asked about transactions just responds with a blank stare. Or does it? LockPtr still needs to be declared a friend; this means at least a trivial change will be needed. Furthermore, Transaction doesn't know the concrete type of the pointee, so it can't use the LockPtr template to create a lock object. Remember, that's why we created the abstract base class Lock. Sigh. It would have been nice to leave ConstPtr blissfully ignorant, but that isn't in the cards.

Some Closing Perspective

There isn't much code involved in implementing the full transaction scheme presented here, but that doesn't make it simple. Changes are required to virtually every class that points to another class, since most pointers have to adhere to the ConstPtr/LockPtr conventions. However, rather than showing the utter futility of trying to do something like this in C++, this just reinforces the value of sticking to two basic C++ principles from the outset:

1. Use smart pointers, even if you aren't sure why you should.
2. Religiously separate out const accesses to things from non-const accesses.

It is an order of magnitude easier to implement this sort of advanced architecture if code has already been factored in this way.

This is part of that Zen of C++ I keep talking about, an understanding not just of how the language addresses the immediate problem, but of how the language accompanies you on the journey through to a complete, robust program. The C++-isms that support this sort of architecture really don't have counterparts in other languages (copy constructors, operator=, operator->, to name a few). These syntactic and semantic oddities end up making complex class libraries more readable and useable. Think of how much more complicated this would all be for a user, for example, if you couldn't overload operator-> in ConstPtr and LockPtr. If you use the right idioms, C++ won't lag behind when the road turns muddy and the weather sours.

Above all, remember that this chapter has been an exercise in seeing just how far the idea of a smart pointer can carry us before we move on to fresh material. The answer is: pretty far. When we add in some of the idioms and design practices of later chapters, these sorts of architectures will become easier to add to existing code.

SECTION 3 —— *Tips on Types*

So much has been written on designing class hierarchies that I hesitate to even broach the subject. Most of what has been written has little to do specifically with C++, so we can skip that part. Of the rest, I think there are a couple of subjects that haven't received the attention they deserve. One is the critical importance of a special kind of class hierarchy to C++ programming: the homomorphic class hierarchy. The other is the idea that a pointer can look to a client exactly like a real, honest-to-goodness object, not a portal to one. Those are the primary subjects of this section. Along the way, as usual, we'll take time to wander onto interesting paths as they cross the main road.

CHAPTER 10

Multiple Dispatch

When I talk about class hierarchies, it is tempting to launch into a rambling discourse on object-oriented design, but I'll resist the temptation and stick to a portion of the subject that plays to C++'s strengths: the homomorphic class hierarchy. This is a long name for a simple idea — a hierarchy of classes all of which have the same public interface, inherited from a common base class. Simple in concept, but the implications of this idiom are enormous.

One subject that comes up immediately is the dispatch of member functions when the only thing you know about the arguments is that they are all derived from some lofty ancestral class. The brute force switch/case techniques that you see in conventional code can usually be replaced by a much more elegant, faster, and easier-to-maintain architecture known as *multiple dispatch*.

This and the next chapter step away from our obsessive focus on pointers, but all you pointer fans out there, don't despair — Chapter 12 combines the two concepts of homomorphism and smart pointers into even smarter pointers, so smart you don't even know they are there.

Homomorphic Class Hierarchies

In a homomorphic class hierarchy, somewhere at the top you will always find an abstract base class that defines the public interface for its descendants. For purely sentimental reasons, I will call this ancestral class Grandpa. Grandpa is usually a *pure abstract class*, that is, one that has no data members and has only pure virtual member functions.

```
class Grandpa {
public: // Nothing private or protected
    virtual void Fn1()=0;
    virtual int Fn2(int)=0;
};
```

Grandpa obviously doesn't need constructors and the pure virtual members ensure that Grandpa will never be instantiated directly. I have a less formal name for a pure abstract class: a *retired* class. This sort of class probably used to do useful things early in the development cycle, but now it mostly just binds together the family abstractly.

This much doesn't guarantee homomorphism. That is determined by the way you derive from Grandpa. Derived classes that do not add any public members are homomorphic with respect to Grandpa. They can have all the private and protected members they want, just no new public ones.

```
class Dad : public Grandpa {
private:
    // Stuff Dad never told me about
protected:
    // Stuff I got from Dad that didn't come from Gramps
public:
    virtual void Fn1();
    virtual int Fn2(int);
};
class AuntMartha : public Grandpa {
private:
    // Private stuff
```

```
protected:
    // Stuff she passed along to my cousins
public:
    virtual void Fn1();
    virtual int Fn2(int);
};
```

You can continue to derive as deeply as you want from here (e.g., class Me : public Dad), as long as no one adds to the public interface.

We'll be seeing lots of examples demonstrating how useful homomorphic class hierarchies can be, but before we do, here is a three-pronged intuitive argument for using the concept.

Substitution of Derived Classes

If you arrived early enough at the object-oriented party you got to name things. A fellow named Liskov got his name on the idea that if a client deals with some base class, it shouldn't care which derived class is actually doing the work. You should be able to substitute an instance of any derived class for an instance of any other derived class and clients of the base class should shrug their shoulders and go about their business as if nothing has happened. This is the Liskov Substitution Criterion, and it is generally agreed among the object-oriented cognoscenti that this is a Good Idea.

Strictly speaking, you don't have to use homomorphism to accomplish this. If derived classes have extra public members, just don't call them from a client of the base class. But wait a minute ... why did you add those public member functions if they aren't meant to be used? If one derived class adds some public members, and another derived class adds different ones, it is a sure bet that eventually you'll run across a spot in your program where the two can't be freely swapped.

The real danger if you don't provide for substitutability is that clients will have to worry about derived classes, not just the base class they know and love. If there are additional public members in Dad, a client of Grandpa will eventually have to ask the object, "Let's

drop the pretences here — just what kind of object are you really?"
This violates a whole book's worth of principles of modularity and
encapsulation.

The easiest way to achieve substitutability is to use homomorphism. At least for interfaces, homomorphism supports substitutability by definition, since clients of Grandpa don't have to worry
about whether there are other member functions out there that they
are supposed to use.

Normal Derivation

It is possible to have impure virtual member functions and data
members in Grandpa and still have full substitutability of the interfaces. However, just because the interfaces are the same, this
doesn't mean the objects are interchangeable. There is the little matter of side effects. Suppose that Fn1() is no longer a pure virtual in
Grandpa.

```
void Grandpa::Fn1()
{
    // code that causes sideeffects
}
void Dad::Fn1()
{
    // code that causes different sideeffects
}
void AuntMartha::Fn1()
{
    Grandpa::Fn1();
    // additional stuff
}
```

A client of Grandpa may rely on Grandpa's side effects. I know, I
know, encapsulation blah blah blah and one should never rely on
side effects, but get real. We call functions to do things like draw on
the screen or create other objects or write things to a file, and without those side effects the functions wouldn't be worth much, would
they? If Grandpa has certain built-in side effects, clients of Grandpa

have a perfect right to expect that all his derived classes will preserve them. Dad always challenged Grandpa's authority, and in his override of Fn1(), he doesn't bother to call Grandpa::Fn1(). This trashes Grandpa::Fn1()'s side effects, and sooner or later that's going to worry a client of Grandpa, who may not want to deal the same way with Dad. AuntMartha, however, calls Grandpa::Fn1() from within her override, thereby preserving any side effects of Grandpa::Fn1(). AuntMartha can now do anything additional within reason, and clients of Grandpa couldn't care less.

An override that calls the base class version of the function is said to *normally derive* from that function. It doesn't matter as much if that call comes first, last, or in the middle of the override, just that it happens at some point. If all overrides in a derived class derive normally, then the entire class is said to derive normally. If all derived classes of a homomorphic base class derive normally, and none of them adds really outrageous side effects of its own, they are substitutable for one another.

The easiest way to enforce this is to make all of Grandpa's member functions pure virtuals. This is a degenerate case of normal derivation; if the base class version is a pure virtual, then by definition side effects (there are none) are preserved.

Encapsulated Derived Classes

We still haven't completed the case for using a pure abstract base class at the top of the hierarchy. We can still achieve substitutability and normal derivation with data members and non-virtual member functions in Grandpa and virtual member functions that are normally overridden by derived classes. Why insist that Grandpa be a pure base class? The answer, in a word, is *encapsulation*. If clients deal only with a pure abstract base class containing only public member functions, those clients are receiving the bare minimum information needed in order to use the class. The rest, including the derived classes themselves, can all be buried discretly inside a .cpp file.

```
// In the .h file
class Grandpa {...};
// In .cpp file(s)
class Dad : public Grandpa {...};
class AuntMartha : public Grandpa {...};
```

This encapsulation of derived classes is one of the rays of true C++ enlightenment, one of those dead giveaways when you look at code that the person who wrote it knew what she was doing. You can make this even stronger by declaring the private classes to be static, thereby limiting their name space to that of the source file in which they appear.

There are some sticky problems with encapsulated derived classes — for example, how can you create instances of classes such as Dad that the client can't see from the .h file — but these are easy to solve with the idioms that follow in this and the next two chapters. Until we say otherwise, we'll continue to publish the derived classes in the .h file, knowing that that is a way station on the track to fully encapsulating them.

Multiple Dispatch

The most commonly used example of a homomorphic class hierarchy is a set of classes that together represent all the different sorts of numbers: integers, complex numbers, real numbers, and so on. The Grandpa class for this might be called Number and might have an interface like this.

```
class Number {
public:
    virtual Number operator+(const Number&)=0;
    virtual Number operator-(const Number&)=0;
    // etc.
};
class Integer : public Number {
private:
    int i;
public:
```

```
    Integer(int x) : i(x) {}
    virtual Number operator+(const Number&);
    // etc.
};
```

This looks easier on paper than it actually is. How can we implement Integer::operator+(Number&) when you and I both know that's not really a Number but some specific derived class inside those parentheses? For every pair of addend types, there is a specific algorithm needed to do the arithmetic. Complex + Integer is different from Integer + Real, which is different from Integer + ArbitraryPrecisionInteger. How is the program to figure out which algorithm to use? If you said something like "Ask the argument to operator+ what its real type is," go to the back of the class.

```
class Number {
protected:
    int type; // Encodes the real type
    int TypeOf() { return type; }
    // etc.
};
// Somewhere in your code
    switch(type) {
        case kInteger:...
        case kComplex:...
        };
```

That's exactly the sort of type knowledge we're trying to avoid. Besides, there aren't really any very elegant ways to directly implement that type knowledge. Have you ever seen how switch/case statements are implemented? It isn't pretty or efficient. Instead, let's leverage the compiler's type knowledge and the miracle of modern vtable technology.

Double Dispatch

The general problem can be represented by a matrix whose rows represent the type of the left-hand side of an operation and whose columns represent possible types of the right-hand side. At each cell of the matrix, there is a specific algorithm that handles that intersection of types. This comes up most often with homomorphic class hierarchies like Number, but in general the types on the left-hand side don't need to be the same as the ones on the right.

There are brute force solutions, such as burying a type code of some sort into each instance, but a more elegant — and usually more efficient — solution is known as *double dispatch*.

```
class Number {
protected:
    // Dispatch functions for operator+
    virtual Number& operator+(const Integer&)=0;
    virtual Number& operator+(const Complex&)=0;
    // etc. for all derived types
public:
    virtual Number& operator+(const Number&)=0;
    virtual Number& operator-(const Number&)=0;
    // etc.
};
class Integer : public Number {
private:
    int i;
protected:
    virtual Number& operator+(const Integer&);
    virtual Number& operator+(const Complex&);
public:
    Integer(int x) : i(x) {}
    virtual Number& operator+(const Number&);
    // etc.
};
Number& Integer::operator+(const Number& n)
{
    return n + *this; // Flip left and right hand sides
}
Number& Integer::operator+(const Integer& n)
{
    // The following is pseudocode
    if (i + n.i is too big for an int) {
        return an ArbitraryPrecisionInteger
```

```
    }
    else return Integer(i + n.i);
}
```

There is a subtle problem with this fragment that we'll return to later, but for now concentrate on the concept. This is a little like one of those 3D puzzle pictures — you have to relax your eyes and stare at the code for a while before the pattern becomes clear. When a client tries to add two Integers, the compiler dispatches to Integer::operator+() because operator+(Number&) is virtual — the compiler correctly finds the derived class implementation. By the time your code in Integer::operator+(Number&) starts, you know what the real type of the left-hand side is, but the right-hand side is still a mystery. That's when the second dispatch in double dispatch comes in: return n + *this;. This flips the left- and right-hand sides, causing the compiler to go scrambling to find n's vtable. But now it is looking for the override of Number::operator+(Integer&), since the actual type of *this is known with certainty to be Integer. This leads to a call to Integer::operator+(Integer&), where the actual type of both sides is known and the arithmetic can finally take place. If you have trouble seeing the pattern here, go take a walk around the block and try again until it comes clear. Think of it this way: Instead of an integer type code, we use the vtable to determine the true type of a Number.

This is not only elegant, it is also probably more efficient than the solutions you were cooking up in your own mind. Have you ever seen the code generated for a switch/case, for example? It isn't pretty and it's a lot less efficient than indexing two vtables in succession.

In spite of the elegance, there is a high price in code size and complexity to pay for double dispatch:

- If you have m derived classes and n operators over them, there are a total of m*(n+1) virtual member functions to maintain in *each* derived class, as well as a like number of pure virtual stubs in the ancestor class. The total number of dispatch functions is thus $(m+1)*m*(n+1)$. That's a big number in all but the most trivial hierarchies.

- If the operator is not commutable — that is, you cannot simply redispatch to the same operator with the arguments reversed — double this number, because you'll have to implement the function with the arguments in both orders. For example, x/y is not the same as y/x; you'll need both operator/ and DivideInto members, the latter with the order of the arguments reversed.
- Clients of the base class see all the gory protected member functions, even though they don't care about them.

Nevertheless, for simple situations double dispatch is a reasonable way to address a problem that is hard no matter how you tackle it. These situations by their nature require lots of little fragments of code. Double dispatch just replaces big, ugly, nonmodular switch/ cases with faster, more modular virtual dispatching.

In most situations, there are ways to reduce the number of member functions, but they involve various degrees of compromise to our strict rules about never asking an object what its real type is. A discussion of some of these tricks follows. The visibility of the derived classes to clients of Number is also correctable at a slight additional cost; it will be discussed in Chapter 12. As in most design problems in C++, if you are faced with one of these matrices of operations, you will have to exercise your good judgment as to when a performance or code size penalty is worth the better modularity.

Heteromorphic Double Dispatch

Double dispatch most commonly arises in situations like this in which both arguments derive from a common ancestor, but that need not be the case. The left- and right-hand sides to an operation might be from different classes with no common ancestor.

One of my favorite case studies of this comes from event processing in graphical user interfaces. You have lots of different kinds of events: mouse activity of various sorts, keyboard events, operating system-generated events, perhaps even exotica like voice recognition or pen strokes. On the other hand, the user interface will typically have lots of different kinds of *views*, *panes*, or *windows* — the terminology depends on the operating system and language you use — including outermost windows with title bars and close boxes, text-editing views, and areas where you can draw pretty pictures. For each intersection of a specific kind of event with a specific kind of view, a unique implementation might be required. This is exactly the same problem we had with operations on Numbers, except that events and views do not have a common base class. Nevertheless, the same double dispatch technique still works.

```
class Event { // A pure virtual base class for events
public:
    virtual void Process(View* v)=0;
};
class MouseClick : public Event {
public:
    virtual void Process(View* v)
        {  v->Process(*this); }
};
class View { // A pure virtual base class for views
public:
    virtual void Process(MouseClick& ev)=0;
    virtual void Process(Keystroke& ev)=0;
    // etc.
};
```

Although at first glance this problem is different from Number, look closer. The implementation of the Process() member function of Event does nothing more than "turn around" the operation by redispatching the other way. Because Event::Process() is virtual, by the time the View class gets the message, the exact type of Event is known, and the compiler will correctly call the right overloaded version of View::Process().

In general, whenever it is tempting to stick in a type code as a data member, so that you can tell with which derived class you are dealing, it is a good idea to first consider whether or not double dispatch, or one of the variations below, can throw the monkey onto the compiler's back.

Higher Order Dispatch

So far, we've only discussed binary functions, but the same technique can be extended to handle functions of any number of unknown argument types. If there are n arguments to the function, you need to dispatch n times. Suppose there is a function that takes three Numbers as arguments, returning a Number& as the result. We can arrange for the first argument to be the left-hand side of operator -> (or .). The remainder is a game of permutations.

```
class Number {
protected:
    // 'this' is the implicit 2nd argument
    virtual Number& fn1(Integer& n1, Number& n3)=0;
    virtual Number& fn1(Complex& n1, Number& n3)=0;
    // etc. for all types in 1st position

    // 'this' is the implicit 3rd argument
    virtual Number& fn2(Integer& n1, Integer& n2)=0;
    virtual Number& fn2(Integer& n1, Complex& n2)=0;
    virtual Number& fn2(Complex& n1, Integer& n2)=0;
    virtual Number& fn2(Complex& n1, Complex& n2)=0;
    // etc. for all permutations
public:
    // 'this' is the implicit 1st argument
    virtual Number& fn(Number& n2, Number& n3)=0;
};
class Integer : public Number {
protected:
    // 'this' is the implicit 2nd argument
    virtual Number& fn1(Integer& n1, Number& n3)
        {   return n3.fn2(n1, *this); }
    virtual Number& fn1(Complex& n1, Number& n3)
        {   return n3.fn2(n1, *this); }
    // etc. for all types in 1st position

    // 'this' is the implicit 3rd argument
    virtual Number& fn2(Integer& n1, Integer& n2)
        {   // the real implementation - all 3 are known
        }
```

```
    // etc. for all permutations
public:
    // 'this' is the implied 1st argument
    virtual Number& fn(Number& n2, Number& n3)
        {  return n2.fn1(*this, n3); }
};
```

As with double dispatch, this is usually faster than the sorts of architectures people usually come up with. It involves three trivial hops among the vtables, which is much faster than hashing or table lookup. However, it is ugly and gets unwieldy in a hurry. If you take every problem with double dispatch and make it grow exponentially, you will get some idea of what maintaining this structure requires.

This technique applies to heteromorphic situations as well, although the result is what I call *grasshopper* code: It jumps all over the place. If you do this in a nontrivial situation, on the day of your code review you might want to bring in a box of donuts or chocolates and be extra nice to everyone on the team. Even if it is the best solution, it is likely to be … er, controversial at the least.

If the function to be performed has more than two arguments, the number of permutations grows faster than weeds in your lawn after a rain shower. If you use multiple dispatch with more than two arguments, you would do well to seriously consider some of the following clustering techniques to reduce the number of permutations.

Dispatch Clusters and Conversions

In real life, you seldom have a unique implementation for each combination of left-hand and right-hand types. For example, in any operation involving a Complex number and something else, you will end up producing a Complex result. Converting the non-Complex argument to Complex reduces the number of dispatch member functions you have to maintain. The general term I use to describe this collapsing of the dispatch matrix is *clustering*. There really aren't any elegant, general-purpose yet blazingly fast clustering techniques available for most problems. More to the point, those techniques have little or nothing to do with C++ syntactic features or idioms. They require either adding type knowledge, a subject we'll return to in the next chapter, or using the sort of if-then-else or switch/case logic we strove so hard to avoid in this section.

These are two basic approaches:

1. Use a class hierarchy to dispatch multiple combinations of different argument types to the same implementation.
2. Form a *conversion hierarchy* and convert one or both arguments to more universal types; then dispatch.

It is easy to confuse these, but they really are different.

Clustering by Base Class. The first approach may involve setting up a class hierarchy that mirrors the clusters, then maintaining dispatch members only for higher levels of the class hierarchy. The compiler will "convert" derived classes to the intermediate-level base classes automatically in order to match the member function signatures. This works best with very shallow hierarchies, since the compiler will yell "Ambiguous!" if a signature matches two base classes.

```
class foo {...};
class bar : public foo {...};
class banana : public bar {...};
void fn(bar&);
void fn(foo&);
fn(*(new banana)); // Ambiguous! Ha, ha, ha, ha!
```

Compilers love this sort of thing, especially since they can lie in wait and not report an error until you actually hit the right combination of types. If f() is also overloaded to accept a banana& there is no problem, because the compiler always prefers an exact match over a conversion, but that would undo the whole point of clustering through automatic conversion to a base class.

Separating Types from Class Hierarchies. The second approach involves some tortured logic, but it converts arguments from more specific to more universal types before dispatching. For example, in any operation involving a Complex, first convert the other argument to type Complex, effectively removing one entire row and column — those involving Complex — from the dispatch matrix. If neither argument is a Complex, check to see whether one is Real and, if so, convert the other one to Real. If neither one is Complex or Real, check for Rational, and so on. This conversion hierarchy — from Integer (or whatever) to Rational to Real to Complex — does not match the class hierarchy, since deriving a lightweight Integer from a top-heavy Complex doesn't make sense. This is actually a very interesting case study in why hierarchies of types — numbers, in this case — often make lousy hierarchies of classes, which are based on strictly shared properties.

We're Not Done Yet

There are clearly some problems with the dispatch techniques just discussed. For one thing, the derived classes cannot reasonably be encapsulated, since they all have to be listed in the dispatch member function interfaces of the base class. In fact, in the interests of avoiding a publicly known type code, we exposed all the derived types for public scrutiny — not a very good tradeoff. For another, what happens to operators like +=? If you do Integer += Complex, the type of the result should be Complex, but we have no way yet to convert the type of something in place.

Both of these problems will be disposed of for homomorphic class hierarchies in Chapters 11 and 12, although the techniques can be generalized to other situations like the Event-View problem. In the meantime, the techniques shown in this chapter are directly useful in situations in which encapsulation is not a prime consideration, but performance is. Two hops through vtables are almost always faster than more conventional approaches.

Finally, did you get a funny twinge each time you saw a member function return a Number&?

```
Number& Integer::operator+(const Integer& n)
{
    // The following is pseudocode
    if (i + n.i is too big for an int) {
        return an ArbitraryPrecisionInteger
        }
    else return Integer(i + n.i);
}
```

Returning a reference to a temporary value is dicey. Many compilers will already have trashed the return value before you can use it. Allocating the return value with operator new instead of on the stack solves the immediate problem, since the value is guaranteed to live after the member function is finished. But alas, that introduces a memory management problem: how and when to delete the return value? To solve this problem, we need both the material in Chapters 11 and 12, and one of the memory management techniques, such as reference counting, which are discussed in the last section of this book.

In sum, this chapter provides enough information to solve simple problems like events and views, but it only lays a foundation on which to build more general solutions.

CHAPTER 11

Factory Functions and Class Objects

The last chapter wandered over the general subject of homomorphic class hierarchies and plunged into multiple dispatch. This chapter continues to explore the terrain of class hierarchies by examining class objects and related subjects.

One problem with the examples in the last chapter is that the derived classes are all visible to clients. Yet, if the derived classes are all buried under several feet of .cpp file, how is a client to create instances of those hidden classes? That is the focus of the early part of this chapter. A *factory function* is a function that encapsulates the use of operator new to create instances of a class. It is generally agreed among the C++ literati that factory functions are a Good Thing, and we'll see why throughout the remainder of the book. If you find yourself at one of those C++ cocktail parties searching for good conversation topics, swizzle your wineglass and casually mention the time you found yourself on a C++ safari and got out of a nasty scrape with a factory function.

We'd like to be able to do a variety of useful things at run time in many programs, such as asking an object what its class is, that are simply not supported by the C++ run-time model. There is a proposed standard called Run Time Type Information (RTTI), but for reasons we'll discuss, it is hardly a thorough or a practical tool today. We will instead look at custom-built solutions revolving around the idea of class objects, including a special case, the exemplar.

Factory Functions

Suppose you bought in to the idea that homomorphism is a good thing to do and ran out and created your own homomorphic class hierarchy.

```
// In Grandpa.h
class Grandpa {...};

// Hidden away in Grandpa.cpp
class Dad : public Grandpa {...};
class AuntieEm : public Grandpa {...};

// In your program somewhere
#include "Grandpa.h"
Grandpa* g = new... oops! How do I create a Dad?
```

Yes, I know the biological answer, but let's stick to C++, shall we? The problem is that we encapsulated Dad out of all existence (sorry, Dad), at least as far as any code outside Grandpa.cpp is concerned. Grandpa's excellent interface will allow us to manipulate any instance of a derived class, including Dad, to our hearts' content, but there is no way to create the instance in the first place!

'Make' Functions

Enter the factory function. By convention, the simplest form is called makeFoo(), where Foo is the name of the class to be generated.

```
class Grandpa {
public:
    static Grandpa* makeDad(); // Creates instance of Dad
    static Grandpa* makeAuntieEm();
};
// In Grandpa.cpp
Grandpa* Grandpa::makeDad()
{
    return new Dad;
}
Grandpa* Grandpa::makeAuntieEm()
{
    return new AuntieEm;
}
```

We still expose the concept that there are specific derived classes, but the actual interfaces of Dad and AuntieEm are nicely tucked away, safe from prying eyes.

Symbol Classes and Overloaded 'Make' Functions

All those makeFoo function names sure seem out of character with C++'s overloaded nature, don't they? Let's take another crack at discriminating which "make" we want.

```
class VariationDad {}; // An empty class declaration
class VariationAuntieEm {};
class Grandpa {
public:
    static Grandpa* make(VariationDad);
    static Grandpa* make(VariationAuntieEm);
};
// In your program
Grandpa* g = Grandpa::make(VariationDad());
```

The phrase VariationDad() creates what is known as an *anonymous instance* of the class VariationDad, that is, an instance that is not attached to any variable in the originating scope. It lives only long enough to make the call, then disappears. The only purpose the instance of VariationDad serves is to tell the compiler which overloaded version of make to call. A class that has no members and is used in this way is a *symbol* class. It plays the role that a symbol data type plays in dynamic languages like Lisp: a string that is precompiled into a more efficient form.

Since the derived classes are encapsulated in the .cpp file anyway, we can improve on this slightly by changing the name of the original Dad to something local to the .cpp file, then simply use Dad instead of VariationDad in the .h file.

Optimization Using Factory Functions

Let's back up a second. Suppose there are no derived classes of Grandpa that the public even cares about enough to discriminate among them in the choice of factory function. There is still a strong case to be made for using one or more factory functions for constructing the instances. One reason is to hide all the logic that decides which derived class to instantiate, depending on the information provided at the point of creation. Put another way, factory functions can be a tool for optimizing your program.

```
class Number {
public:
    static Number* make(); // Constructs a default number
    static Number* make(int);
    static Number* make(double);
    static Number* make(string); // Such as "-1.23"
};
// In the .cpp file
class Integer : public Number {...};
class Real : public Number {...};
class ArbitraryPrecisionInteger : public Number {...};

Number* Number::make()
{
    return new Integer(0);
}
Number* Number::make(int x)
{
```

```
    return new Integer(x);
}
Number* Number::make(double x)
{
    return new Real(x);
}
Number* Number::make(string s)
{
    // pseudocode
    if (a small integer)
        return new Integer(atoi(s));
    if (a big integer)
        return new ArbitraryPrecisionInteger(s);
    if (real)
    // etc.
}
```

This is something you can't do with a constructor. By the time the compiler starts looking for a constructor with a matching signature, you have already told it what class to instantiate. Furthermore, this technique decouples the structure of the derived classes from the arguments to the factory function.

Localizing Using Factory Functions

One of the more powerful uses of factory functions is in isolating code that must be changed when a program is ported from one machine or environment to another. The public interface, as expressed through the base class, stays the same, but hidden away in the .cpp file lies a custom derived class that implements code specific to the platform.

```
class Window {
public:
    static Window* make();
    // The homomorphic interface follows
};
// In window.cpp for the Windows OS
class MS_Window : public Window {...};
Window* Window::make()
```

```
{
    return MS_Window();
}

// or in window.cpp for the Mac OS
class Mac_Window : public Window {...};
Window* Window::make()
{
    return Mac_Window();
}
```

To switch from one platform to another, you just recompile and relink a single .cpp file, window.cpp, and otherwise all clients of the Window class are ignorant of the localization that's taken place. (This assumes that you are up to creating a truly generic, homomorphic representation of graphical user interface windows, a task that has daunted even the most stouthearted of designers.)

Junkyard Functions

I don't know what to call these, since *factory* doesn't really have an antonym, so I'll use the term *junkyard functions* to describe functions that destroy instances of a class. The basic idea is to make the destructor protected or private, then provide a function that encapsulates the use of operator delete.

```
class Grandpa {
protected:
    virtual ~Grandpa();
public:
    static Grandpa make();
    static void destroy(Grandpa*);
};
// In grandpa.cpp
void Grandpa::destroy(Grandpa* g)
{
    delete g;
}
```

This may not make much sense right now, but when we start talking about custom memory management, junkyard functions can be very useful. For now, just tell your boss and co-workers that you're doing it because it lends an aura of symmetry to your programs. They'll give your office or cubicle a wide berth, so you'll be much more productive for a while.

Double Dispatch Revisited: Intermediate Base Classes

Armed with factory functions, we can easily improve the encapsulation of double dispatch.

```
// In grandpa.h
class Grandpa {
public:
    // Factory functions and homomorphic interface
};
// In grandpa.cpp
class RealGrandpa : public Grandpa {
// An intermediate homomorphic base class
protected:
    // Double dispatch functions
};
class Dad : public RealGrandpa {...};
class AuntieEm : public RealGrandpa {...};
```

The factory function(s) mean we can hide the derived classes. By adding the intermediate base class RealGrandpa, we can also completely hide all the gory details of double dispatch inside the .cpp file as well. No more protected member functions in the .h file!

Copy Constructors and operator= … Not!

Presumably, Grandpa is a pure homomorphic base class with at least one pure virtual member function. This prevents a client from directly instantiating Grandpa. If you use a factory function with a class that is instantiable, it is a good idea to make the constructors protected so that only the factory function can create instances.

While we're on the subject, it should be apparent after a little thought that you really don't want a client of a homomorphic base class to use the copy constructor or operator=. If someone wants to clone an instance, provide a version of "make" that copies this.

```
class Grandpa {
public:
    virtual Grandpa* makeClone()=0;
};
```

This is not a static member function, because it must be custom for each derived class. Assignment is more problematic. If you override operator= for the left-hand side, you are left wondering what to do about the right, whose type is unknown. One practical solution is to take away the whole idea of assignment in these situations by making operator= private. Another is to use a variation on the theme of double dispatch: make operator= virtual, and in each derived class have the implementation turn around and call a virtual AssignTo() member function that is overloaded for each derived class. It's ugly, but it works.

Class Objects

A class object is one whose primary responsibility is to create instances of the type it represents. In terms we've already introduced, a class object is an object whose primary member functions are factory functions for some class. There are other duties we'll assign to class objects later on, such as describing the structure of an instance, but the best way to proceed is to plunge right in with an example.

```
class GrandpaClass { // Class object for Grandpa
public:
    Grandpa* make(); // Creates instances of Grandpa
};
class Grandpa {...};
```

All the variations of factory functions apply to class objects as well, including tucking away encapsulated derived classes, optimizations, and transparent localization. "OK," you ask, "what good is it?" For one thing, it gets rid of all those static member functions and sticks to a purer object-oriented treatment in which everything gets done by sending a message to an object. These style points do add up, as simple as each seems taken in isolation. For another, it provides a convenient way to keep track of other information about instances and classes.

Class Information

Information about a class can be readily stored in the class object. This is best done through a homomorphic base class for class objects.

```
class Class {
protected:
    Collection<Class> base_classes;
    Collection<Class> derived_classes;
    String class_name;
    Class() {} // Makes this an abstract base class
public:
    // Accessor functions to retrieve name & etc.
};
```

The information to be stored varies tremendously according to both your application's needs and just how seriously hooked you got that week you spent hacking in Smalltalk.

Class Name and Instantiate by Name. The most basic information a class object can provide is the name of the class as a character string of some sort. Optionally, you may choose to maintain a dictionary of all class objects, indexed by class name. If you do this and there is a universal interface to the factory function, it is easy to implement a feature not directly supported by C++ known as *instantiate by name*.

```
// In client code somewhere
Class* c = gClasses.Find("Grandpa");
???* g = (Grandpa*)c->make(???);
```

As you can see, there are some problems that limit the utility of this approach. If you already knew the thing was going to be a Grandpa, you would have had no reason to use instantiate-by-name — it is hard to determine what class to cast down to, and there is no room in this scheme for providing separate signatures for the factory functions of derived classes. There are still a couple of situations in which this technique is extremely useful, however. Suppose you have written out an object as a byte stream and are now reading it back in. If the first n bytes are the class name as a character string, you can properly find the right class object to use to create the instance. It is customary to finish the implementation by providing all Classes with a make(istream&) or its equivalent. The code then becomes this.

```
// In the stream-reading code
cin<<className;
Class* c = gClasses.Find(className);
BaseClass* obj = c->make(cin);
```

You still need some abstract mother-of-all-base classes — BaseClass in this example —to make this work, but the rest is relatively easy.

Class Hierarchy. There are various ways to store information about the class hierarchy, but all amount to data structures of Class instances. One technique, illustrated above, is to have each Class maintain two collections, one of its base classes and another of classes derived from it. (Of course, *it* should be in quotes here; we're really talking about the hierarchy of the classes the Class objects represent. Separating "class" from Class is guaranteed to give you a headache, but seems to be considered great sport and a sign of mastery by Smalltalk and Lisp aficionados.) Another technique is to maintain one global data structure of pairs (base, derived), indexed both ways. In some situations, this needs to be a triplet (base, derived, sequence) so that base classes are maintained in the order of their declaration in the represented class.

Descriptions of Data Members. There is occasionally justification for having Class objects smart enough to pick apart instances of the class represented and describe their structure. This begins with data members. The most straightforward implementation of this is to have the Class return an iterator, which in turn returns an offset-Class pair representing the offset of the data member within the instance and the Class of the member. It makes sense to enumerate three subsets of the data members:

1. All data members, including basic types like ints. In order to do this you will have to create dummy derived classes of Class to represent the primitive types.
2. Only nonbasic data members that naturally have a Class anyway.
3. Only pointers and references to other objects.

The last variation is extremely important in certain advanced garbage collection algorithms.

Descriptions of Member Functions. In even more rare cases, you may want a Class object to be able to describe the set of member functions of the class it represents. This is dangerously close to forcing yourself to playact at being a C++ compiler, so don't go overboard with this one. Again, an iterator is the best representation. For each function, you can choose to return anything from as simple as the function name to its address and the names, types, and order of its arguments and the type of the return value. Some problems are just not C++ material; if you find yourself wanting to do something like this, think seriously about using a truly dynamic language.

Collections of Instances. Another handy thing to do with Class objects is to maintain a collection of all instances of the class. This can be either one collection for each Class or a single global data structure of pairs (Class, instance). If the latter is used and the collection is indexed in both directions, it is extremely useful for debugging ("Show me all instances of Class x") and can also be used to answer questions like "What is the class of this object?" without physically storing the address of the Class object inside every instance. That will only work with the outermost instances created by the factory functions; nested objects as data members or base classes will not end up in any such registry.

Statistics. This runs the gamut: a running count of the number of instances currently in memory, the total number created since the program started, statistical profiles of how and when instances are created … the possibilities are limited only by how much time you have to dabble in this. If you are paid by the hour, this is a great way to spend your time; it's easy to make a case for any one statistic. If not, be sure there is a positive payback on the overall investment of your time.

More about Junkyard Functions

Having rambled on at great length about all the neat things you can do with Class objects, let's return to the junkyard function. Many of the ideas presented in the preceding section, such as hidden collections of instances and statistics, can only be implemented if you have a hook into both the time when instances are created and the time when they are destroyed.

It is of course possible to implement these sorts of statistics using static data members, factory functions, and so on, within the target class itself, but the Class object techniques presented above provide much better modularity. Take an existing class. Add a Class object class. Sprinkle in a factory function or two. Stir in a junkyard function. Simmer over a brew of statistics. Voilá! You've added all that administrative stuff without modifying the original class. Clients have to be aware of the changes, but if there aren't any clients when you start, and the class to be managed is substantial or comes without source code, you've accomplished a great deal without side effects to the most critically constrained code.

Finding the Class of an Object

Given an object, it is common to wish to know its Class. That sounds simple, but it is actually a very deep subject. Remember that an object can be potentially created on the stack, on the heap, embedded as a data member or base class inside another object, or using factory functions. Here are some basic strategies.

Embedded Pointer to Class Object. The most obvious strategy is to bury a pointer to the Class object inside every object, nested or not.

```
class Object { // The mother of all real classes
protected:
    static ObjectClass s_my_class;
    Class* my_class; // == &s_my_class;
public:
    Object() : my_class(&s_my_class) {}
    Class* My_Class() { return my_class; }
};
class Foo : public Object {
protected:
    static FooClass s_my_class;
public:
    Foo() { my_class = &s_my_class; }
};
```

All classes (little *c*) derive from a common ancestor Object that defines the protocol for obtaining the Class (big *C*) object. It is perfectly legal to use the same data member names at multiple levels of a class hierarchy, as is the case with s_my_class here. The compiler picks the one in the immediate scope. Furthermore, constructors execute base-then-data-member-then-derived, so the last constructor will leave my_class set to the correct value. In this scheme you can always obtain the Class object, no matter how much derived-to-base typecasting you do.

The overhead here is the four bytes needed to store the pointer. No virtual member functions are required, so no vtable is added to a class that otherwise doesn't need one. Some extra CPU cycles are required for the redundant construction of my_class, but that won't be significant for most applications. The worst overhead is all that code — and the discipline to always stick to convention — embodied in the constructors.

A cleaner variation involves Class object factory functions setting the Class pointer.

```
class Object {
friend class Class;
private:
    Class* my_class;
public:
    Class* My_Class() { return my_class; }
};
class Class {
protected:
    void SetClass(Object& obj)
        { obj.my_class = this; }
};
class Foo : public Object {...};
class FooClass : public Class {
public:
    Foo* make() {
        Foo* f = new Foo;
        this->SetClass(f);
        return f;
        }
};
```

This is a little better, since classes derived from Object are blissfully ignorant of all these shenanigans … or are they? The problem with this approach is that it won't work for instances of Foo declared on the stack or nested as data members inside other classes. This is one of many situations in which you have to make a tough choice: Should you restrict a class to have only instances on the heap, or should you put up with even more complicated solutions to already complicated problems?

A variation on this theme is to control the allocation of memory and stuff the address of the class object directly above the real object in memory, rather than making it a data member of an ancestral class. This requires techniques of memory management that we'll get to in Section 4.

External Data Structures. As mentioned previously, it is also possible to maintain a global collection of instance-Class pairs. This is not as outrageous as it may seem, especially if the Class information is only needed for debugging and will be turned off in production mode. Done carefully, it can also apply to such nested objects as data members or instances allocated on the heap, although you will need support from the class (little *c*) constructor and destructor.

Custom Memory Spaces. Another solution we will explore in Chapters 15 and 16 is to physically separate objects into separate parts of memory according to their class. This simply won't work with nested objects, and it is a complicated solution all around, but it can have impressive performance and space characteristics.

Exemplars

In *Advanced C++ Programming Styles and Idioms,* James Coplien has advocated a special kind of class object called an *exemplar*. Put simply, an exemplar is a class object that is an instance of the class it represents. Got it? This stuff gives me a headache.

```
class Exemplar {}; // A symbol class
class Foo {
private:
    Foo(); // Along with all other constructors but one
public:
    Foo(Exemplar); // The exemplar constructor
    Foo* make(); // Factory functions of the exemplar
};
extern Foo* foo; // The exemplar itself
```

The details aren't really important. The point is that one instance — pointed to by the variable foo — acts as the class object for the class Foo. In the implementation of factory functions, one checks to make sure that this is equal to the exemplar, because a factory function should not be called for any other instance of the class.

You can do anything with an exemplar that you can do with a class object. These are the tradeoffs:

- With an exemplar you don't have to create an extra class to represent the Class.

- With an exemplar you don't have to declare things to be friends (typically a class object must be a friend of the class it represents).

- With a true class object it is much easier to model class hierarchies.

- With a true class object it is easier to set up a homomorphic interface for the sorts of descriptive information just discussed.

- With a class object the distinction between things that apply to the exemplar/class object and things that apply to real instances is much clearer.

All in all, class objects are more flexible and only moderately more difficult to implement than exemplars are.

CHAPTER 12 — *Invisible Pointers*

Advanced C++ usage is like one of those old *Twilight Zone* episodes. Someone drives a car off the road. After waiting a while for someone to come by, she decides to go for help. But no matter what direction she takes, no matter how carefully she checks her course, she ends up coming right back to the scene of the wreck. So it is with pointers: You keep coming back to the wreck. Er, maybe I should think up a more inspirational metaphor than a wreck.

In the meantime, this chapter circles back once more to the subject of pointers, this time in the light of homomorphic class hierarchies. I call the variations discussed here *invisible* because in most cases you can arrange for a client to be completely oblivious of the fact that there's a pointer there in between it and the target object. A special case of invisible pointer has also been called the "envelope-letter paradigm" by James Coplien; this is a more general treatment.

Basic Concepts

If homomorphism is good for other sorts of classes, it should be good for pointers, right? The concept is simple: The pointer and the pointee both derive from the same pure abstract base class.

```
class Foo {
public:
    virtual void do_something()=0;
    virtual void do_something_else()=0;
};
class PFoo : public Foo {
private:
    Foo* foo;
public:
    virtual void do_something() { foo->do_something(); }
    virtual void do_something_else()
        { foo->do_something_else(); }
};
class Bar : public Foo {
// All that derived stuff
};
```

PFoo uses delegation, rather than overloading operator->. This code fragment only scratches the surface. There are lots of details to be attended to, starting with ways to hide both pointers and pointees from clients.

Encapsulated Pointers and Pointees

One of the biggest advantages of homomorphic pointers is that both the pointer and the pointee can be encapsulated in a .cpp file. Look at the code fragment just shown. The pointer does not add anything to the public interface already presented by Foo, so clients do not need to see PFoo or the derived classes to which it points. In fact, if this is done with care, it is possible to make clients think they are dealing with the pointee when, in fact, you've jammed a pointer in the middle. Hence the name *invisible pointer*.

```cpp
// In foo.h
class Foo {
public:
    static Foo* make(); // Factory function
    virtual void do_something()=0;
    virtual void do_something_else()=0;
};
// In foo.cpp
class PFoo : public Foo {
private:
    Foo* foo;
public:
    PFoo(Foo* f) : foo(f) {}
    virtual void do_something() { foo->do_something(); }
    virtual void do_something_else()
        { foo->do_something_else(); }
};
class Bar : public Foo {
// All that derived stuff
};
Foo* Foo::make()
{
    return new PFoo(new Foo);
}
```

One can easily envision slipping PFoo into an existing body of code — provided you took the precaution of designing it to use a homomorphic class hierarchy and encapsulated such derived classes as Bar. You did do that, didn't you? This is one of those Zen issues, something you do because it keeps the world in balance, not because you see an immediate use. One day, out of the blue, you run across the need to slip in a smart pointer, and because the world is nicely balanced already it's no problem.

Factory Functions

Of course, factory functions are needed any time you encapsulate the derived classes. In the previous code fragment, we changed the factory function to create two objects, the pointer and the pointee.

Notice that the pointer's constructor does not create the pointee. There is a very good reason for this. Presumably, we want to recycle the same pointer class PFoo with all the derived classes of Foo. That means that someone outside of the pointer class — the factory function — must decide what to instantiate and stuff inside the pointer.

In the early chapters on smart pointers we emphasized templates and generated pointer classes that paralleled the pointee classes. Templates no longer serve any real purpose with invisible pointers.

The entire discussion of factory functions and class objects from the preceding chapter applies equally to invisible pointers. You can optimize, localize, and socialize to your heart's content. In general, the pointer class itself is not involved in any of this activity.

References to Pointers

It is not necessary to return Foo* from the factory function. A Foo& will do as well.

```
class Foo {
public:
    static Foo& make(); // Factory function
    virtual void do_something()=0;
    virtual void do_something_else()=0;
};
// In foo.cpp
class PFoo : public Foo {
private:
    Foo* foo;
public:
    PFoo(Foo* f) : foo(f) {}
    virtual void do_something() { foo->do_something(); }
    virtual void do_something_else()
        { foo->do_something_else(); }
};
class Bar : public Foo {
// All that derived stuff
};
Foo& Foo::make()
```

```
{
    return *(new PFoo(new Foo));
}
```

The only problem with this is that copying with the copy constructor, as we shall see in a moment, is a no-no, yet people armed with a & invariably try to copy the object. The temptation to copy is much weaker with *'s. Other than that, the choice is a matter of taste.

Non-master Pointers

It is possible to implement either master or non-master pointers within the invisible pointer paradigm. The treatments of various problems differ quite a bit, depending on the result of this design decision. Following are the details for non-master pointers.

Copying. A client cannot really copy the pointer, because it doesn't know what its true class is. The technique of the previous chapter, a special virtual variation on *make* for cloning an object, works well. For a non-master pointer, it is sufficient to simply copy the address of the pointee.

```
class Foo {
private:
    Foo(const Foo&) {}
public:
    virtual Foo* makeClone(); // Copying
};
// In foo.cpp
class PFoo : public Foo {
private:
    Foo* foo;
public:
    PFoo(Foo* f) : foo(f) {}
    virtual Foo* makeClone()
        { return new PFoo(foo); }
};
Foo* Foo::makeClone()
{
```

```
        return NULL; // Irrelevant to all but pointers
}
```

It is not necessary to implement makeClone() for anything but the pointer class, so a stub implementation is provided in the ancestral class so that every derived class does not have to override it.

Assignment. operator= obviously won't work either without special care, since the client doesn't know the actual type of the pointer. Because we're dealing with non-master pointers, it makes sense to keep assignment consistent with the way copying works; that is, assignment only affects the pointer, not the pointee. This is easily implemented with a virtual operator= for the pointer and a stub for the pointee, as with copying.

```
class Foo {
public:
    virtual Foo& operator=(const Foo&);
};
// In foo.cpp
class PFoo : public Foo {
private:
    Foo* foo;
public:
    virtual Foo& operator=(const Foo& f)
        {
        foo = f.foo;
        return *this;
        }
};
Foo& Foo::operator=(const Foo&)
{
    return *this;
}
```

Looking Forward: Garbage Collection. Because derived classes are encapsulated, the use of non-master pointers leads to a tough design problem: How do you know when to delete the pointee? In the memory management chapters, we will tackle that problem head-on, but it is worth setting the stage by summarizing the two basic strategies:

1. In the pointee, maintain a count of how many pointers point to it at any given time. When the count goes from 1 to 0, have the pointee delete itself.

2. Implement a scavenging scheme in which it is possible to locate all pointers and pointees. Check off all pointees that are pointed to by at least one pointer; then delete any pointees that aren't checked.

Reference counting is of limited use, but this is a problem tailor-made for it. Scavenging is a subject that will absorb a lot of brain cells in Chapter 16.

Master Pointers

Invisible pointers are most often master pointers; that is, there is a one-to-one correspondence between a pointer and a pointee. I know it's been a while since we've dealt with master pointers, so a brief summary of what we need to do to maintain master pointer semantics is appropriate here:

1. When the pointer is destroyed, the pointee is also destroyed.
2. When the pointer is copied, the pointee is also copied.
3. When the pointer is assigned to, it is changed to point to a copy of the pointee of the right-hand side.

It is not enough to assign the pointee of the right-hand side to the pointee of the left-hand side, since they may not be of the same class.

Destruction. The destructor of the ancestral class must be virtual, and the destructor of the pointer must destroy the pointee.

```
class Foo {
public:
    virtual ~Foo() {}
};
// In foo.cpp
```

```
class PFoo : public Foo {
private:
    Foo* foo;
public:
    virtual ~PFoo() { delete foo; }
};
```

Copying. Copying invisible master pointers picks up where we left off with non-master pointers. Each derived class must override the makeClone() member function.

```
class Foo {
protected:
    Foo(const Foo&) {}
public:
    virtual Foo* makeClone()=0; // For copying
};
// In foo.cpp
class PFoo : public Foo {
private:
    Foo* foo;
public:
    PFoo(Foo* f) : foo(f) {}
    virtual Foo* makeClone()
        { return new PFoo(foo->makeClone()); }
};
class Bar : public Foo {
protected:
    Bar(Bar&); // Copy constructor
public:
    virtual Foo* makeClone();
};
Foo* Bar::makeClone()
{   return new Bar(*this);
}
```

We finally get to use a real copy constructor. The pointer makes a copy, not just of itself, but of the pointee as well. The pointee, in turn, uses its own copy constructor to do the heavy lifting. Notice that the copy constructor of Foo was changed to protected to enable this.

Assignment. Assignment of invisible master pointers is similar to assignment of any other kind of master pointer. Again, we pick up where we left off with invisible non-master pointers.

```
class Foo {
public:
    virtual Foo& operator=(const Foo&);
};
// In foo.cpp
class PFoo : public Foo {
private:
    Foo* foo;
public:
    virtual Foo& operator=(const Foo& f)
        {
        if (this == &f) return *this;
        delete foo;
        foo = f.foo->makeClone();
        return *this;
        }
};
Foo& Foo::operator=(const Foo&)
{
    return *this;
}
```

It is not necessary to override operator= in any of the pointee classes. Even if we did, it wouldn't do any good, because the pointee on the left-hand side might not be of the same class as that of the right-hand side. It seems grubby, but the most practical thing is to trash the old left-hand side's pointee and to replace it with a fresh copy of the right-hand side's pointee.

Double Dispatch — Again

Many problems are elegantly solved by invisible pointers. One of them is a better encapsulation of double dispatch, including solving that nasty += problem. We need to combine double dispatch with the concept of a malleable type, discussed in the ancient past in Chapter 6.

Double Double Dispatch

OK, let's try double dispatch, invisible pointer style. This is a straightforward extension of the techniques used without pointers.

A First Try. Here is a first crack at arithmetic with invisible pointers. It works, but has limitations that will be noted and corrected in due course. To avoid the problems involved in returning references to temporary values, discussed at the end of Chapter 11, I will switch to using operator new and worry about the garbage collection issues later.

```
// In number.h
class NBase; // Clients needn't know anything about this
class Number {
protected:
    Number(const Number&) {}
    Number() {}
public:
    virtual NBase& operator+(const NBase&) const=0;
    virtual Number& operator+(const Number&) const=0;
    // etc.
};
// In number.cpp
class Integer;
class Real;
class PNumber : public Number {
private:
    NBase* number;
protected:
    virtual NBase& operator+(const NBase& n) const
        { return *number + n; } // #2
public:
    PNumber(NBase* n) : number(n) {}
    virtual Number& operator+(const Number& n) const
```

```
            { return *(new PNumber(&(n + *number))); } // #1
};
class NBase : public Number {
// An intermediate base class
// Conventional double dispatch within NBase
public:
    virtual NBase& operator+(const Integer&) const=0;
    virtual NBase& operator+(const Real&) const=0;
    // etc.
    virtual NBase& operator+(const NBase&) const=0;
    virtual Number& operator+(const Number& n) const
        { return Integer(0); } // Stub - not called
};
class Integer : public NBase {
private:
    int value;
protected:
    virtual NBase& operator+(const Integer& i) const
        { return *(new Integer(value+i.value)); } // #4
public:
    Integer(int i) : value(i) {}
    virtual NBase& operator+(const NBase& n) const
        { return n + *this; } // #3
};
class Real : public NBase {...};
```

As with the original double dispatch, it's best to relax your eyes and slowly move the page away from your nose until the code comes into focus. Here is a blow-by-blow description of what happens when a client tries to add two Numbers (actually, two PNumbers, but the client doesn't know that). We'll assume two Integers:

1. The left-hand pointer's PNumber::operator+(const Number&) is called. This flips the arithmetic around, dispatching to the right-hand side's pointer with the left-hand pointee as argument. Before it does, however, it creates a PNumber to wrap the result.

2. The right-hand pointer's PNumber::operator+(const NBase&) is called. This delegates to its pointee's operator+.

3. The right-hand pointee's Integer::operator+(const NBase&) is called. This flips the arithmetic once more.

4. The left-hand pointee's Integer::operator+(const Integer&) is called, and it finally does the actual work of computing the sum.

There are a total of four dispatches involved, two for the pointers and two for the pointees, hence the name *double double dispatch*. There are no typecasts required, at the cost of having to publish the existence of NBase on the front page of the newspaper.

Reducing to Three Dispatches. If we permit the code to "know" that both the original left- and right-hand sides are PNumbers and typecast accordingly, the whole thing could be reduced to three dispatches: one to PNumber's operator+(const Number&) and two for the normal double dispatch from there. The first PNumber would deduce that the right-hand side is also a PNumber, typecast from Number downward to PNumber, then directly access its pointee. This bypasses PNumber::operator+(const NBase&). This has the added advantage that you can, if you are careful, remove all reference to NBase in the .h file.

The problem with this is that some idiot might, against all your warnings to the contrary, derive from Number outside of your own carefully crafted hierarchy. That means that not all Numbers need necessarily be wrapped in PNumbers. The technique just shown prevents anyone from deriving from Number outside the .cpp file and even works properly with unwrapped derived classes — Numbers not encased in PNumbers — provided they implement the double double dispatch properly.

How Long Is the Result Valid? As implemented above, the client must remember to get rid of the Numbers by calling delete &aResult. This is a severe restriction that complicates nested arithmetic, among other things, since all intermediate results must be pointed to by a variable for later deletion. This is one reason that it has been proposed to the ANSI committee, and all but accepted, that compilers should guarantee that a temporary value on the stack be valid until the largest enclosing expression is completely evaluated. If your compiler follows that rule then the key line of code

```
    { return *(new Integer(value+i.value)); } // #4
```

can be rewritten as

```
    { return Integer(value+i.value); } // #4
```

The creation of the PNumber is similar. The value returned will continue to be valid throughout whatever expression you are evaluating. Any reference that needs to live beyond the enclosing expression should be obtained by calling makeClone(), which will allocate the PNumber on the heap, or by doing an assignment to some other Number using the virtual operator= for invisible master pointers described earlier in this chapter. Some garbage collection techniques, which we'll discuss in Section 4, can be used to handle these annoying little memory leaks.

Self-Modification and Malleability

As with any smart pointer, an invisible master pointer can be treated as a malleable type. If you simply replace the pointee with some other derived class, you have effectively changed the type of the overall combination as seen by a client. This is the key to the += problem, which requires self-modification of the left-hand side as well as a possible change of types on the fly. If you add a Complex right-hand side to an Integer left-hand side, the type of the left-hand side has to change.

```
// In number.h
class NBase; // Clients needn't know anything about this
class Number {
protected:
    Number(const Number&) {}
    Number() {}
public:
    virtual NBase& AddTo(const NBase&) const=0;
    virtual Number& operator+=(const Number&) const=0;
    // etc.
```

```
};
// In number.cpp
class Integer;
class Real;
class PNumber : public Number {
private:
    NBase* number;
protected:
    virtual NBase& AddTo(const NBase& n) const
        { return number->AddTo(n); } // #2
public:
    PNumber(NBase* n) : number(n) {}
    virtual Number& operator+(const Number& n) const {
        number = &(n.AddTo(*number)); // #1 - replacement
        return *this;
        }
};
class NBase : public Number {
// An intermediate base class
// Conventional double dispatch within NBase
public:
    virtual NBase& operator+=(const Integer&) const=0;
    virtual NBase& operator+=(const Real&) const=0;
    // etc.
    virtual NBase& AddTo(const NBase&) const=0;
    virtual Number& operator+(const Number& n) const
        { return Integer(0); } // Stub - not called
};
class Integer : public NBase {
private:
    int value;
protected:
    virtual NBase& operator+=(const Integer& i) const {
        if (value + i.value is small enough) {
            value += i.value;
            return *this;
            }
        else {
            ArbitraryPrecisionInteger api(value);
            api += i.value;
```

```
            delete this;
            return api;
            }
        }
public:
    Integer(int i) : value(i) {}
    virtual NBase& AddTo(const NBase& n) const
        { return n += *this; } // #3
};
class Real : public NBase {...};
```

Everything is as before, except that the +'s are now +='s, and the double dispatch now goes to +=(left,right) and to AddTo(right,left) so that we can discriminate between the two arrangements of the arguments. This is important, because ultimately we only want to replace the pointee of the left-hand side with the new value. That is done in two places:

1. PNumber::operator+=(const Number&) automatically replaces number with whatever new value it gets back.

2. Integer::operator+=(const Integer&) returns itself if it didn't have to change type; otherwise it returns a new object of a different type after deleting itself.

I call the second of these a *replacement function* for obvious reasons. The peculiar — some would say, smelly — attribute of a replacement function is that the address of the object before the call cannot be counted on to be valid after the call. Obviously you should only use this when you can stuff the logic into some hole so deep and dark that no one can mess it up, but if you have such a case this idea tremendously simplifies otherwise messy algorithms.

This example is safe as long as PNumber acts as a master pointer and as long as it can be guaranteed that no object derived from NBase can exist without a PNumber pointing to it. That will be the case here with everything hiding inside the .cpp file.

This is a lot of code for such a simple problem. I'm not going to pretend that all this effort is worthwhile in all projects. It is mostly for situations in which you spend a lot of time creating a highly reusable class hierarchy and can afford the investment in improved modularity. I present it here in keeping with the spirit of this book, to push the envelope of C++ and toss out brain teasers to occupy even the mightiest of C++ experts.

Multiple Double Dispatch

Multiple dispatch and all variations thereon also have counterparts in the world of invisible pointers, but if you seriously consider them for a real-world project, consider getting a life instead.

Applications of Invisible Pointers

We will talk in the remaining chapters about memory management, but it isn't a bad idea to look ahead here at the sorts of memory management strategies that are facilitated by invisible pointers.

Caching

We talked about this in the context of ordinary smart pointers, but caching takes on added importance with invisible pointers. An invisible pointer can store an on-disk address to the pointee and read it in at the last second before delegating to it. This takes place transparently to the client, making it possible to experiment with the scheme without upsetting lots of code.

Distributed Objects and Proxies

While we're at it, why bother with a disk when there's another machine available? Invisible pointers are the perfect vehicle for making it transparent to a client whether the object they're talking to is local to the same machine and process or flung over a wide area network somewhere in Tibet. When an invisible pointer is used to delegate to a remote object, it is called a *proxy* for that object.

Advanced Distributed Architectures

In certain distributed architectures, you want proxies to contain locally cached images of the remote object. This minimizes network traffic for objects that don't change often. One architecture used in conjunction with this strategy is called a *master token* approach: In order to update an object, you must first obtain the master copy from whatever process and machine currently holds it. You can do all this transparently, using invisible pointers, by distinguishing const from non-const member functions. In fact, invisible pointers make a great laboratory for experimenting with various strategies to find the one that works best. The techniques that implement malleable types also allow replacement on the fly of one object representation by another.

Managing Memory

For all the time it consumes in real-life programming, remarkably little has been written about how C++ idioms can simplify memory management. This section delves into this mysterious subject, starting with the simplistic and proceeding to the ridiculously complex. Throughout, the emphasis is on ways to fold, spindle, and mutilate C++ syntax to hide or take advantage of memory management techniques; the techniques are the subject of a book in themselves. Take out your incense and start waving!

CHAPTER 13

Overloading New and Delete

Let's take a breather from the idea of pointers for a while and talk about memory management. It has been estimated that a typical C++ programmer — if there is such a thing — spends 50 percent of her time managing memory. (The program's, not hers.)   When should an object be deleted? How do you make sure no one is pointing at an object's old address after it is gone? How do you cajole decent performance out of frequently used classes, given the one-size-fits-all default memory management used by the compiler? Unlike languages like Smalltalk and Lisp, C++ does little to help by default. Fortunately, the language leaves some pretty powerful trapdoors; those who know their way around backstage can always find ways to coerce decent performance and — dare I say it? — Smalltalk-caliber memory management when the need arises.

Memory management is one of the most arcane of all subjects in computer science, the sort of thing brilliant people at great universities think about so hard they don't notice when they've bumped their heads against a post. I will make no attempt to provide an in-depth treatment of the general subject. As in the rest of this book, we'll stick to showing how C++ syntax and idioms provide a framework for plugging in whatever algorithms and data structures you want to implement. However, even the brief samples in this and the following chapters should prove useful for all but the most complex problems.

This chapter starts with the essential plumbing: overloading operators new and delete. That is followed by a series of simplistic but very useful memory management tricks commonly used in C++. More elaborate techniques built on ideas from this chapter will be found in the succeeding chapters.

Overloading New and Delete

It is surprising to most people that operators new and delete can be overloaded like any other operators. The easiest way to learn how is by example.

A Simple Free List

Here is a simple example. operator delete adds the deallocated space to a free space list, and operator new first tries to allocate from the list, only deferring to the global operator new if the free space list is empty.

```
class Foo {
private:
    struct FreeNode {
        FreeNode* next;
        };
    static FreeNode* fgFreeList;
public:
    void* operator new(size_t bytes) {
        if (fgFreeList == NULL)
            return ::operator new(bytes);
        FreeNode* node = fgFreeList;
```

```
        fgFreeList = fgFreeList->next;
        return node;
        }
    void operator delete(void* space) {
        ((FreeNode*)space)->next = fgFreeList;
        fgFreeList = (FreeNode*)space;
        }
};
```

This is not a complete code fragment, as we will discuss in a moment, but it illustrates the basic technique of overloading operators new and delete for a specific class. operator new takes a single argument, the amount of space to allocate, and returns the address of the space allocated. operator delete accepts as its argument the address of the space to reclaim. Don't bother trying to make either virtual; the compiler will just laugh at you. The compiler knows exactly what the class is when it calls operator new, so it doesn't need a vtable. When operator delete is called, the destructor determines which class's operator delete is used; if you need to guarantee that a derived class operator delete will be called, you have to make the destructor virtual, not operator delete. Derived classes of Foo will inherit these overloads, so their allocation and deallocation are also affected. In fact, it is not uncommon to create an abstract base class that does nothing more than something like what was just shown, then use it as a mixin for classes to be managed in that way.

```
class Bar : public Baseclass, public Foo {...};
```

Here Bar presumably inherits all of its type characteristics from Baseclass, but multiply inherits from Foo to pick up the custom memory management.

Minimum Size Constraints. Before you jump on your compiler, there are a few problems to iron out with this code fragment. For one thing, it presumes that an instance of Foo is at least as many bytes as a Foo::FreeNode*. This is not guaranteed for a class like this that has no data members and no virtual member functions. It will have some size — in many compilers, two bytes — so that it can have a unique address, but that may be fewer bytes than a pointer to a FreeNode. You must guarantee that Foo is not less than the size of a pointer by making sure there is either a vtable or at least a pointer's worth of data members.

Derived Classes That Add Data Members. Another problem is that this will not work with derived classes that add data members. Consider this class hierarchy.

```
class Bar : public Foo {
private:
    int x;
};
```

Each instance of Bar is at least a couple of bytes bigger than an instance of Foo. If you delete an instance of Foo, and then try to immediately allocate an instance of Bar, kablooie! The space allocated comes up that same couple of bytes short. A brute force solution is to make operator new smart enough to intercept only allocations of the right number of bytes. We will talk about more sophisticated approaches later.

```
class Foo {
public:
    void* operator new(size_t bytes) {
        if (bytes != sizeof(Foo) || fgFreeList == NULL)
            return ::operator new(bytes);
        FreeNode* node = fgFreeList;
        fgFreeList = fgFreeList->next;
        return node;
        }
};
```

This only fixes the allocation side of things. Deallocation needs to be changed to match this strategy. An alternative form of operator delete has a second argument, the number of bytes to deallocate. On the surface, this seems to provide a graceful way out.

```
class Foo {
public:
```

```
    void* operator new(size_t bytes); // as above
    void operator delete(void* space, size_t bytes) {
        if (bytes != sizeof(Foo))
            ::operator delete(space);
        ((FreeNode*)space)->next = fgFreeList;
        fgFreeList = (FreeNode*)space;
        }
};
```

Now only real Foos and derived classes that are identical in size will be put into the free list or taken from it. Not bad, but there is a problem. How will the compiler handle this code?

```
Foo* foo = new Bar;
delete foo; // What size does the compiler use?
```

Bar is bigger than Foo, so Foo::operator new delegates to the default global operator new. But, as you've probably already guessed in disgust, the compiler gets it wrong when deallocation time rolls around. The size passed to Foo::operator delete is based on the compiler's best guess of the real type, which may or may not be correct. In this case, you've told the compiler it's a Foo, not a Bar, and the compiler grins and plays along. Patching this up requires an understanding of the exact sequence of destruction used with a statement like delete foo;. First, destructors are called from the derived class up the line. Second, operator delete is called by the code surrounding the derived class destructor. This means that if your destructor is not virtual, you are subject to this hokiness, but if your destructor is virtual, the size argument to operator delete will always be correct — reason number 2,438 to make your destructors virtual unless you have a really, really good reason not to do so.

A Working Free Space List Class. Taking all this together, the following code will always work properly with a compiler that uses vtables.

```
class Foo {
private:
    struct FreeNode {
```

```
        FreeNode* next;
        };
    static FreeNode* fgFreeList;
public:
    virtual ~Foo() {}
    void* operator new(size_t bytes) {
        if (bytes != sizeof(Foo) || fgFreeList == NULL)
            return ::operator new(bytes);
        FreeNode* node = fgFreeList;
        fgFreeList = fgFreeList->next;
        return node;
        }
    void operator delete(void* space, size_t bytes) {
        if (bytes != sizeof(Foo))
            ::operator delete(space);
        ((FreeNode*)space)->next = fgFreeList;
        fgFreeList = (FreeNode*)space;
        }
};
```

The vtable pointer ensures that each Foo is at least as big as the next-in-list pointer (FreeNode*), and the virtual destructor makes sure that the size passed to operator delete will be correct.

Again, this is not a practical memory management strategy — it takes its ball and bat and goes home when a derived class is used — but it illustrates a number of basic principles of overloading operators new and delete.

Inheriting operators new and delete

If you overload operators new and delete for a class, derived classes inherit those overloads. There is nothing to stop you from overloading new and/or delete again in one of those derived classes.

```
class Bar : public Foo {
public:
    virtual ~Bar(); // Foo::~Foo must be virtual as well
    void* operator new(size_t bytes);
```

```
    void operator delete(void* space, size_t bytes);
};
```

This works as long as the destructor is virtual. If it is non-virtual, a sequence like the following would call the right operator new, but the base class operator delete.

```
Foo* foo = new Bar;
delete foo;
```

Even though it works, this sort of overridden overloaded operator is usually bad form and is not something to brag about in a circle of C++ experts. Unexpected side effects can crop up all over the place when a derived class changes the way its base class expects to manage memory. If you want to use more than one memory management strategy in a single class hierarchy, it is better to mix the strategy you want directly into the concrete derived classes, using multiple inheritance, than to inherit one strategy and then say, "Ha, ha, ha, I was just kidding," in a derived class.

Arguments to operator new

operator new can be overloaded to accept additional arguments beyond just the size. These overloads take away the default signature void* operator new(size_t), so if you want that to stay you'll have to manually wire it in.

```
#define kPoolSize 4096
struct Pool {
    unsigned char* next; // Next byte to allocate
    unsigned char space[kPoolSize];
    Pool() : next(&spacc[0]) {}
    };
class Foo {
public:
    void* operator new(size_t bytes)
        { return ::operator new(bytes); }
    void* operator new(size_t bytes, Pool* pool) {
        void* space = pool->next;
        pool->next += bytes;
```

```
            return space;
        }
};
void f()
{
    Pool localPool;
    Foo* foo1 = new Foo; // Uses default operator new
    Foo* foo2 = new(&localPool) Foo; // Uses overload
}
```

Here the client, not the class, directs where the object is to be placed. This is a fragment of a complete strategy. For example, how is operator delete to know whether the space came from the global pool used by the default operator new, or from the custom pool used by the overloaded operator new? The basic idea, though, is simple: Give the client of a class some control over where instances get placed. This means that allocation can be done on an object-by-object basis, rather than the same way for all instances of a class.

It is legal to overload operator new with any new and creative signatures you like, as long as they are all distinct and as long as the first argument to each is a size_t representing the number of bytes needed. These can either be global overloads or member overloads of specific classes. When the compiler sees arguments between the new and the class name, it prepends the size and searches for a matching signature.

Split-Phase Construction

This idiom is due to James Coplien, who calls it a "virtual constructor." What does the following overloaded operator new do?

```
class Foo {
public:
    void* operator new(size_t, void* p) { return p; }
};
```

The answer, seemingly, is "Nothing; this is a waste of time." Or is it? What happens in this code fragment?

```
union U {
    Foo foo;
    Bar bar;
    Banana banana;
    };
U whatIsThis;
```

A C++ compiler has no way of knowing which constructor to call for whatIsThis, Foo::Foo(), Bar::Bar(), or Banana::Banana(). Clearly it can't call more than one, because these members all share the same space in memory, yet absent any instructions from you it can't figure out which one to use. As in so many other cases with C++, the compiler punts; it signals an error and refuses to accept a union whose members have constructors. If you want to have one spot in memory initialized in any of several different ways, you'll have to figure out how to fool the compiler. The "no op" constructor just described is the best thing.

```
unsigned char space[4096];
Foo* whatIsThis = new(&space[0]) Foo;
```

This effectively does something you aren't supposed to be able to do in C++: call a constructor. No space allocation or deallocation takes place, because the operator new does nothing. However, the C++ compiler will go ahead and assume that this is a new object and *call the constructor anyway*. If you later change your mind and want to use the same space for some other object, you can call this tricky operator new again to reinitialize it.

Any time an object is allocated using operator new, the compiler uses a two-phase process:

1. Allocate space for the object.
2. Call the object's constructor.

This code is buried in the executable code generated by the compiler, and under ordinary circumstances, you can't do the second step without the first. The virtual constructor idiom throws a bag over the compiler's head and allows you to get around this limitation.

Changing the Type of an Object on the Fly. If you later decide you've had enough of the Foo and want to turn that space into a Banana, assuming Banana also has the same overloaded operator new, you can change the type on the fly.

```
Banana* b = new(&space[0]) Banana;
```

Poof! It's now a Banana. This is called the *virtual constructor* idiom. And yes, it is in full conformance with the language specification.

Limitations. You must make sure of two things when you use this idiom:

1. The space passed to operator new must be adequate to construct the class.
2. All clients holding the object's address must know about the change!

It would be pretty embarassing if you changed the type of that Foo to Banana, only to have some other client object call one of Foo's member functions after the change.

Split-Phase Destruction

Normally, the compiler uses a two-step process to get rid of an object passed as an argument to operator delete:

1. Call the destructor.
2. Call operator delete to reclaim the space.

Many times you'll shake your head and say, "If only I could call the destructor but leave the space alone." For example, you used a memory pool when you allocated the object, and now you want to avoid having part of your locally created pool returned to the main free store. In the same way that we split the two-phase construction process, we can split the two-phase destruction process by directly invoking destructors. Unlike the shenanigans required to split the construction process, splitting the destruction process is easy — just call the destructor as if it were a member function.

```
void f()
{
    Pool localPool;
    Foo* foo1 = new Foo; // Uses default operator new
    Foo* foo2 = new(&localPool) Foo; // Uses overload
    delete foo1; // Allocated using default operator new
    foo2->~Foo(); // Call destructor directly
}
```

localPool is a big block of space local to a function. Because it is allocated on the stack, when f() exits it will be popped off the stack. Allocation is lightning fast, since local objects are allocated from the bottom of the pool upward. Deallocation is even faster, because the whole pool gets trashed at the same time. The only problem is that the compiler will not automatically call the destructors of objects allocated inside localPool. You have to do that yourself, using the technique just shown.

Any time a single class's objects can be allocated in more than one way, you will have to use this split-phase destruction trick. In this example, foo1 is allocated one way, foo2 another, even though they are both from the same class. If all objects in a class are allocated identically, simply overloading operator delete for the class will do the same thing without nearly as much extra work.

Who Controls Allocation?

That's enough about mechanics; now let's talk about architecture. There are three basic strategies for determining where an object gets placed in memory and how its space ultimately gets reclaimed:

1. Global allocation and deallocation
2. Class-specific allocation and deallocation
3. Client-directed memory management

The latter breaks down further. The client code may or may not determine where things go; class objects may or may not make those decisions; and master pointers may or may not do the heavy lifting.

Global Allocation and Deallocation

By default, objects are allocated by the global operator new and are deallocated by the global operator delete. You can overload these to provide your own custom memory management scheme, but that is considered poor form:

- It is very difficult to combine separately written libraries each of which overloads the default operators new and delete.

- Your overloads affect not just your code, but also code written by others, including libraries for which you have no source code.

- Any class-specific overloads overload your global overloads, which is the C++ equivalent of requesting both milk and lemon in your tea; if you want to do it in the privacy of your own home or office, fine, but I wouldn't advise it at one of those C++ cocktail parties.

- Users can change your supposedly global strategy by overloading operators new and delete in specific classes. You don't really have as much control as you may think you gained by overloading the default global operators.

Class-Specific Allocation and Deallocation

Overloading operators new and delete as member operators provides a slightly finer level of control. The changes apply to that class and its derived classes only, so side effects are generally minimal. This works best when the custom memory management scheme is separated into a mixin class, then combined into the concrete classes using multiple inheritance. This is not feasible for some memory management schemes, but the burden should be on the architect to demonstrate why it should *not* be done using mixins.

If class-specific allocation is done and you might derive from the affected class, it should be a foregone conclusion that you will make the destructor virtual so that the same class can also deallocate. Derived classes should not overload the overloads.

Client-Directed Memory Management

As in the code fragments above, it is possible to have client code direct where objects should be placed. This is generally done using an overloaded operator new with additional arguments beyond the size_t. This opens new vistas in memory management: Objects from a single class can be managed on an object-by-object basis, rather than class by class. Unfortunately, this strategy throws the entire burden back on the client to also manage deallocation. This is complicated, and the modularity is poor. Change the arguments to your custom operator new, for example, and you may have to change every piece of client code that uses it. At a minimum you'll have time to go for a walk around the block while everything recompiles. Despite all these problems, this strategy is easy to implement, very efficient, and works well in simple situations.

Class Objects and Factory Functions

It is also possible to have the class object or factory function(s) decide where to put the object. This can be as simple as providing one strategy for the entire class or deciding which strategy to use on the basis of the arguments provided to the factory function. When more than one strategy is used, invariably you end up using an invisible pointer strategy, discussed in the next section. In fact, the two ideas work very nicely together.

Master Pointer-Based Memory Management

OK, I lied; we will talk about smart pointers in this chapter after all. You can refine client-directed memory management by encapsulating the various strategies into smart master pointers. Extending the local pool architecture illustrates the basic idea, which can be adapted to almost any object-by-object management scheme.

Specialized Master Pointers. The simplest strategy is to create a specialized master pointer class or template that knows all about the local pool and uses a globally overloaded operator new.

```
struct Pool {...}; // As before
void* operator new(Pool* p); // Allocates from pool
template <class Type>
class PoolMP {
private:
    Type* pointee;
    PoolMP(const PoolMP<Type>&) {} // No copying...
    PoolMP<Type>& operator=(const PoolMP<Type>&)
        { return *this; } // or assignment
public:
    PoolMP(Pool* p) : pointee(new(p) Type) {}
    ~PoolMP() { pointee->~Type(); }
    Type* operator->() const { return pointee; }
};
```

A client can choose to use PoolMP whenever it wants to do local pool-based allocation and deallocation. The destructor of the master pointer calls the destructor of the pointee but does not deallocate its space. Because the master pointer does not keep track of the original pool, copying and assignment cannot be supported, because the master pointer has no idea into which pool to allocate the new copies. Despite these drawbacks, this is basically a no-cost pointer.

It might be argued that copying and assignment should be supported, but using the default operators new and delete. In that case, the copy constructor and operator= are as for any normal master pointer.

Backpointers to the Pool. Copying and assignment within the pool can be supported at the cost of remembering the address of the pool.

```
template <class Type>
class PoolMP {
```

```
private:
    Type* pointee;
    Pool* pool;
public:
    PoolMP(Pool* p) : pointee(new(p) Type), pool(p) {}
    ~PoolMP() { pointee->Type::~Type(); }
    PoolMP(const PoolMP<Type>& pmp)
        : pointee(new(pool) Type(*pointee)) {}
    PoolMP<Type>& operator=(const PoolMP<Type>& pmp) {
        if (this == &pmp) return *this;
        delete pointee;
        pointee = new(pool) Type(*pointee);
        return *this;
        }
    Type* operator->() const { return pointee; }
};
```

This costs an extra four bytes of space, but no extra CPU cycles over a normal master pointer.

Coexisting with Normal Master Pointers. This is pretty limiting so far. The PoolMP interface exposes all sorts of stuff that is better left to the classes in the know. Furthermore, if you want to intermingle objects allocated to the pool and objects allocated another way — perhaps by the default mechanism — things get really clumsy. At the cost of adding a vtable, we can encapsulate a lot more of the differences in memory management strategies.

```
template <class Type>
class MP {
protected:
    MP(const MP<Type>&) {} // No copying allowed
    MP<Type>& operator=(const MP<Type>&)
        { return *this; } // No assignment, either
    MP() {} // Derived class use only
public:
    virtual ~MP() {} // Leave deallocation to deriveds
    virtual Type* operator->() const=0;
};
template <class Type>
```

```
class DefaultMP : public MP<Type> {
private:
    Type* pointee;
public:
    DefaultMP() : pointee(new Type) {}
    DefaultMP(const DefaultMP<Type>& dmp)
        : pointee(new Type(*dmp.pointee)) {}
    virtual ~DefaultMP() { delete pointee; }
    DefaultMP<Type>& operator=
        (const DefaultMP<Type>& dmp)
        {
        if (this == &dmp) return *this;
        delete pointee;
        pointee = new Type(*dmp.pointee);
        return *this;
        }
    virtual Type* operator->() const { return pointee; }
};
template <class Type>
class LocalPoolMP : public MP<Type> {
private:
    Type* pointee;
    Pool* pool;
public:
    LocalPoolMP(Pool* p)
        : pointee(new(p) Type), pool(p) {}
    LocalPoolMP(const LocalPoolMP<Type>& lpmp)
        : pointee(new(lpmp.pool) Type(*lpmp.pointee)),
          pool(lpmp.pool) {}
    virtual ~LocalPoolMP() { pointee->Type::~Type(); }
    LocalPoolMP<Type>& operator=
        (const LocalPoolMP<Type>& lpmp)
        {
        if (this == &lpmp) return *this;
        pointee->Type::~Type();
        pointee = new(pool) Type(*lpmp.pointee);
        return *this;
        }
    virtual Type* operator->() const { return pointee; }
};
```

Now you can intermingle the use of DefaultMP and LocalPoolMP by simply telling clients that they are all MP<Type>&'s. Copying and assignment are supported for those that interact with the derived classes but is disallowed for those that only know about the base class. There is one subtlety in this code. LocalPoolMP::operator= always uses new(pool) rather than new(lpmp.pool). This is safer in case the two master pointers come from different scopes and different pools.

Invisible Pointers. Once you've paid the price of admission to this master pointer class hierarchy, why not go all the way and make the pointers invisible? You have to implement the pointer classes separately for each pointee class, rather than using a generic template, but that is a small price to pay for the flexibility that results.

```
// In foo.h
class Foo {
public:
    static Foo* make(); // Uses default allocation
    static Foo* make(Pool*); // Uses pool
    virtual ~Foo() {}
    // pure virtuals for the class follow
};
// In foo.cpp
class PoolFoo : public Foo {
private:
    Foo* foo;
    Pool* pool;
public:
    PoolFoo(Foo* f, Pool* p) : foo(f), pool(p) {}
    virtual ~PoolFoo() { foo->~Foo(); }
    // overrides of class members, delegating to foo
};
class PFoo : public Foo {
// A normal invisible pointer
};
class ConcreteFoo : public Foo {...};
Foo* Foo::make()
```

```
{
    return new PFoo(new ConcreteFoo);
}
Foo* Foo::make(Pool* p)
{
    return new PoolFoo(new(p) ConcreteFoo, p);
}
```

This is much cleaner for the client. The only time that client code has to know anything about pools is when the object is created using make(Pool*). All other users of the resulting invisible master pointer have no idea whether or not they are dealing with a pool-based object.

Stack-Based Wrappers. For the ultimate in encapsulation, add the following to the architecture just described:

- Make Pool itself a pure abstract base class with encapsulated derived classes, factory functions, etc.

- Provide a static Foo::makePool(). make(Pool*) will still work with other sorts of Pools, but makePool() allows Foo to pick the factory function of Pool that is optimal for storing Foos, for example, by passing the size of instances.

- Recycle the old MP template from earlier chapters — with the operator Type*() option — to make the whole thing roll itself up when the pool and pointers leave scope.

The resulting interface looks something like this, with a fragment of client code and no virtual operator=.

```
// In foo.h
// Bring in the pure abstract base class declaration
#include "pool.h"
class Foo {
private:
    Foo(const Foo&) {}
    Foo& operator=(const Foo&) { return *this; }
public:
    static Pool* makePool(); // Create Foo-optimized pool
    static Foo* make(); // Does not use a pool
```

```
      static Foo* make(Pool*); // Use the given pool
      // etc.
};
// Client code
void g(Foo*);
void f()
{
    MP<Pool> pool(Foo::makePool());
    MP<Foo> foo(Foo::make(pool));
    foo->MemberOfFoo(); // Uses operator->()
    g(foo); // Uses operator Type*()
    // Exiting scope - first foo, then pool are deleted
}
```

Perspective

This is a nice way to end the chapter, with a clever, efficient encapsulation of a very complex design problem. The only point of vulnerability here is in the call to g(), which must promise not to maintain a persistent pointer to its argument. That sort of analysis must be part of any use of temporary pool architectures, anyway; the encapsulation of the solution is key here.

Look past the focus on pools, temporary or otherwise, and you will see a variety of generic strategies for using master pointers to support and encapsulate memory management in C++.

CHAPTER 14

Basic Memory Management

This chapter presents a number of simple strategies for managing memory. If you skipped the previous chapter, go back and read it. Everything you will see in this and later chapters depends on a thorough grasp of the basic material already covered.

The first set of strategies all have one thing in common: client code must decide when to delete things and reclaim their space. Sometimes this control is indirect, but until a client takes some specific action, nothing gets reclaimed.

The second set of strategies all revolve around the idea of reference counting. This is the first example of automatic garbage collection, a theme that will be made more general in the final chapters. Reference counting is extraordinarily useful, but as we will see, it comes with some pretty severe restrictions as well.

Finally, we'll talk about a general concept that will form the foundation of more sophisticated approaches: the memory space. This is really just another way of thinking about the low-level techniques, casting them in the light of architecture rather than optimization.

Building Blocks

One of the most basic principles of custom memory management in C++ has got to be: "Consider something really stupid; it just might work." Even if it doesn't work by itself, it might provide something to build on.

Block-at-a-Time Deallocation

When performance is limited by allocation and deallocation of objects, sometimes the simplest way to fix the problem is to start doing everything in blocks. Allocate from the bottom of a block to the top, and reclaim storage a block at a time, rather than an object at a time.

Do-Nothing Deletion. A large class of programs is designed to run quickly and then go away. This is especially true in a Unix environment, where shell scripts are the glue that holds together lots of tiny, short-lived programs. Often allocation of new objects is the most serious performance bottleneck in such programs. A simple strategy for optimizing is to allocate objects from the bottom of huge blocks up, then *never delete them*.

```
struct Pool {
    static Pool* gCurrentPool; // Pool to allocate from
    enum {block_size=8096}; // Pick your favorite size
    unsigned char* space; // Space to allocate next
    size_t remaining; // Bytes remaining in this block
    Pool()
        : space((unsigned char*)calloc(block_size,'\0'))
        , remaining(block_size) {}
    void* Allocate(size_t bytes) {
        if (bytes > block_size)
            return ::operator new(bytes); // Too big
        if (gCurrentPool == NULL || bytes > remaining)
            gCurrentPool = new Pool;
        void* memory = space;
        space += bytes;
```

```
        remaining -= bytes;
        return memory;
        }
};
class Foo {
public:
    void* operator new(size_t bytes) {
        if (Pool::gCurrentPool == NULL)
            Pool::gCurrentPool = new Pool;
        return Pool::gCurrentPool->Allocate(bytes);
        }
    void operator delete(void*) {}
};
```

Talk about fast! Allocations take just a few machine cycles, and deallocations are close to instantaneous. Obviously, this won't win you any prizes at the local programming contest, but I've seen it bail out some projects with severe performance problems with a few hours' work. At a minimum, it can be the basis for determining where your efforts at optimization are best spent, since it can quickly rule out allocation and deallocation as a factor. Applied class by class, it can diagnose which classes are causing the most trouble.

Note the use of calloc(), rather than ::operator new, to allocate the blocks. Most C++ compilers allocate from calloc() or a native operating system call in large blocks, then manage the objects within them. If you use ::operator new to allocate blocks, it is likely that you'll have duplicated overhead and fragmentation, because your blocks have to live inside the default memory manager's blocks. Better to bypass ::operator new with this sort of strategy.

This strategy also works well in longer-lived programs that initially allocate lots of objects from a given class, then rarely if ever delete them. If you overload operators new and delete on a class-by-class basis, you can do this optimization for only those classes that have this characteristic.

Generational Garbage Collection. Many algorithms look something like this.

```
void Eval(Structure s)
{
    // Allocate local objects
    Eval(s.SomePart()); // Evaluate a substructure
    // Delete local objects
}
```

Walking trees, evaluating recursive expressions in languages like Prolog, and lots of other recursive algorithms have this basic structure. Making the local objects stack-based may help speed up allocation and deallocation, but often that isn't practical. An alternative is to allocate a pool that is local to Eval() and trash it en masse when Eval() exits. Within the scope of Eval(), all temporary objects get allocated into that pool.

```
void* operator new(size_t size, Pool* p)
{
    return p->Allocate(size);
}
template <class Type>
class PoolP { // A pointer that uses a pool
private:
    Type* pointee;
public:
    PoolP(Pool* p) : pointee(new(p) Type) {}
    ~PoolP() { pointee->Type::~Type(); }
    // Remaining master pointer stuff
};
void Eval(Structure s)
{
    Pool p; // Declared on the stack!
    PoolP<Foo> foo(&p); // Use the pool
    Eval(s.SomePart()); // Will use its own pool
    f(p, s); // Instead of f(s); f will use the same pool
    // Destructor of p deallocates everything at once
}
```

Pool is any variation on a memory pool, but presumably a really dumb one that simply allocates bottom-to-top and doesn't bother to reclaim space. The smart pointer PoolP will call the destructor of the pointee, but not deallocate its space. There are lots of variations on this:

- Bypass PoolP. Either have the pool itself call destructors of the objects it contains from its own destructor (they will all need a common base class and a virtual destructor for this) or don't bother calling destructors. (Gasp! Did I say that? But often it *is* workable; just don't brag about it at a C++ cocktail party.)

- Designate a "current pool" in a global variable or static class member, then overload operator new to use whatever the current pool is. This avoids having to pass the current pool to all those subfunctions like f(), just described.

- Provide some way to move or copy objects out of the local pool into a place where they can live beyond the scope of Eval(). This is beyond this chapter, maybe beyond this book, but the "handles everywhere" techniques of the next chapter can be bent to this purpose.

The last variation is used in memory-management strategies so advanced your head hurts *before* you hit that post. Fortunately, all the pain comes from proving whether or not the object has to be moved because it is reachable from something that will outlive the block; this really isn't a C++ issue but one of algorithms and data structures.

Hidden Information

Most memory managers actually allocate a few extra bytes in operator new, so that when operator delete is called, you can be sure of knowing the correct size, regardless of whether or not the destructor is virtual.

```
void* Foo::operator new(size_t bytes)
{
    size_t real_bytes = bytes + sizeof(size_t);
    unsigned char* space =
        (unsigned char*)::operator new(real_bytes);
    *((size_t*)space) = real_bytes;
```

```
      return space + sizeof(size_t);
}
```

Now you can access the size information in operator delete or whenever you want to know the exact size. There are a number of considerations to keep in mind with this strategy.

Redundant Overhead. Depending on your operating system and compiler, this technique may already be used behind the scenes. If you add the size information yourself, it may duplicate overhead already there. This is very likely to be the case if you delegate to ::operator new on an object-by-object basis, described earlier. This technique is mostly useful in conjunction with block-oriented allocation schemes, reducing the overhead of ::operator new or calloc or whatever to per block, not per object.

Optimizing Grain Size. One big advantage of this technique is that you can allocate more than the space requested. How's that? It's an advantage to allocate extra unused space? Well, basically, yes, as long as you are reasonable about it. One approach is to always allocate in n-byte increments, where n can vary from 4 to a large number. This makes it more likely that after you deallocate that 17-byte object someone else will be able to reuse the space for, say, an 18- or 19-byte object. More sophisticated approaches always allocate in powers of two, or, if you're into bumping your head against posts just like the memory-management pros, Fibonacci numbers. These are called *buddy systems*, since from any allocated chunk you can find its buddy, or the other half of whatever larger block it was allocated from, based solely on its size and starting address. This allows efficient recombination of adjacent deallocated chunks. If you are interested in this sort of thing, Chapter 16 discusses some of the bare essentials of the power-of-two buddy system in the context of automatic scavenging.

Other Information. In addition to the size of the block, you can store other information, such as:

- the address of the class object for the object
- flags for the block, such as the following "zombie flag"
- statistical information, such as a timestamp for the point of creation of the object

Free Lists

The simplistic free list shown in earlier chapters is useful only for a single size of object at a time. It didn't work very well with derived classes that add data members, for example, because they are of various sizes. The list itself was constrained to only one size; virtual destructors were required in order to have the correct size passed to operator delete. It is easy to create more general free lists.

A simple extension is to store not just the address of the next-in-list pointer in each node of the free list, but the size of the block as well. This allows blocks of arbitrary sizes to be stored together in a single list. To allocate space, just search the list until you find a block big enough to suit your purposes. This requires that you store the block size as hidden information even after allocation so that the full block is recovered when the object is deallocated. This is a pretty dumb strategy unless you expect the list to remain very small, because the search time grows linearly with the size of the list, but it's a starting point for discussion.

A more efficient representation is a collection of free lists, with each list representing blocks of a single size. Here is one simplistic but useful implementation.

```
class MemManager {
private:
    struct FreeList { // A list for one particular size
        FreeList* next; // Next FreeList
        void* top_of_list; // Top of this free list
        size_t chunk_size; // Size of each free block
        FreeList(FreeList* successor, size_t size)
            : next(successor)
```

```
                , top_of_list(NULL), chunk_size(size) {}
        };
    FreeList* all_lists; // List of FreeLists
public:
    MemManager() : all_lists(NULL) {}
    void* Allocate(size_t bytes);
    void Deallocate(void* space, size_t bytes);
};
void* MemManager::Allocate(size_t bytes)
{   for (FreeList* fl = all_lists;
            fl != NULL && fl->chunk_size != bytes;
            fl = fl->next) {
        if (fl->top_of_list != NULL) {
            void* space = fl->top_of_list;
            fl->top_of_list= *((void**)(fl->top_of_list));
            return space;
            }
        return ::operator new(bytes); // Empty list
        }
    return ::operator new(bytes); // No such list
}
void MemManager::Deallocate(void* space, size_t bytes)
{   FreeList* fl = NULL;
    for (fl = all_lists; fl != NULL; fl = fl->next)
        if (fl->chunk_size == bytes) break;
    if (fl == NULL) { // No list of that size
        fl = new FreeList(all_lists, bytes);
        all_lists = fl;
        }
    *((void**)space) = fl->top_of_list;
    fl->top_of_list = space;
}
```

Allocate() and Deallocate() are called from the overloaded operators new and delete, respectively. This is a very simplistic treatment, but it works fine. You can choose to use it with any combination of classes, and it will work with derived classes that add data members. It can also be used with master pointer-based memory management. There are various improvements one might consider adding to the basic works:

- Constrain chunks to multiples of some number of bytes or powers of two or Fibonacci numbers.

- Use a more efficient data structure than a linked list of free lists, perhaps a binary tree or even an array if the range of sizes is small.

- Provide a Flush() member function that deallocates everything in the free lists under low memory conditions.

- In Allocate(), if there is no space of the desired size in the free list, preallocate an array of chunks of that size rather than one at a time.

Reference Counting

The basic idea of reference counting is to keep track of how many pointers there are to an object. When the count goes to zero, delete the object. Sounds simple, doesn't it? Within narrow constraints, it really is as simple as it sounds, but reference counting has rather nasty limits that restrict its usefulness.

A Reference-Counting Base Class

We will start with an abstract base class from which a class can derive if it wishes to be reference counted. The base class has a data member that keeps track of the number of times the Grab() member function has been called minus the number of times Release() has been called.

```
class RefCount {
private:
    unsigned long count; // Reference count
public:
    RefCount() : count(0) {}
    RefCount(const RefCount&) : count(0) {}
    RefCount& operator=(const RefCount&)
        { return *this; } // Doesn't change the count
```

```
virtual ~RefCount() {} // Placeholder
void Grab() { count++; }
void Release() {
    if (count > 0) count--;
    if (count == 0) delete this;
    }
};
```

As long as client code calls Grab() and Release() properly, this is perfectly safe. Whenever a client takes the address of an object derived from RefCount, or copies such an address, it calls Grab(). Whenever it can guarantee that such an address will no longer be used, it calls Release(). When the count goes to zero, poof! No more object!

This suffers an obvious flaw; it relies too much on programmers' following the rules. We can do better.

Reference-Counting Pointers

Let's build on the RefCount base class by creating a modified smart pointer template for use with anything derived from RefCount.

```
template <class Type>
class CP { // For "counting pointer"
private:
    Type* pointee;
public:
    CP(Type* p) : pointee(p) { pointee->Grab(); }
    CP(const CP<Type>& cp) : pointee(cp.pointee)
        { pointee->Grab(); }
    ~CP() { pointee->Release(); }
    CP<Type>& operator=(const CP<Type>& cp) {
        if (this == &cp) return *this;
        if (pointee == cp.pointee) return *this;
        pointee->Release();
        pointee = cp.pointee;
        pointee->Grab();
        return *this;
        }
```

```
    Type* operator >() { return pointee; }
};
```

If all client code accesses reference-counted classes through this or similar templates, reference counting is automatic. Every time a new copy of the pointer is made, the call to Grab() takes place automatically. Every time a pointer is destroyed, its destructor decrements the count. The only danger is if a client bypasses the smart pointer. That can be countered by using factory functions of the target class.

```
class Foo : public RefCount {
private:
    Foo(); // Along with any other constructors
public:
    static CP<Foo> make(); // Creates an instance
    // Interface to Foo follows
};
```

This ensures that Foo will only be accessed through the reference-counting pointer. Notice that this is not a master pointer, but a plain, run-of-the-mill smart pointer.

Reference-Counted Master Pointers

If you don't want to modify the concrete class to have it derive from RefCount — perhaps it's one of those terribly performance- and space-sensitive classes or maybe it is part of an off-the-shelf class library — don't despair. You can shift the reference counting to a master pointer.

```
template <class Type>
class CMP { // "Counting master pointer."
private:
    Type* pointee;
    unsigned long count;
public:
    CMP() : pointee(new Type), count(0) {}
    CMP(const CMP<Type>& cmp)
        : pointee(new Type(*(cmp.pointee))), count(0) {}
    ~CMP() { delete pointee; } // Regardless of count
```

```
            CMP<Type>& operator=(const CMP<Type>& cmp) {
                if (this == &cmp) return *this;
                delete pointee;
                pointee = new Type(*(cmp.pointee));
                return *this;
                }
            Type* operator->() const { return pointee; }
            void Grab() { count++; }
            void Release() {
                if (count > 0) count--;
                if (count <= 0) {
                    delete pointee;
                    delete this;
                    }
                }
        };
```

This is basically equivalent to mashing together the old master pointer template with the RefCount base class. Now we've succeeded in avoiding putting the reference count itself into the concrete class, but at the cost of reintroducing reliance on those all-too-imperfect programmers.

Reference-Counting Handles

Enter the reference-counting handle. This is to the CMP template what CP was to RefCount; that is, it automatically calls the Grab() and Release() member functions in its constructors, destructor, and operator=.

```
template <class Type>
class CH { // For "counting handle"
private:
    CMP<Type>* pointee;
public:
    CH(CMP<Type>* p) : pointee(p) { pointee->Grab(); }
    CH(const CH<Type>& ch) : pointee(ch.pointee)
        { pointee->Grab(); }
    ~CH() { pointee->Release(); }
    CH<Type>& operator=(const CH<Type>& ch) {
```

```
        if (this == &ch) return *this;
        if (pointee == ch.pointee) return *this;
        pointee->Release();
        pointee = ch.pointee;
        pointee->Grab();
        return *this;
        }
    CMP<Type> operator->() { return *pointee; }
};
```

If this is used in conjunction with counted master pointers, you can pick and choose which instances of a class to reference count and which instances to manage in some other way.

Problems with Reference Counting

It all seems so easy; it's a shame to throw a wet blanket over the party. Reference counting suffers from a very common problem: circular graphs. Picture the following situation: Object A has done a Grab of object B, and object B has Grabbed A. Neither A nor B is reachable from any other object. By all rights, both A and B should be deleted, but neither will be because their reference counts will never go to zero. Bummer.

This sort of circularity comes up all the time. It can apply to entire subgraphs of objects, not just two at a time. A points to B points to C points to D points to A, but no one outside this group points to any of them. The whole complex ends up riding a sort of high-tech Flying Dutchman, doomed to sail through memory for all eternity. There are a couple of strategies for breaking circularity, neither of them very general, but they may bail out reference counting for your case. In general, though, when you run into a circular reference problem, it is time to consider using one of the more sophisticated approaches of the last two chapters. There is a very easily approached point of diminishing returns from reference counting.

Decomposition. Suppose you have A Grab B, but then B grabs some component of A:

```
class A {
private:
    Foo* foo;
    B* b;
};
```

If you arrange for B to Grab at the member foo, there is no more problem. When the last reference to A goes away, its reference count goes to 0, because B hasn't incremented it. This requires some fancy footwork, and the design is heavily dependent on the particular objects, but it is surprising how often it can resolve a circularity problem.

Strong Versus Weak Handles. Suppose A's reference to B involved a Grab, but B's reference to A didn't? Then at the moment when the last reference to A by the outside world went away, the pair would both be reference counted out of existence. This is the idea behind distinguishing *strong* from *weak* handles or counting pointers. The CH template just described would be considered the strong handle, since it maintains the reference count. A normal handle template — with no Grab and Release calls — would be considered weak. If you can design your object architecture in such a way that no subgraph based solely on strong handles is circular, then the whole reference-counting scheme is back on track. The most common situation in which this applies is a whole/part hierarchy, in which parts are deleted when the whole is. The whole maintains strong references, the parts weak ones.

Reference Counting and Master Pointers

That said, one of the most common and powerful uses of reference counting is in the management of master pointers. This subject has been glossed over in earlier chapters. Handles live on the stack and so are garbage-collected automatically by the compiler. Master pointers, however, usually have to be allocated on the heap for the same reasons that objects are. How do you know when to delete a master pointer? Reference counting makes it easy.

Circularity is not a problem: Because a master pointer does not keep any references to its handles, the reference is one-way. The handles are copied and passed around, and they remain four bytes wide with no virtual member functions and only trivial inlines. A few extra cycles are eaten up when you Grab and Release, but those are minor compared with what you would have to do otherwise to manage the master pointers. The extra few bytes for the count in the master pointer don't matter all that much; these are being allocated on the heap, anyway, where granularity of allocation is generally much bigger than four bytes.

You might want to return to earlier chapters and consider the use of a reference-counting scheme like this one wherever you see a master pointer at work. This will be a key to more advanced memory management in the remaining chapters.

Memory Spaces

All these tricks form a foundation upon which to build, but they are not really architectures. For more advanced memory management, more advanced concepts are needed to organize the work. In simple memory-management situations, you will treat all available memory as a single chunk to be allocated from. This can either be done directly by asking the operating system to hand you a huge chunk of memory at startup, or indirectly by ultimately delegating back to ::operator new and ::operator delete.

In the final two chapters, we will take a more sophisticated approach to the problem by dividing available memory into *memory spaces*. A memory space is a concept; it can be implemented if you use almost any of the block-oriented memory-management schemes described earlier. For example, within one memory space you might use a buddy system, in another a freelist approach. This abstract base class describes the concept.

```
class MemSpace {
public:
    void* Allocate(size_t bytes)=0;
    void Deallocate(void* space, size_t bytes)=0;
};
```

(If your compiler supports exception handling, these member functions should both be declared to throw exceptions.) Some memory spaces might not need to be told the size of returning chunks in Deallocate(), and there may be other member functions for particular schemes, but this is the minimal interface. Presumably, one would also maintain a global data structure, a collection of all MemSpaces, for reasons to be discussed shortly. This collection should be able to efficiently answer the question "Inside what memory space does this address lie?" Given an object's address, you need to find the memory space in which it lives.

The choice of memory space can be made using any of the techniques described in the previous chapter.

- Global overloads of operators new and delete (not generally recommended)
- Class-specific overloads of operators new and delete
- Client-directed use of operator new with arguments
- Master pointer-based use of operator new with arguments

There are many reasons that you might partition memory in this way. Following are a few common strategies for deciding which objects should go together in a memory space.

Partitioning by Class

We spoke in an earlier chapter about class objects, but never addressed head-on this question: How does one determine the class object of a given object? The simplest answer is: Add a data member that points to the class object. That involves a fair amount of overhead to maintain, both in space and constructor code. There are two additional options, however:

1. Have a master pointer maintain the pointer to the class object on behalf of the object. This is the same basic overhead, but better encapsulated.

2. Put all objects of a given class into a single memory space and point to the class object from the beginning of the memory space, as is shown in the figure.

The latter requires far less overhead, provided that given the address of an object you can efficiently determine the beginning of the memory space in which it lives, perhaps using the collection of memory spaces mentioned previously.

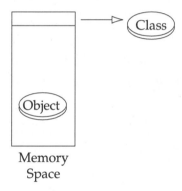

Memory
Space

At first glance, it may seem silly to go to so much trouble over such a simple problem. Why not just add the extra data member pointing to the class object? There are at least two reasons:

1. The class you are managing may be an off-the-shelf class for which you have no source code or that you don't want to change for other reasons.

2. The class may be a trivial object-oriented wrapper around a primitive data type like an int. The extra bytes for the pointer to the class object, not to mention the vtable needed for the inevitable virtual member functions to access it, may be very significant overhead.

Partitioning by Size

It may be prudent to group together all objects of a given size or range of sizes into a single memory space to optimize their allocation and deallocation. Most memory-management strategies tend to work better with certain size ranges than with others. For example, if you allocate lots of large, irregularly sized objects, a power-of-two scheme will probably leave you with lots of unused fragmentary space, yet power of two works extremely well for relatively small objects or for those close to a power of two in size. In extreme cases, an entire memory space may be filled with objects of identical size. Such a space can be very efficiently represented and is easy to manage.

Partitioning by Usage

An alternative strategy is to partition the objects according to use. In a threaded server application, for example, we might separate objects by client. Infrequently used objects might live in one space and highly volatile objects in another. Objects that may be cached on disk may be managed separately from objects that stay in memory at all times. This can be done one class at a time or object by object.

Partitioning by Accessibility

An important reason for separating into various memory spaces is to keep separate track of objects accessible from the stack, from other processes, or purely internally from the heap. This is a key to scavenging and compacting garbage-collection schemes, as we will see in the final chapters.

In the next two chapters, we will use this approach quite a bit. Objects that we can move about from place to place will be separated from objects that must stay put. Master pointers accessible from the stack will be put into one space, and master pointers accessible from other processes will go somewhere else.

Stack Versus Heap Spaces

Finally, we can consider the stack itself to be a form of memory space, and pools allocated on the stack a special case. This approach was used earlier in this chapter for pools local to a particular function's scope. We will continue to look at the stack as a special beast in the next two chapters.

CHAPTER 15

Compacting Memory

Routine memory management in C++ requires that you wave some incense, sacrifice a rubber chicken or two to the operating system, then delete your object. If all goes well, the object will be properly deinitialized and deallocated, and no one will ever again attempt to use it. Hah! We all know how well that works in real life.

One of the principal attractions of dynamic languages like Small-talk and Lisp has nothing to do with the languages and everything to do with the fact that they do the deletion for you, safely and automatically. This is a tremendous saving of time and energy, not to mention rubber chickens. Can the same be done in C++? The answer is neither yes nor no, but rather "It depends on how much you are willing to invest in the solution."

This chapter opens the fun and games by showing how to shove objects around in memory in order to minimize fragmentation of free space. I hope these algorithms won't set people rolling on the floor laughing when you describe them. At the same time, we will be setting the stage for the full-blown scavenging algorithms of the next chapter.

Enumerating Pointers

Moving beyond reference counting and customized operators new and delete, most memory-management strategies involve combinations of two techniques: detecting when an object can no longer be accessed so that it can be automatically deallocated (scavenging) and moving objects around in memory (compaction). These, in turn, both depend on being able to do something that is simple in many other languages but devilishly difficult in C++: finding all the pointers to objects.

Enumerating pointers in a C++ program is hard because the compiler doesn't leave around instructions for doing it. Furthermore, C++ allows a program to take the direct address of portions of objects, so that some pointers actually point into the middle of larger objects.

Mommy, Where Do Pointers Come From?

There is an incredible variety of ways to get a pointer in C++. Some of them have to do with the way objects are represented in memory, some of them have to do with inheritance, and others have to do with data members. Taking the address of an object is the obvious way to get a pointer. Now let's look at some of the not-so-obvious ones.

Addresses of Data Members. Given an object, it is perfectly legal in C++ to take the address of a data member and mail it to yourself or some other object.

```
class Foo {
private:
    int x;
    String y;
public:
    int& X() { return x; } // A reference to x
    String* Name() { return &y; } // Address of y
};
```

Each instance of Foo looks something like this diagram (this is technically compiler-dependent, but they all tend to work this way).

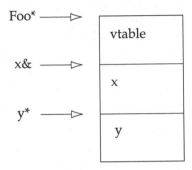

Generally, the first few bytes are occupied by a pointer to the vtable for the object's class, followed by the data members in their order of declaration. If you take the address of a data member, as either a reference or an explicit pointer, that produces a pointer into the middle of the object.

Addresses of Base Classes. Inheritance also provides endless hours of amusement in the form of pointers.

```
class A {...}; // One base class
class B {...}; // Another base class
class C : public A, public B {...}; // Multiply derived
```

Under single inheritance, typecasting from derived* to base* leaves the address the same even though the compiler thinks the type has changed. Under multiple inheritance, things aren't so simple.

```
C* c = new C;
A* a = c; // Typecast from derived to first base
B* b = c; // Typecast from derived to second base
cout << c << endl;
cout << a << endl;
cout << b << endl;
```

This may look like a simple piece of code, but in fact the compiler pulls a really slimy trick. When you cast from C* to A*, the pointer stays the same. When you cast from C* to B*, however, the compiler actually *changes the address*. This is because of the way the object is laid out in memory. (This is all compiler-dependent, but it applies to every compiler I've used.)

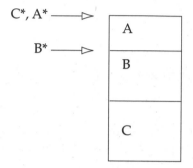

The compiler lays out the object in order of the declaration of the base classes, followed by the derived class. When the compiler typecasts from C* to A*, it is as if the compiler threw a cloak over the B and C components of the object, fooling client code into thinking it is dealing with a real, dyed-in-the-wool A.

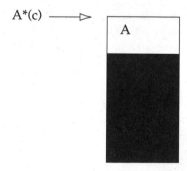

The vtable at the beginning of the object ensures that C's implementations of virtual member functions declared in A will be reached, but their offsets are the same as A's. When the compiler works with a C*, it knows the complete layout of the entire object and can deal with A, B, and C in their proper places. However, when the complier typecasts to the second or a succeeding base class under multiple inheritance, the address must be changed in order to allow client code to think it is dealing with a real B.

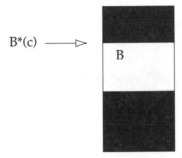

There are actually two vtable pointers, one at the beginning of the object that includes all virtual member functions declared initially in either A or C, and one at the beginning of the B component containing virtual member functions originally declared in B. This means that typecasting from derived to base in C++ can, in some circumstances, result in a pointer to within an object just like those pointers to data members we talked about earlier. It also leads to some stupid C++ pet tricks, like these.

```
C* anotherC = C*(void*(B*(c)));
anotherC->MemberOfC();
```

See the problem? The typecast B*(c) moves the pointer. This is cast to void*. The cast back to C* results in code that thinks the C begins at the wrong place. Without the cast to void*, this would work, since the compiler can figure out what the offset from a B* to a C* is. In fact, this sort of cast from base* to derived* is done all the time when a client calls a virtual member function of B overridden in C. But when it casts from void* to C*, the compiler just makes the naive assumption that the programmer knows what she is doing.

Remember this: At some point in every C++ programmer's career she spends a sleepless night trying to figure out why her object is apparently so screwed up, only to have some guru come along, diagnose it as one of these class-to-void-to-class problems, generally in a loud voice and accompanied by uproarious laughter. But I digress.

Virtual Base Classes. If you use them, you can pretty well kiss good-bye any compaction or scavenging scheme that requires objects be moved around in memory. Here is a code fragment and a diagram that shows how it is represented in memory.

```
class Base {...};
class A : virtual public Base {...};
class B : virtual public Base {...};
class Foo : public A, public B {...};
```

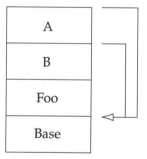

Yuck. The compiler is so ashamed of what it has to do to implement Base as a virtual base class that it hides it waaay down under the Foo. A and B each have pointers to the instance of Base ... yes, that's right, pointers, as in direct memory addresses. You don't have access to these pointers and, therefore, cannot hope to update them if you try to move the object around in memory.

Pointer to Member. The idea of a pointer to member is that a member can be uniquely identified, not by its direct address, but by the address of the object that contains both it and the offset of the member within that object. If you haven't used pointer to member before, clear your head before reading this code fragment.

```
class Foo {
private:
    int x;
public:
    static int& Foo::*X() { return &Foo::x; }
};
Foo* f = new Foo; // Create an instance
int& Foo::*pm = Foo::X(); // Calculate offset of an int
int& i = f->*pm; // Apply the offset to an instance
```

The function X() returns not a reference to an int, but rather the offset of some int within instances of class Foo. Foo::X() is declared static, since it does not apply to any specific instance but rather to the class as a whole. The phrase return &Foo::x; takes the offset of a specific member, x. The line int& Foo::*pm = Foo::X(); declares a variable, pm, that holds the offset of an int member of Foo. It is initialized to the offset returned by Foo::X(). The offset is finally applied to a specific instance to calculate the address of a specific int in the statement int& i = f->*pm;. i now contains the address of a data member — x — of a specific instance. Note that pm by itself is useless until you combine it with an object.

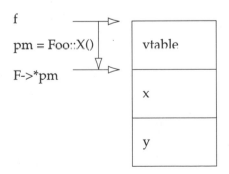

All those int&'s could have been int*'s without anything being changed. Both end up indirectly taking the address of some part of an object just as if you had taken the explicit address of a data member. (Pointer to member can also be used to indirectly point to a member function, not just a data member, but that isn't relevant to a discussion of memory management. Besides, this stuff is giving me another headache.)

Implications. The implications of all this for memory management are profound. If you want to move an object, you have to make sure you move the outermost enclosing object, since it may be a data member whose address you have. Furthermore, if you move an object, you have to update all pointers, not just to the object itself, but to all enclosed data members and base classes as well.

If you want to determine whether or not an object is referenced from anywhere, you have to look not just for pointers to the beginning of the object, but also to data members and base classes.

Finding Pointers

OK, now that we know all the different kinds of pointers we might have to deal with, how do we go about finding them all? In order to move an object, you have to update all pointers to it. In order to figure out whether an object is reachable, you have to be able to enumerate all pointers.

Custom Pointer Spaces. One brute-force solution is to put all the pointers someplace where you can easily find them. This, in turn, implies that all the pointers must be smart pointers and that all smart pointers are stored in custom memory spaces. Those memory spaces must be arranged in such a way that you can enumerate their contents, that is, iterate over the set of smart pointers. Classes should replace all those *'s with references or handles to smart pointers, since the pointers themselves must reside in the separate memory space. In the code fragment that follows, P and H are standard pointers and handles, respectively, except that P is arranged to store pointer instances in a custom memory space. The technique works equally well with invisible pointers, provided one of the custom memory space techniques is used to put them in a safe and well-known place. P will usually be a master pointer, but it does not have to be.

```
template <class Type>
class P { // A carefully managed pointer
private:
    Type* pointee;
public:
    void* operator new(size_t); // Uses custom mem space
    void operator delete(void*); // Uses custom mem space
    // Usual smart pointer stuff here
};
template <class Type>
class H { // A handle
private:
    P<Type>* ptr;
public:
    // The usual handle stuff
};
class Foo {
private:
    P<Bar>& bar; // Reference to smart pointer to a Bar
    // OR
    H<Bar> bar; // Handle to a Bar
};
```

In the first version, we store a reference to the smart pointer, which presumably is stored somewhere else. In the second version we use the handle idiom, a smart pointer to a smart pointer. The handle itself lives in the object, but the pointer it points to lives in the custom pointer space used by P's operators new and delete. If the pointer space is implemented cleverly, you can enumerate all pointers directly from it. Moving an object is then easier, though still not easy, since the pointers to it can all be found in the pointer space. A full implementation of this technique appears later in this chapter.

Hidden Collections of Pointers. Another option is to maintain hidden collections of smart pointers.

```
template <class Type>
class P {
private:
    static P<Type>* head; // Head of list of MPs
    static P<Type>* tail; // Tail of list
    P<Type>* next; // Next in list
    P<Type>* previous; // Previous in list
    Type* pointee;
public:
    P(); // Stuff 'this' into list
    P(const P<Type>& p); // Stuff 'this' into list
    ~P(); // Remove 'this' from list
    P<Type>& operator=(const P<Type>& p); // Leave list
        // alone, but copy p.pointee
    // Usual smart pointer stuff follows
};
```

You have to use some care to manage the linked list properly in the copy constructor and operator=, but this is otherwise pretty straightforward. Using this template, a class needn't store references to smart pointers; it can directly embed them.

```
class Foo {
private:
    P<Bar> bar; // Pointer automatically goes into
                // hidden collection
};
```

The appropriate constructor of P will be called whenever a Foo is constructed and will automatically stuff bar into the hidden collection. When a Foo is destroyed, the destructor of P will be called to remove bar from the collection. Of course, one could use data structures other than a doubly linked list. Also, as we will see later, it is useful to use a generic base class for all those type-specific pointers and to store them all together in a single collection. The just described code will generate a separate collection for each type of pointer.

Parse the Instances. A more radical approach is to use normal, everyday pointers, but to provide some way to walk through all pointers embedded in an instance.

```
class Foo {
private:
    Bar* bar;
};
```

This would be allowed in this scheme, provided a very complex architecture was in place to find that Bar* given a Foo. Implementing this requires code that knows about the structure of each instance — specifically, where to find data members that are addresses or may recursively contain addresses — and the ability to accurately tell the type of each thing pointed to. For example, it would do no good to find bar if you didn't then know whether it is really a Bar at the other end or some class derived from Bar. That derived class may add additional pointers not present in Bar.

This sort of parsing will be discussed further, but if this were a car commercial, you would see a disclaimer at the bottom of the screen: "Professional stunt driver on a closed track. Do not try this at home." Nevertheless, there are lots of situations in which the simplistic approaches don't work, so in the next chapter we'll dive feet-first into this scheme.

Stack Variables. Of course, not all pointers are data members of objects. Some are variables on the stack. The custom space approach obviously won't work for stack variables unless they are really references or handles to smart pointers stored elsewhere. Hidden collections, however, will work equally well for stack- or heap-based pointers, provided you have exception handling that properly unwinds the stack. The only variable that requires special handling is this, which is set up by the compiler, not your own smart pointer-based code. Stack variables greatly complicate the instance-parsing approach, since we also have to design a separate scheme for finding or at least avoiding collisions with them.

Handles, Handles Everywhere

One strategy for compaction and scavenging in C++ that borrows a page from dynamic languages is to refer to all objects through handles.

```
class Foo {
private:
    H<Bar> bar; // Handle to a Bar
public:
    H<Bar> GetBar() { return bar; }
};
```

Here, H is a handle template like those we discussed in earlier chapters. Each H<Bar> is a smart pointer to a master pointer to a Bar. Member functions that indirectly expose the data member, such as GetBar(), return copies of the handle. The master pointers, in this version at least, all live in a custom pointer space, so they are easy to find.

Here is one simple implementation of compaction using handles, although by no means the only one possible.

Outline of the Architecture

The first stab at the architecture revolves around the following principles:

- Because we are mixing different types into one set of master pointers, we use an abstract base class VoidPtr for master pointers. The concrete master pointers come from a template derived from this base class.

- The master pointers live in a custom pointer space that allows easy enumeration of the pointers.

- Each master pointer maintains a reference count and deletes itself when the count goes from 1 to 0. Its destructor, in turn, calls the destructor of the pointee and, depending on the algorithms being used, may or may not attempt to reclaim the object's storage at that time.

- All data members and variables use handles to master pointers, rather than direct pointers to other objects.
- Memory is reclaimed only when the portion of the heap being managed is compacted. In other words, when we need more memory, we will shove active objects down in the heap to make room at the top. Allocation is always bottom-up.

This is only a compaction architecture. No attempt is made to resolve circularity problems or to scavenge objects that are no longer reachable but have not been deleted. That will come in the next chapter.

Master Pointers

As in most memory-management strategies, we will need to store lots of different kinds of master pointers in one enumerable structure. This argues for a common abstract base class for all master pointers. Here are our requirements for the master pointers:

1. Maintain a reference count.
2. Put them all in a custom memory space that allows enumeration.
3. In the destructor, call the pointee's destructor. Depending on the scavenging algorithm used, we may or may not attempt to reclaim storage at the same time. For this example, we needn't bother reclaiming the object's storage.

VoidPtr Base Class. Here is an abstract base class that these requirements implements.

```
class VoidPtrPool; // Used to allocate, deallocate,
                   // enumerate VoidPtrs
class VoidPtr {
friend class VoidPtrPool;
private:
    unsigned long refcount; // Reference count
protected:
    void* address; // Address of pointee
```

```
      size_t size; // Size in bytes of pointee
      VoidPtr() : address(NULL), size(0), refcount(0) {}
      VoidPtr(void* addr, size_t s)
          : address(addr), size(s), refcount(0) {}
  public:
      static VoidPtrPool* pool;
      virtual ~VoidPtr() { size = 0; address=NULL; }
      void* operator new(size_t) {
          if (pool == NULL)
              pool = new VoidPtrPool;
          return pool->Allocate();
          }
      void operator delete(void* space)
          { pool->Deallocate((VoidPtr*)space); }
      void Grab() { refcount++; }
      void Release() {
          if (refcount > 0) refcount--;
          if (refcount <= 0) delete this;
          }
  };
```

Master Pointer Template. The actual master pointer is a template derived from VoidPtr. This chiefly exists to implement operator-> and the virtual destructor that knows which destructor to call for the pointee. I have chosen to disallow copying and assignment. Copying a handle will copy the address of the master pointer, not the master pointer or pointee themselves. Therefore, there is no real need to support copying and assignment of the master pointer. As usual, there are lots of variations on the theme of constructors. Here I have chosen to have the master pointer's constructor create the pointee.

```
template <class Type>
class MP : public VoidPtr {
private: // To disallow them
    MP(const MP<Type>&) {}
    MP<Type>& operator=(const MP<Type>&) {return *this;}
public:
    MP() : VoidPtr(new Type, sizeof(Type)) {}
```

```
    virtual ~MP() { ((Type*)address)->Type::~Type(); }
    Type* operator->() { return (Type*)address; }
};
```

Handle Template. The handle template is the same as the reference-counting handle of early chapters.

```
template <class Type>
class Handle {
private:
    MP<Type>* pointer;
public:
    Handle() : pointer(new MP<Type>)
        { pointer->Grab(); }
    Handle(const Handle<Type>& h) : pointer(h.pointer)
        { pointer->Grab(); }
    Handle<Type>& operator=(const Handle<Type>& h) {
        if (this == &h) return *this;
        if (pointer == h.pointer) return *this;
        pointer->Release();
        h.pointer->Grab();
        return *this;
        }
    MP<Type>& operator->() { return *pointer; }
};
```

This is used in code for variables that refer to objects.

```
class Bar {
private:
    H<Foo> foo;
public:
    void f();
};
void Bar::f()
{
    Handle<Foo> f; // Equivalent to Foo* f = new Foo;
    f = foo; // Uses operator=(Handle<Type>(foo));
    foo = f; // Uses operator H<Type>(f)
}
```

Master Pointer Pool. For the sake of simplicity, we'll assume that derived classes of VoidPtr are identical in size to VoidPtr itself; that is, they add no data members. That simplifies matters; VoidPtrPool can now be a simple linked list of arrays of VoidPtr. The array structure is called VoidPtrBlock.

```
struct VoidPtrBlock {
    VoidPtrBlock* next; // Next block in list
    VoidPtr slots[BLOCKSIZE]; // Array of slots
    VoidPtrBlock(VoidPtrBlock* next_in_list)
        : next(next_in_list) {
        // Arrange new slots into linked list
        for (int i = 0; i < BLOCKSIZE-1; i++)
            slots[i].address = &slots[i+1];
        slots[BLOCKSIZE-1].address = NULL;
        }
    ~VoidPtrBlock() { delete next; }
    };
class VoidPtrPool {
private:
    VoidPtr* free_list; // Free list of VoidPtrs
    VoidPtrBlock* block_list; // Head of list of blocks
public:
    VoidPtrPool() : block_list(NULL), free_list(NULL) {}
    ~VoidPtrPool() { delete block_list; }
    VoidPtr* Allocate();
    void Deallocate(VoidPtr* vp);
};
VoidPtr* VoidPtrPool::Allocate()
{
    if (free_list == NULL) { // Allocate another block
        block_list = new VoidPtrBlock(block_list);
        // Add to free list
        block_list->slots[BLOCKSIZE-1].address=free_list;
        free_list = &block_list->slots[0];
        }
    VoidPtr* space = (VoidPtr*)free_list;
    free_list = (VoidPtr*)space->address;
    return space;
}
```

```
void VoidPtrPool::Deallocate(VoidPtr* vp)
{
    vp->address = free_list;
    free_list = (VoidPtr*)vp->address;
    vp->size = 0;
}
```

There is nothing tricky about this. When a new block is allocated, its slots are formed into a linked list, which is glommed on to the top of the free list. When the free list is empty and someone wants another master pointer, allocate a new block, then allocate from the free list, which is by then repopulated.

Master Pointer Iterator. To enumerate all the master pointers, we provide an iterator class called VoidPtrIterator. VoidPtrPool returns one such iterator, enumerating all of the currently active pointers, that is, all pointers not on the free list. We declare this as a pure abstract base class, because in the next chapter we will use the same interface to enumerate pointers embedded inside objects.

```
class VoidPtrIterator {
protected:
    VoidPtrIterator() {}
public:
    virtual bool More() = 0;
    virtual VoidPtr* Next() = 0;
};
```

The iterator itself is very straightforward. It simply loops through the blocks, looking for pointers that have a nonzero size.

```
class VoidPtrPoolIterator : public VoidPtrIterator {
private:
    VoidPtrBlock* block;
    int slot; // Slot number within current block
    virtual void Advance() { // Find next in-use slot
        while (block != NULL) {
            if (slot >= BLOCKSIZE) {
                block = block->next;
                slot = 0;
```

```
                          }
                  else if (block->slots[slot].size != 0)
                     break;
                  slot++;
                  }
            }
     public:
        VoidPtrPoolIterator(VoidPtrBlock* vpb)
              : block(vpb), slot(0) { Advance(); }
        virtual bool More() { return block != NULL; }
        virtual VoidPtr* Next() {
            VoidPtr* vp = &block->slots[slot];
            Advance();
            return vp;
            }
     };
```

We also add the following member function to VoidPtrPool.

```
     VoidPtrIterator* iterator()
        { return new VoidPtrPoolIterator(this); }
```

Finally, we have to declare VoidPtrPoolIterator to be a friend of VoidPtr, so that it can see the size member in this code. Looking ahead, we will be using this iterator for other purposes in Chapter 16; that is why Advance() is declared virtual, so that derived classes can add their own further filtering. Any time we find a slot with a size of zero, we skip it. Otherwise, this is simply enumerating the slots in the arrays that make up the pointer blocks.

Variations

Before describing the compaction algorithms themselves, let's look at other ways we might have set things up. None fundamentally affects the architecture or algorithms involved, just the C++ idioms used to implement them.

Invisible Master Pointers. Rather than use handles and master pointer templates, one could instead have the real master pointers multiply derive from VoidPtr and a homomorphic base class.

That is, the master pointers become invisible pointers, as is described in earlier chapters. This brings into play all the machinery that goes with the invisible pointer idiom, such as factory functions.

```
class Foo {
public:
    static Foo* make(); // Returns ptr-pointee pair
    virtual void Member1()=0;
    // etc. for the public interface
};
// In foo.cpp
class FooPtr : public Foo, public VoidPtr {
public:
    FooPtr(Foo* foo, size_t size) : VoidPtr(foo, size) {}
    virtual ~FooPtr() { delete (Foo*)address; }
    virtual void Member1()
        { ((Foo*)address)->Member1(); }
    // etc. for remaining public member functions
};
class RealFoo : public Foo {...};
Foo* Foo::make()
{
    return new FooPtr(new RealFoo, sizeof(RealFoo));
}
// In client code
class Bar {
private:
    Foo* foo; // Actually an invisible pointer
public:
    Bar() : foo(Foo::make()) {}
};
```

This provides better encapsulation of the use of master pointers. It also allows the factory functions to decide which instances to manage this way and which ones to manage using normal invisible pointers or even directly without pointers at all. This works fine, as long as you are careful to allocate enough space for FooPtr in VoidPtrPool. Remember that because of the multiple inheritance it is at least a vtable pointer larger than VoidPtr.

Class Objects. Another variation is to insist that all objects derive from a common ancestor class that is capable of returning the class object for the object, or at least the object's size. With this variation, you needn't store the size of the instance in the pointer, since the class object can return it. If you are willing to put up with some type coercion in the handles, this also makes it possible to avoid the second-tier templates used for the master pointers. Everything can be stored in terms of CommonBase* in VoidPtr, rather than void*. This gets rid of the size data member, the need for the template derived from VoidPtr, and the virtual destructor in VoidPtr and, therefore, the four-byte vtable address. If the objects being managed already have vtables and this won't force you into using multiple inheritance, there is no cost on the other side.

Special Case Optimizations

If a data member's address is never taken, it can be stored as an embedded object. This is not entirely in the control of the programmer that designs the class, as the following illustrates.

```
void f(int);
class Foo {
private:
    int x; // Address never taken, so stored directly
public:
    void Fn() { f(x); }
};
```

Seems safe enough, right? Now suppose the author of f() changes its interface to this.

```
void f(int&);
```

All of a sudden, your carefully crafted optimization comes crashing down on your roof. Another problem with embedded objects is that you have to verify not just that the object's address is never taken, but that no recursively embedded member's address is taken.

```
class Bar {
private:
    Foo foo;
};
```

You may be able to prove that none of Bar's member functions takes the address of foo, but you have to go one step further and verify that all of Foo's member functions are safe, too. The same logic must be applied to base classes. The point here is that this form of optimization needs to be done with a view to the whole program, not just to the class under construction.

Baker's Algorithm

One compaction approach is to waste gobs — specifically, half — of memory in the interests of speed and a compaction algorithm that can be interwoven a little at a time with regular processing. This is known as Baker's Algorithm.

Divide the memory pool being managed into two halves, called A and B. At any one time, one of these is the *active* half, the half into which new objects are allocated. Memory is allocated from a half bottom-to-top, with no attempt made to reclaim space from deleted objects at the time they are deleted. Instead, from time to time, you copy all active objects from one half to the other, compacting them down to the bottom of the new half as you go. An active object is one that has a master pointer — a VoidPtr, that is — pointing to it from master pointer land.

Object Spaces

The halves are represented as custom memory spaces for the objects. HalfSpace represents one half, Space the whole enchilada as seen by clients.

HalfSpace. Each half looks in isolation like a normal memory space with a custom Allocate() member function. There is no need for Deallocate().

```
class HalfSpace {
private:
    unsigned long next_byte; // Next byte to allocate
    unsigned char bytes[HALFSIZE];
public:
    HalfSpace() : next_byte(0) {}
    void* Allocate(size_t size);
    void Reinitialize() { next_byte = 0; }
};
void* HalfSpace::Allocate(size_t size) {
    // Round up to a word boundary
    size = ROUNDUP(size);
    if (next_byte + size >= HALFSIZE)
        return NULL; // Not enough room
    void* space = &bytes[next_byte];
    next_byte += size;
    return space;
}
```

Space. The overall memory pool is a pair of halves. It, too, has an Allocate() member function that under normal circumstances simply delegates to the active half. If that half does not have enough room, it first switches halves and copies active objects across by calling Swap(). This scheme relies on the previous material, a custom, enumerable pool of VoidPtrs.

```
class Space {
private:
    HalfSpace A, B;
    HalfSpace* active;
    HalfSpace* inactive;
    void Swap(); // Swap active spaces, copy objects
public:
    Space() : active(&A), inactive(&B) {};
    void* Allocate(size_t size);
};
```

```
void* Space::Allocate(size_t size) {
    void* space = active->Allocate(size);
    if (space != NULL) return space;
    Swap();
    space = active->Allocate(size);
    if (space == NULL)
        // exception - out of memory
    return space;
}
void Space::Swap()
{
    if (active == &A) {
        active = &B;
        inactive = &A;
        }
    else {
        active = &A;
        inactive = &B;
        }
    active->Reinitialize();
    // Iterate over all VoidPtrs to find active objects
    VoidPtrIterator* iterator=VoidPtr::pool->iterator();
    while (iterator->More()) {
        VoidPtr* vp = iterator->Next();
        if (vp->address >= inactive &&
            vp->address < inactive + sizeof *inactive) {
            void* new_space = active->Allocate(vp->size);
            if (new_space == NULL)
                // exception - out of memory
            memcpy(new_space, vp->address, vp->size);
            vp->address = new_space;
            }
        }
    delete iterator;
}
```

The whole thing rests on that while loop in Space::Swap(). For each object still living in the other, previously active, half, we copy it to the newly active half. The reasons for checking that the address is in the range of the old half will soon become apparent.

operator new. Of course, we also have to have an overloaded operator new that uses this structure.

```
void* operator new(size_t size, Space* space)
{
    return space->Allocate(size);
}
```

Master Pointers. Finally, the master pointers must use this space when they allocate the objects.

```
template <class Type>
class BMP : public VoidPtr {
private: // Disallow copying and assignment of pointers
    BMP(const MP<Type>&) {}
    BMP<Type>& operator=(const BMP<Type>&)
        {return *this;}
public:
    BMP() : VoidPtr
        (new(object_space) Type, sizeof(Type)) {}
    virtual ~BMP() { ((Type*)address)->Type::~Type(); }
    Type* operator->() { return (Type*)address; }
};
```

object_space is a global variable, or maybe a static data member of VoidPtr, that points to the Space to be managed.

Incremental Copying

Unless you like steaming coffee cup cursors, there is a problem with this algorithm. The Swap() process takes place at an unpredictable time and will likely take quite a while to finish. This results in unpredictable response times for the user, which is just slightly more annoying to a user than a hardware failure. Fortunately, Baker's Algorithm is easy to adapt so that it takes place incrementally in the background.

The Bay Bridge in San Francisco employs a full-time painting crew. The crew starts painting from one end of the bridge and keeps painting for a couple of years until it gets to the other side. By then, it's time to start over again at the beginning. Painting takes place continuously, except for the occasional earthquake or demonstration against the day's politically incorrect. That is basically the way to turn Baker's Algorithm into an incremental compaction scheme. Here is another pass at the Space class. Swap() is divided into two pieces, one of which switches active halves, the other of which is called repeatedly to copy one object at a time.

```
class Space {
private:
    VoidPtrIterator* iterator; // Stores state of copying
    HalfSpace A, B;
    HalfSpace* active;
    HalfSpace* inactive;
    void Swap(); // Swap active spaces, copy objects
public:
    Space() : active(&A), inactive(&B), iterator(NULL)
        { Swap(); }
    void* Allocate(size_t size);
    void Copy1();
};
void* Space::Allocate(size_t size) {
    void* space = active->Allocate(size);
    if (space == NULL)
        // exception - out of memory
    return space;
}
void Space::Swap() {
    if (active == &A) {
        active = &B;
        inactive = &A;
        }
    else {
        active = &A;
        inactive = &B;
        }
    active->Reinitialize();
    delete iterator;
    iterator = VoidPtr::pool->iterator();
}
```

```
void Space::Copy1()
{
    if (!iterator->More())
        Swap(); // Start over going the other way
    else {
        VoidPtr* vp = iterator->Next();
        if (vp->address >= inactive &&
            vp->address < inactive + sizeof *inactive) {
            void* new_space =
                active->Allocate(vp->size);
            if (new_space == NULL)
                throw(OutOfMemory());
            memcpy(new_space, vp->address, vp->size);
            vp->address = new_space;
            }
        }
}
```

Copy1() must be called as often as possible, but it can be woven in with normal processing. New objects are allocated into the active half, interleaved with the copied objects, but that does no harm. Since we check to make sure the object is currently in the inactive space before we copy, objects allocated into the active half are left unchanged.

External Objects

Suppose you need to pass the address of an object to a system call that doesn't know anything about your handles and master pointers. That object had better not move about until the system call completes!

```
SystemCall(&aString); // Better not move aString until
                      // system no longer has its address
```

How you get the address of the object in the first place is not obvious, since the master pointers and handles we've talked about so far do not provide any direct access to object addresses. But assuming you've added that capability, you've got to proceed cautiously.

Your first instinct might be to put a flag into the master pointer, indicating that the object isn't allowed to move. However, that would throw a really rotten tomato into the compaction algorithm, because you then have to step carefully around the object in order to avoid copying over it. A better solution is to actually pick up the object and move it out of the compacting space as long as it needs to remain fixed.

```
class Space {
public:
    void Externalize(VoidPtr* vp) {
        void* space = ::operator new(vp->size);
        memcpy(space, vp->address, vp->size);
        vp->address = space;
        }
    void Internalize(VoidPtr* vp) {
        void* space = Allocate(vp->size);
        memcpy(space, vp->address, vp->size);
        ::operator delete(vp->address);
        vp->address = space;
        }
};
```

Externalize() moves the object outside the compacted space; Internalize() brings it back. The Copy1() algorithm works fine, because it does not attempt to move anything that does not fall within the inactive half.

This technique can also be used when you need to pass the address of a data member or, for that matter, this, to some member function or global function. You may be interfacing between your classes and code from an off-the-shelf class library, for example, which doesn't know anything about your fancy conventions for compaction.

Beyond the burden of proving when external code has stopped using your object, this variation can cause problems if passing addresses to external functions is common, since copying the entire object in and out of a memory space is likely to prove expensive.

Care and Feeding of Baker's Algorithm in C++

There are severe restrictions needed in order to use the algorithms just described. Think of Baker's Algorithm for C++ objects as that kitten your kid brought home and swore to always, forever feed and take care of. In other words, prepare to take on a management chore despite the best of everyone's intentions to follow the rules.

Operation Queues and 'this'. If this exists at the time Copy1() is called, the object it points to may be moved from one half to another, while this continues to merrily refer to the old copy. We took care of all other stack variables by making them handles that had to take a U-turn through a master pointer to get to the object. The brute-force alternative that works, but is not much better, is to call Copy1() as the last thing a member function does.

```
class Foo {
public:
    void Fn() {
        // Code that does something meaningful
        VoidPtr::pool->Copy1();
        }
};
```

Of course, this is only safe if whatever calls Fn() won't use its own this after Fn() returns. I don't know about you, but I have enough trouble sleeping at night without having to worry about whether one of the 2,435 programmers using my class libraries has screwed this up.

A better approach is to arrange for Copy1() to be called from some top-level event loop. You don't really want any member functions of scavenged objects on the stack at the time Copy1() is called. This results in what I call *inside-out* architectures; a member function does not do something itself, but rather creates and posts an *operational* object to some master queue. This is a common feature of class libraries.

```
class Operation {
friend void MainLoop();
private:
    static Queue<Operation> OperationQ;
public:
    virtual void DoSomething()=0;
    void Post() { OperationQ.Push(this); }
};
void MainLoop()
{
    Operation* op;
    while ((op = Operation::OperationQ.Pop()) != NULL) {
        op->DoSomething();
        object_space->Copy1();
        }
}
```

Now when an object wants to get something done, rather than do it right away, it creates an Operation derived class and Pushes it onto the queue. If the processing requires iteration, that Operation object keeps reposting itself to the queue at the end of each call to DoSomething() until the iteration is complete. Here is the outline of an example of the conventional and inside-out approaches.

```
// Old-style way to do something
void Foo::SomeOperation()
{
    for (...)
        OnePass();
}
```

If this is a lengthy operation, you are stuck with two uncomfortable choices: don't do any scavenging and compaction until Foo::SomeOperation() is done, thereby voiding much of the benefit of all that effort you went to to manage memory; or indirectly call Copy1() during Foo::SomeOperation(), which is unsafe. Here is another way to handle the problem using an operation queue.

```
// Inside-out with operation queues
class FooSomeOperation : public Operation {
```

```
public:
    virtual void DoSomething() {
        // Perform one pass
        if (not done yet)
            this->Post(); // Repost for next round
        delete this;
        }
};
void Foo::SomeOperation()
{
    Operation* op = new FooSomeOperation(args);
    op->Post();
    // op->DoSomething will do the work
}
```

It is now guaranteed that Copy1() will never be called at a time when FooSomeOperation::DoSomething() is on the stack. This sort of operation queue comes in handy for so many other reasons that it is a near-standard feature of object-oriented class libraries. There are as many variations on the theme as there are class libraries, such as prioritizing the operations or allowing blocking of some operations until others complete, but they all share the same basic property of unloading most of the stack before periodic maintenance takes place.

Addresses of Data Members. The same problem arises if the address of a data member is taken, even by a member function of the object being managed. That is why we insisted on using handles everywhere, remember? If you use the inside-out approach, there will be no problem as long as the address of a data member is taken, used, then forgotten during one cycle. Even if you don't go to the trouble of using an inside-out architecture, if you can prove that the address is not retained to the next call of Copy1(), you can selectively lift the restriction that handles be used everywhere.

Multiple Inheritance. Multiple inheritance is safe as long as you adhere to the care and feeding of this according to the guidelines just given. The fact that this dances about as you call members of the second or third base class does not present any new problems; they are the same this problem in disguise. Obviously, you must never return the address of yourself cast to a base class, but then, handing out this isn't particularly safe, either.

Volatile Objects. An object whose address — as opposed to the address of its master pointer — is passed outside your control, as to a system call, must first be moved outside of scavenged space. The easiest way to manage that is to create an Operation that moves it, and then makes the system call once it is safely in its new location.

Compaction in Place

The obvious drawback of Baker's Algorithm is that it wastes half of the memory. A less obvious drawback is that it forces all objects to be copied from one spot in memory to another on each pass. Memory-to-memory copying can itself become a performance bottleneck. Both of these problems can be addressed using a different approach known as *compaction in place*. There is only one space, where before we had two halves, and objects are stuffed down within that space to compact memory. This diagram shows a before and an after image of the compacted space.

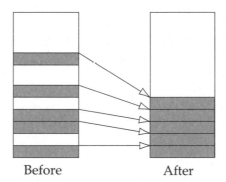

Before   After

The objects must be copied in just the right order, bottom to top, or they end up walking all over one another. This can be arranged in two ways: sort the master pointers at the time enumeration starts or store them in sorted order in the first place. Maintaining the master pointers in a doubly linked list sorted by address of pointee actually turns out to be quite easy, providing you are willing to spend the extra couple of words for the next and previous pointers. The master pointer template and handles are identical to the ones we've used so far. The VoidPtr base class is enhanced to maintain instances in a linked list.

VoidPtr Base Class

Objects are always allocated from the bottom of the memory space to the top; if we always add a new VoidPtr to the tail of the linked list, the list will always be sorted by increasing order of pointee address. The constructors that follow are set up to directly manipulate the VoidPtr-Pool::tail data member. The destructor unlinks the instance from the list. Otherwise, VoidPtr is unchanged. Below are the changes to VoidPtr.

```
class VoidPtr {
private:
    // New data members to maintain the list
    VoidPtr* next; // Next in list
    VoidPtr* previous; // Predecessor in list
protected:
    // Modified constructors
    VoidPtr() : address(NULL), size(0), refcount(0)
        , next(NULL), previous(NULL) {}
    VoidPtr(void* addr, size_t s)
        : address(addr), size(s), refcount(0)
        , next(NULL), previous(pool->tail->previous) {
        pool->tail->next = this;
        pool->tail = this;
        }
public:
    // Modified destructor
    virtual ~VoidPtr() {
        if (size != 0) { // An active pointer - unlink
            if (previous != NULL)
```

```
                previous->next = next;
            if (next != NULL)
                next->previous = previous;
            if (pool->tail == this)
                pool->tail = previous;
            }
        size = 0;
        address=NULL;
        }
};
```

Master Pointer Pool

Changes to the pool of master pointers, VoidPtrPool, are similarly trivial.

```
class VoidPtrPool { // As before, plus the following
friend class VoidPtr; // Allows access to "tail"
private:
    // Additional data members to maintain list
    VoidPtr head; // A dummy VoidPtr that points to
                  // the list of active pointers
    VoidPtr* tail; // Tail of list
public:
    // Revised constructor
    VoidPtrPool() : block_list(NULL), free_list(NULL)
        , tail(&head) {}
};
```

This is otherwise identical to the VoidPtrPool used for Baker's Algorithm, with the addition of the linked list of active VoidPtrs.

Master Pointer Iterator

The pointer iterator is now trivial. It simply walks the list from head to tail — that is, from low to high memory address.

```
class VoidPtrPoolIterator : public VoidPtrIterator {
private:
    VoidPtr* next;
```

```
public:
    VoidPtrIterator(VoidPtr* first) : next(first) {}
    virtual bool More() { return next != NULL; }
    virtual VoidPtr* Next() {
        VoidPtr* vp = next;
        next = next->next;
        return vp;
        }
};
VoidPtrIterator* VoidPtrPool::iterator()
{
    return new VoidPtrPoolIterator(&head.next);
}
```

Compaction Algorithm

The compaction algorithm is now so simple that it almost isn't worth bothering to show it.

```
class Space {
private:
    unsigned long next_byte;
    unsigned char bytes[SPACESIZE];
public:
    Space() : next_byte(0) {}
    void* Allocate(size_t size);
    void Compact();
};
void* Space::Allocate(size_t size) {
    // Round up to word boundary
    size = ROUNDUP(size);
    if (next_byte + size > SPACESIZE) {
        Compact();
        if (next_byte + size > SPACESIZE)
            // exception - out of memory
        }
    void* space = &bytes[next_byte];
    next_byte += size;
    return space;
}
```

```
void Space::Compact()
{
    next_byte = 0;
    VoidPtrIterator* iterator = VoidPtrPool::iterator();
    while (iterator->More()) {
        VoidPtr* vp = iterator->Next();
        void* space = Allocate(vp->size);
        if (space < vp->address) // Make sure it must move
            memmove(space, vp->address, vp->size);
    }
    delete iterator;
}
```

Optimizations

There are many ways to make this more efficient for normal cases. One easy optimization is to store a *low water mark* designating the lowest object that has been deleted. This low water mark is the lowest VoidPtr in the active list that is above something that has been deleted. It is stored as a VoidPtr* data member alongside the head and tail of the list. The destructor of VoidPtr checks to see if the address of the pointee is less than the address in the current low water mark; if so, it replaces the low water mark with its successor. Start the compaction from there, since nothing below needs to be moved. In other words, don't start from the head of the list; start somewhere in the middle — specifically, at the low water mark.

This technique is particularly valuable given a peculiar characteristic of compaction in place. It has been observed that the older an object gets, the less likely it is to be deleted anytime soon. Old objects in this scheme end up clustered at the bottom of the pool. This makes for a nice, big block of objects that seldom need to be moved, since the low water mark is always above them. This minimizes memory-to-memory copying.

Another optimization is to assemble contiguous objects into a single memmove. The overhead of doing several memmoves rather than one big one is not large, but this squeezes a few more cycles out.

Incremental Compaction in Place

This algorithm is also easy to adapt for incremental background compaction. The technique is simple: Keep the VoidPtrIterator around as a data member of the Space and use it to shove down one object each time you call the Copy1() member function. The details are straightforward, as long as you are careful about deletions during a compaction run. Remember that you are iterating over the list of VoidPtrs at the same time that one of them is removed from the list. This is a simple case of the threaded iterator problem discussed in Chapter 8.

Everything said about external objects using Baker's Algorithm applies equally to compaction in place. The address pointed to by the VoidPtr should be checked against the range of addresses in the compacting memory space, and objects can be freely moved into and out of the memory space.

Because this chapter is already incredibly long and this sort of compaction is seldom really needed, the details are left as an exercise for the reader.

Closing Perspectives

Compaction is usually not really what's bugging a C++ programmer, so take all of this with a grain of salt. If you can make reference counting work properly, compaction can be a nice addition to the mix, but otherwise this chapter serves mainly to set up the scavenging techniques of the next chapter. It also reveals much about the outer edges of the language, since C++ is fundamentally not designed to allow objects to be picked up and moved about.

In the next chapter, we'll see this "handles everywhere" strategy and raise it. It is not possible to do truly generalized memory management with arbitrary, off-the-shelf classes, but that won't stop us from seeing just how far the language will allow us to go before it reaches out and thrashes our keyboard-callused fingers.

CHAPTER 16

Scavenging

This is the final chapter of the book, and if you've stayed with me so far, you have my admiration and sympathy. I've probably ruined you for any real-life projects short of controllers for nuclear power plants or expeditions to Mars. But since we've come this far, let's go out with a bang … oops, a poor choice of words in connection with nuclear plants and spaceships. Let's just say that some of you will someday need to do real scavenging in C++ and that this chapter points the way. For the rest, treat this chapter as a final intellectual romp through the meadow of C++ memory management and idioms.

Reachability

The first thing to do is to detect which objects can be reached and which cannot, and the first question to answer is: Reached from where? This section lays out the basic options for walking inward from a well-defined perimeter. That will be followed by two specific scavenging architectures that use these techniques.

The Perimeter

Scavenging techniques beyond reference counting require starting from some outer perimeter of the object graph. Designing that perimeter is itself somewhat tricky.

Stack Variables. If you strip away all the object-oriented gobbledygook from a C++ program, you are left with code fragments. Those code fragments allocate local variables, which is the most common way to reach an object.

```
void f()
{
    Foo* foo = new Foo; // foo is reachable
}
```

The variables on the stack can directly (that is, without involving another object) get at an object in any of several ways:

- this is an implicit pointer to an object that is reachable from the method code.
- A variable can contain a pointer (*) or reference (&) to an object.
- A variable can be an object.
- A variable can contain information needed to look up an object.

In addition, an object can be reached from a stack-based variable indirectly. For example, if this has a Bar* data member, the Bar pointed to is indirectly accessible from within any member function of this.

External Pointers. If you pass the address of an object or one of its data members to a system call or coprocess or anywhere outside your carefully crafted scavenging code, that object is directly accessible.

```
class String {
private:
    char* str;
public:
```

```
    operator char*() { return str; }
};
strcpy(aString, bString); // Uses operator char*
```

The conversion operator is used here to call strcpy(char*, char*). During the execution of strcpy, both strings are directly accessible from the code that implements strcpy, which is not in your control. This is fairly benign, since strcpy can be thought of as an atomic unit of processing. Not so if you pass a reference to a functor to, say, a database function as an object-oriented callback function. You will go on about your merry business until the phone rings, but in the meantime, don't trash that functor!

Indexed Collections. This is an odd case. Suppose that a collection of objects is indexed by, say, a very large integer.

```
template <class Type>
class Array {
public:
    Type* operator[](LargeInt);
};
```

One could argue that all the objects in the collection are reachable if the collection is reachable, but that isn't always a very satisfactory answer. Often, you want to know whether an object in the collection can ever be accessed by its index; that is, does any object other than the collection have the index of object X? If not, then only the collection has X's address, and you may well want to get rid of it. We won't go further with this hot potato in this chapter, other than to note the problem in passing. It most commonly occurs when objects get cached on disk and in distributed object systems.

The Interior

Once you have identified all the objects that can be directly reached, the next problem is to identify objects that are indirectly reachable from the perimeter. Any object can potentially access another object. Objects refer to each other in constrained ways.

Data Members. One object can be literally embedded inside another as a data member, or a data member may be a pointer or reference to some other object.

Arguments to Member Functions. One object can potentially gain access to another through arguments to its member functions. This is really a special case of the stack variable just discussed.

```
void Foo::f(Bar* b)
{
    b->member_of_Bar();
}
```

Base Classes. A base class in C++ is really treated as if it were an embedded object. This is especially true under multiple inheritance and with virtual base classes, as discussed in the previous chapter. Given the address of one object, you may refer to several different logical objects within it — some data members, others base classes. Those objects will not, in general, share the same memory address as the enclosing object.

Parsing the Instances

Scavenging algorithms generally start on the perimeter, then for each object on the perimeter, enumerate the objects it contains and points to, then for each of those objects, enumerate, and so forth recursively until you have stopped reaching new objects. This requires some way, given an object, to find its embedded objects and pointers/references.

In Smalltalk and other dynamic languages, this would be the job of the class object, to describe the structure of instances. In C++, there are several options. The first two solutions that follow are quite practical, and the third is a desperation ploy only to be used on a closed track by a professional stunt driver.

Virtual Member Functions. If all objects descend from a common base class, that base class can declare a virtual member function that enumerates pointers and embedded objects. Each class then overrides the function, but only if it adds data members or uses multiple inheritance to combine base classes.

Class Objects. You can also roll your own class objects, as is described in earlier chapters, and train them to enumerate embedded objects and pointers inside instances.

Ingenious Pointers. As a last resort, by using smart pointers you can ask the pointer to an object to describe the object.

```
class Foo {
private:
    Bar* bar;
};
class PFoo { // A smart pointer to a Foo
private:
    Foo* foo;
public:
    FunctionThatEnumeratesPointersInfoo();
};
```

I say this is a last resort, because it risks having the pointer misguess the actual type of the thing pointed to. Clearly, we can ensure that foo here is really a Foo* if PFoo is a master pointer, but what do you do when you get to bar? How do you know it is really a Bar and not something derived from it? If Bar does not have the self-describing virtual member function just shown, and it doesn't return a class object, the only chance is to bury smart pointers everywhere and hope for the best.

```
class Bar {
};
class PBar { // A smart pointer to a Bar
};
class Foo {
private:
    PBar bar;
};
```

```
class PFoo { // A smart pointer to a Foo
private:
    Foo* foo;
public:
    FunctionThatEnumeratesPointersInfoo();
};
```

Now we start with one smart pointer, PFoo, and recursively find another one, PBar. Each of these smart pointers knows its way around the inside of the object to which it points. These pointers have transcended *smart*, so I call them *ingenious* (a cynic might say, *foolish*).

Walking the Object Graph

For the following discussion, we will pick the virtual function technique of enumeration from the previous list, although the discussion that follows would apply equally well to class objects. There are two basic strategies for the actual enumeration: use recursive functions and functors, or use iterators.

Recursive Functions and Functors. This is everyone's knee-jerk reaction: set up a callback mechanism, pass in the function or functor to call for each reachable object, then step back while the recursive walkthrough takes place.

```
class Functor { // The callback 'function'
public:
    virtual void Apply(MotherOfAllClasses*)=0;
};
class MotherOfAllClasses {
public:
    // Apply fn to each reachable object
    virtual void EachObject(Functor& fn);
};
```

EachObject() calls fn.Apply(this), then calls EachObject() for each embedded object or object pointed to by a data member. EachObject() also calls Base::EachObject() for each base class, thereby including base class members in the enumeration. Depending on the algorithm, you may put a "mark bit" in MotherOfAllClasses to indicate that the object has previously been seen, although, as we shall see, that is not always required.

Iterators Everywhere. A better approach is to have each object return an iterator over objects embedded inside it, including base classes, or directly pointed to by data members.

```
class MOAOIterator { // "MotherOfAllObjectsIterator"
public:
    virtual bool More()=0;
    virtual MotherOfAllObjects* Next()=0;
};
class MotherOfAllObjects {
public:
    virtual MOAOIterator* EachObject();
};
```

The code involved in this is obviously more complicated than the virtual member function approach in the last section. However, the "iterators everywhere" technique has one huge advantage: It allows things to be done incrementally. Using the recursive function approach, there is no good way to pop up for air every millisecond or so and let other code run. When you use iterators, as long as you are careful, that is no big deal. This is the technique we will adopt from here on.

Scavenging with Baker's Algorithm

Bet you wondered what good Baker's Algorithm was, didn't you? In the last chapter, it was billed as a compaction algorithm, but what's the point of compacting memory if you have to waste 50 percent of it to do the compaction? Now we'll find out the real magic of Baker's Algorithm — its use as a scavenging architecture.

For the moment, we won't worry about externally accessible objects and will concentrate on stack variables as being the collective perimeter.

Since we are now scavenging, there is no reason to rely on reference counting everywhere. However, reference counting still plays an important role: It is used to count the handles on the stack that refer to a given master pointer. A master pointer with a reference count greater than zero is directly reachable from the stack and, therefore, is on the perimeter. We will use strong handles for stack variables and weak handles for references from one object to another as data members. The VoidPtr and other data structures from the previous chapter are untouched with one exception: VoidPtr::Release() does not delete the master pointer when the count goes to zero. Remember: A zero reference count does not mean the object isn't reachable, just that it's not directly reachable from the stack.

Weak Handle Template

The weak handle is straightforward.

```
template <class Type>
class WH {
friend class Handle<Type>;
private:
    BMP<Type>* pointer;
public:
    WH() : pointer(new BMP<Type>
                    (new(object_space) Type)) {}
    BMP<Type>& operator->() { return *pointer; }
};
```

This is used in data members that refer to other objects.

```
class Foo {
private:
    WH<Bar> bar; // Creates Bar + MP<Bar> on construction
};
```

Strong Handle Template

The strong handle template is identical to the weak handle except that it maintains the reference count of the pointer.

```
template <class Type>
class SH {
private:
    BMP<Type>* pointer;
public:
    SH() : pointer(new BMP<Type>(new Type))
        { pointer->Grab(); }
    SH(const SH<Type>& h) : pointer(h.pointer)
        { pointer->Grab(); }
    SH(const WH<Type>& h) : pointer(h.pointer)
        { pointer->Grab(); }
    operator WH<Type>() { return WH<Type>(pointer); }
    SH<Type>& operator=(const SH<Type>& h) {
        if (this == &h) return *this;
        if (pointer == h.pointer) return *this;
        pointer->Release();
        h.pointer->Grab();
        return *this;
        }
    BMP<Type>& operator->() { return *pointer; }
};
```

This is used in code for variables that refer to objects. Because of the constructor accepting H<Type> and the operator H<Type>(), it can also be used to assign to or from data members that are weak handles.

```
class Bar {
private:
    WH<Foo> foo;
public:
    void f();
};
void Bar::f()
{
    SH<Foo> f; // Equivalent to Foo* f = new Foo;
    f = foo; // Uses operator=(SH<Type>(foo));
    foo = f; // Uses operator WH<Type>(f)
}
```

Master Pointer Iterators

Remember VoidPtrIterator? VoidPtrPool returns one such iterator, enumerating all of the pointers with a nonzero reference count. That is unchanged, except that the interpretation of the reference count is now different. Before, a nonzero reference count meant that the object should not be scavenged. Now, a nonzero reference count has a narrower meaning, that of an object directly reachable from the stack. These will all be saved because they are on the perimeter, but we will also save objects with zero reference counts if they are reachable indirectly.

For the interior, we need to walk through the handles in each object on the perimeter, then recursively walk inward until we have visited all reachable objects. That requires parsing the objects using one of the techniques just described. We will use the virtual member function/iterators everywhere combination for this example. We can recycle the old VoidPtrIterator interface for this.

```
class VoidPtrIterator {
protected:
    VoidPtrIterator() {}
public:
    virtual bool More() = 0;
    VoidPtr* Next() = 0;
};
```

The pool must support two kinds of iterators now. One iterator enumerates pointers that are on the perimeter, that is, those with a nonzero reference count. A second iterator walks through pointers to objects that are in a specified half. In place of VoidPtrPool::iterator() from the previous chapter, we now have the following.

```
// Add to the class VoidPtrPool
class VoidPtrPool {
public:
    VoidPtrIterator* Reachable()
        { return new ReachableIterator(this); }
    VoidPtrIterator* InRange(void* low, void* high)
```

```
        { return new RangeIterator(this); }
};
```

Perimeter Pointers. The pool will return one type of iterator that walks through directly reachable pointers, those that have a non-zero reference count. This is a one-line change to VoidPtrPoolIterator, skipping over the zero-refcount slots in Advance(). It is implemented as a derived class of VoidPtrPoolIterator.

```
class ReachableIterator : public VoidPtrPoolIterator {
protected:
    virtual void Advance() { // Find next in-use slot
        do VoidPtrPoolIterator::Advance();
        while (block != NULL
            && block->slots[slot].refcount == 0);
    }
public:
    ReachableIterator(VoidPtrBlock* vpb)
        : VoidPtrPoolIterator(vpb) {}
};
```

Unreachable Pointers. At the end of a pass, we will need to sweep through the master pointers, finding all that still point to the inactive half. These are the unreachable objects. The following iterator handles that, using another trivial override of VoidPtrPoolIterator.

```
class InRange : public VoidPtrPoolIterator {
private:
    void* low; // Low address in range
    void* high; // High address in range
    virtual void Advance() { // Find next in-use slot
        do VoidPtrPoolIterator::Advance();
        while (block != NULL
            && (block->slots[slot].address < low
                || block->slots[slot].address >= high));
    }
public:
    InRange(VoidPtrBlock* vpb, void* low_addr,
        void* high_addr)
```

```
                 : VoidPtrPoolIterator(vpb), low(low_addr)
                 , high(high_addr) {}
       };
```

Enumerating Pointers within Objects. Each object will return another VoidPtrIterator that enumerates pointers directly reachable from the object. This must be custom-built for each class. Here is an example.

```
class MotherOfAllObjects { // Everyone derives from this
public:
    virtual VoidPtrIterator* Pointers() = 0;
};
template <int Entries>
class VoidPtrArrayIterator : public VoidPtrIterator {
private:
    VoidPtr* ptrs[Entries];
    int next; // Next slot to visit
public:
    VoidPtrArrayIterator() : next(0) {
        for (int i = 0; i < Entries; i++)
            ptrs[i] = NULL;
        }
    VoidPtr*& operator[](int slot) { return ptrs[slot]; }
    virtual bool More() { return next < Entries; }
    virtual VoidPtr* Next() { return ptrs[next++]; }
};
// A sample class and iterator
class Foo {
private:
    WH<Bar> bar;
public:
    virtual VoidPtrIterator*Pointers() {
        VoidPtrArrayIterator<1>* iterator =
            new VoidPtrArrayIterator<1>;
        iterator[0] = bar.Pointer();
        return iterator;
        }
};
```

This VoidPtrArrayIterator is the quick and dirty version, not what you would use in a real project, but it gives the idea. It could do with a good dose of range-checking and throwing exceptions if it is asked to return a VoidPtr* of NULL. Foo::Pointers() shows the generic way to use VoidPtrArrayIterator. For each class, you change the size of the array to match the number of WH<Widget>s and add one line per handle of the form iterator(index++) = widget.Pointer(). This template handles all the simple cases in which we don't have to worry about base classes. If Foo has a base class or two lying around, it will have to arrange to nest iterators over its own and its base class's pointers.

Enumerating Pointers

It is now time to bring all this together in an algorithm that walks through all the accessible objects. Any time we encounter an object that currently resides in the inactive half, we copy it to the active half and change the address in the master pointer to the new copy. If an object is found that is already in the active half, it has presumably already been copied, so we don't bother to look further at it. For the moment, we will simply ignore objects that live outside both halves.

The interface to Space is a slight modification to that used for compaction. We will have to maintain a stack of iterators, rather than just one, as we walk through the object graph. There is also a new member function, Scavenge(), that is called at the end of each cycle through a half. We will assume the existence of the given Stack template.

```
template <class Type>
class Stack {
public:
    Push(Type*);
    Type* Pop(); // Returns NULL if stack is empty
};
class Space {
private:
    VoidPtrIterator* iterator; // Topmost iterator
```

```
        Stack<VoidPtrIterator> iterator_stack;
        HalfSpace A, B;
        HalfSpace* active;
        HalfSpace* inactive;
        void Scavenge(); // Destroy unreachable objects
        void Swap(); // Swap active spaces
public:
        Space() : active(&A), inactive(&B), iterator(NULL)
            { Swap(); }
        void* Allocate(size_t size) {
            void* space = active->Allocate(size);
            if (space == NULL) throw(OutOfMemory());
            return space;
            }
        void Copy1();
};
```

Details on the three key routines — Scavenge(), Swap(), and Copy1() — follow.

Scavenge. Scavenge() is called after one complete pass. It walks through all the master pointers, looking for objects that have been left in the inactive half. Those are the unreachable objects. For each one, it deletes the pointer, which in turn calls the object's destructor.

```
void Space::Scavenge()
{
    VoidPtrIterator* vpi
        = VoidPtr::pool->InRange(inactive,
            inactive + sizeof *inactive);
    while (vpi->More()) {
        VoidPtr* vp = vpi->Next();
        delete vp; // Calls pointee's destructor in turn
        }
    delete vpi;
}
```

Swap. Swap() is called to switch active halves. It calls Scavenge() first to complete the previous pass, then resets everything so that the next call to Copy1() will start copying back the other way.

```
void Space::Swap()
{
    Scavenge(); // Destroy objects in the inactive half
    if (active == &A) {
        active = &B;
        inactive = &A;
        }
    else {
        active = &A;
        inactive = &B;
        }
    active->Reinitialize();
    iterator = VoidPtr::pool->iterator();
}
```

Copy1. Copy1() visits a single object. If it is in the inactive half, it is copied to the active one. If it is not in the inactive half, we assume for present purposes that it is in the active half and, therefore, has already been moved.

```
void Space::Copy1()
{
    if (!iterator->More()) {
        // This iterator is done, delete it and pop
        delete iterator;
        iterator = iterator_stack.Pop();
        if (iterator == NULL) // Done!
            Swap(); // Start over going the other way
        }
    else {
        VoidPtr* vp = iterator->Next();
        if (vp->address >= inactive &&
            vp->address < inactive + sizeof *inactive) {
            // Reachable and needs to be moved
            void* new_space =
                active->Allocate(vp->size);
            if (new_space == NULL)
                // exception - out of memory
            memcpy(new_space, vp->address, vp->size);
            vp->address = new_space;
```

```
                    iterator_stack.Push(iterator);
                    iterator = vp->address->Pointers();
                    }
                    // else it has already been moved
                }
        }
```

Optimizations

The algorithm just described can potentially come to a screeching halt every time Scavenge() is called. Two approaches can be used separately or in combination to optimize further:

1. Scavenge() can be made incremental, rather than operating as a single unit. To do this, you must modify Copy1() to call its incremental scavenging counterpart until scavenging is finished.

2. You can separately keep track of a list of master pointers in use by each half, rather than enumerating everything in the VoidPtr-Pool in order to find them. As each object is moved from the inactive to the active half, its master pointer is moved out of the inactive half's list and into the active half's list. At the end of a compaction pass, this leaves a list of only master pointers that need to be scavenged for the inactive half.

It is unlikely that either of these optimizations will prove worthwhile in a real project, especially the latter, since it requires significantly more overhead in space and time to maintain the lists.

External Objects

Objects that do not live in the scavenged space complicate matters slightly. Objects in the scavenged space may point to these "external" objects. That is no problem in itself, since only objects in the inactive half get moved. The problem arises when external objects then point back to internal ones. Presumably, they use handles, but that still adds to the complexity of the scavenging/compacting algorithm. Here are the adjustments that are needed:

1. Each external object must also be able to enumerate pointers and adhere to the "handles everywhere" convention, at least for references to internal objects.

2. Each external object must be able to mark itself as having been visited during a given pass.

3. In Copy1(), if an object is external and unmarked, it is marked and its iterator is pushed, but the object itself does not get moved.

Multiple Spaces

It is not that difficult once the basic structure is in place to mix and match objects managed in the scavenged space with objects managed in other ways. The key is that all have to cooperate in the pointer walk. Beyond that, it is easy to tell how an object should be managed according to its address.

In-Place Scavenging and Compaction

The same variations from the previous chapter that were used to turn "handles everywhere" into in-place compaction can be used to do this sort of scavenging in place, rather than things having to be copied all over the place. There are two variations on the theme: with and without compaction. Both use a mark-and-sweep algorithm, with one pass to determine what is reachable and the second pass to do the scavenging and, if desired, compaction. This algorithm presumes that a "mark bit" is added to the VoidPtr class:

1. Unmark all VoidPtrs that are not on the free list.

2. Mark all VoidPtrs with a nonzero reference count; that is, mark those directly reachable from the stack.

3. For each newly marked VoidPtr, mark all VoidPtrs embedded in the objects to which they point. This uses the same iterators used for Baker's Algorithm.

4. Repeat step 3 until no more objects can be marked.

5. Delete all VoidPtrs that are unmarked and are not on the free list; that, in turn, will call the destructor of the object pointed to. If you are not going to do compaction, this is also the time to reclaim the space occupied by those objects.

6. If you are doing compaction, walk through all VoidPtrs that are marked in increasing order of memory address pointed to, shoving the objects down to compact fragmented space.

This is more difficult to do incrementally, but if you are careful, it can be arranged. The key is to observe that no object can become reachable once it becomes unreachable. You can decide not to scavenge an object that starts out reachable when the pass begins but becomes unreachable during the pass. Such an object will be reclaimed on the next romp through memory.

Do You Really Want to Call Destructors?

You may or may not really want to call destructors of objects that are no longer reachable. Do you want them calling member functions of other objects, reachable or not? Presumably, they don't delete other objects; that was the point of doing scavenging, so there isn't much left for their destructors to do. On the other hand, sometimes objects have to do other things in their destructors, such as release system resources or close files. Hmm, I don't have a ready answer for that one. You'll have to make the call on a case-by-case basis.

Professional Stunt Drivers Only

Bet you flipped to this section first, didn't you? In fact, I'll bet you're still in the bookstore weighing whether or not to buy this book and saw this section title in the table of contents. Come on, 'fess up — I'm the same way myself. For you real C++ hotshots who like to live on the edge, let's take a look at how far you can go to manage memory with more conventional-looking classes than those that result from "handles everywhere." I don't think more than a small handful of readers will ever need to do any of what follows, and those that do should be pretty good C++ programmers. You also should have bought the book and read the few hundred pages that lead up to this section.

What follow are scavenging ideas that do not move objects in memory and, with the exception of the first, do not require any special programming conventions. Details are only sketched here, since the code depends heavily on the data structures you choose to implement the architectures. Besides, only those who can turn these ideas into code should be licensed to do so.

Mother of All Objects Approaches

I'll start with, then quickly dismiss, approaches that build on the Mother of All Objects idea. Instead of returning an iterator over VoidPtr*'s, the virtual member function can return an iterator over void*&'s or MOAO*&'s. This makes sense until you stop and ask yourself why you bothered to abandon "handles everywhere." The probable reason was that you had little or no control over the classes. Maybe you inherited (a little C++ humor) a class library someone else wrote, and you don't want to rewrite everything to use handles, handles, and more handles. Maybe you just don't think it's practical to explain such a complex architecture to your customers or colleagues. Maybe you just don't like turning C++ into Smalltalk, at least as far as interobject references are concerned. Whatever it was that drove you to this section, it just doesn't make sense to reject handles everywhere but leave in place requirements to derive everything from a common base class, enumerate pointers, and dance lightly around addresses of data members and base classes. On to stuff for the real power programmer in you.

The architecture that follows is organized into four themes:

1. Organizing memory
2. Finding the perimeter
3. Walking the interior
4. Scavenging

Organizing Memory

There are a few key questions you'll want to be able to answer quickly, and answering them requires that memory be in a reasonably organized state:

1. Given a spot in memory, does it contain a memory address or some other sort of value, for example, a bank account number?

2. Given an address, does it point to a valid object or just a random location?

3. Given the address of an object, is it the enclosing object or a data member or base class?

In order to answer these and other questions, you will want to make your memory space pretty smart. Here is one approach that builds on the power-of-two buddy system. This is certainly not the only system; it is just an example.

Memory Blocks. The memory to be managed starts with a short header. In that header is the following information:

- the physical block size
- whether or not this block is in use
- the logical block size

All memory starts out as a single block. When a block gets divided, it is always divided in half. Blocks continue to be recursively divided this way until you have a block whose size is the smallest power of two big enough to contain the object being allocated. When you deallocate, it is easy, given a block's starting address and size, to find its companion block; this allows efficient recombination of adjacent free blocks.

The three questions are answered as follows.

Is a Value an Address? Given a four-byte (in most machines) value, is it a memory address? The answer is presumed to be yes if it points to within the entire managed space; that is, the initial, undivided block.

Is an Address That of an Object? The answer is presumed to be yes if the address lies within the logical extent of an in-use block. The logical extent starts after the header and ends after the logical size. This requires that you search down the binary tree of memory to find the smallest block that encloses the address. If the address is outside managed memory or points to within an unused block or points at or into a block header, it cannot be the address of an object.

Does an Address Point to a Top-Level Object? If an address exactly corresponds to the spot immediately following the header of an in-use block, it points to a top-level (enclosing) object. If it points to somewhere in the interior of an object, it must point to a data member or base class component of the enclosing object.

Performance. If managed memory is N bits long and you never allocate fewer than 2^M bits at a time, it takes at most $N-M$ probes into block headers to answer all three of these questions. If N is 20 (one megabyte) and M is 4 (16 bytes minimum block size), for example, it takes at most 16 probes. This is not a trivial amount of overhead, so fine-tuning block sizes is important — larger blocks mean more fragmentation but fewer probes.

Finding the Perimeter

Lifting the "handles everywhere" restriction means allowing code like this.

```
class Foo {
private:
    Bar* bar;
};
Foo* f = new Foo;
```

It also means allowing pointers to base classes (remember the magical dancing this trick C++ pulls) and pointers to data members. This obviously makes it much more difficult to figure out what's reachable and what isn't, starting with finding the perimeter. Following are two options.

Smart Pointers. The best bet is still smart pointers on the stack, even if they aren't handles. You can enumerate these pointers by maintaining a hidden collection: Each constructor of the smart pointer adds it to the collection, while the destructor removes it.

Walking the Stack. This is going to sound really bizarre, but you can approximate the perimeter, erring on the conservative side, by simply scanning the stack for values that correspond to object addresses. There is always the chance that you will encounter some variable that holds your Aunt Millie's telephone number in Nebraska, which just happens to be the same as the address of some object in memory. This is called *pointer aliasing*. The result is that an object may be marked as reachable when it really isn't. This is seldom harmful beyond not reclaiming a few bytes that aren't really in use. (Think about it—that random "address" on the stack not only has to happen to point to the right spot to cause a problem, it has to be the *only* pointer to an otherwise unreachable object. Don't lose sleep over it.)

Marking Objects. Once you have determined that a stack value points into a valid object, the next step is to mark that object. A mark bit should be part of the block header, so the only real trick is to make sure that you can efficiently find the largest enclosing object. This requires that you walk down the memory tree until you find the header for the smallest enclosing block.

Walking the Interior

Once you have enumerated the perimeter by one of these methods, the next thing is to waltz through the interior. Once again, there are two major choices: parse the object or treat all values as potential pointers.

Parse the Object. You can custom-tailor code to enumerate only pointers within each object. This can use the virtual member function approach, class objects, or even have smart pointers enumerate the pointers in the objects to which they point, but in any case, you'll have to custom-engineer a lot of code into your classes.

Use Brute Force. A second approach is to scan the entire logical size of each marked object for potential object addresses. This is identical to what you did to the stack earlier, with the same annoying but harmless pointer aliasing. Once again, every time you find a value that corresponds to some object's address, mark the object and include it in your recursion.

External Objects. If you manage more than one memory space, you may run into objects that live outside the main space being scavenged, but inside some other space of your own choosing. The fact that an object is external doesn't let you off the hook — that object may point right back into managed space. If that space isn't organized to efficiently enumerate pointers (e.g., it doesn't have object headers), you are on your own to decide how to proceed.

Scavenging

Once you have determined which objects are reachable by completing the mark phase, what's next? Compaction isn't practical without handles and master pointers, because there isn't a single place to update with the new address of a moved object. It is possible — barely — to make a second pass through memory, updating all the pointers in the same way you marked objects as reachable, but before you do that buy some stock in a high-performance RISC workstation manufacturer, because you're going to be sending some business their way. A more practical solution is to scavenge in place.

Unless you can promise that all objects descend from a common ancestor — in which case why are you using such a bizarre and imprecise architecture? — it just isn't practical to call destructors. For all you know, that may be an int or a char* you're looking at; it isn't even guaranteed to have a vtable! Remember that this is, when all is said and done, C++ and not Smalltalk or Lisp.

Incremental Scavenging

Mark-and-sweep algorithms are inherently difficult to make incremental, but it can be done with care. Details are unfortunately beyond the scope of this book, but they have little to do with C++ and everything to do with the particular algorithms you choose.

Closing Perspectives

The last two chapters have basically shown you how to do what C++ isn't supposed to be designed to allow. The techniques for memory management potentially use combinations of everything discussed earlier in the book, from simple smart pointers to homomorphism to class objects to reference counting. But what does all this really mean, beyond the high intellectual sport of it all?

First, there is no better way to understand the outside envelope of C++ or to master its idioms than to delve into memory management. Even if you don't need custom memory management for your project, you will benefit from a good understanding of what the limits of the language are and how things look in memory. If nothing else, it will make you a much better debugger, since you'll understand thoroughly what's going on in the memory representation of objects.

Second, the day may come when you really do need industrial-strength, down-and-dirty memory management. When that day arrives, you'll be prepared. And when that day arrives, remember that these chapters were not designed so much to solve those kinds of problems as to show how to implement in C++ whatever algorithm you dig out of a dusty academic tome. The approaches shown here aren't bad, but they only scratch the surface of the subject.

Third, there is no better way to impress people at those C++ cocktail parties than to wait until everyone has settled into a mellow mood, swizzle around your martini, and say, "Why, I remember back in the summer of '95, when we set out to implement a scavenging, compacting garbage collection scheme in a C++ project...." Have fun!

Java Vs C++

You're probably wondering if all the clamor about Java is simply hype to make you buy another development language, upgrade your hardware, and buy another round of books. You've probably heard reviewers in your favorite trade publications refer to Java as another version of C++. If so, then why would you, as a master of C++, need to bother with this "new" language.

Java is simply a *dialect* of C++. Some have called Java a cleaned-up version of C++ that eliminates the confusing features of C++ rarely used and poorly understood. So, you probably know a lot about Java without having to open a book. However, there are facets of Java that can punch holes in your self-confidence. This appendix explores some of these differences.

Forget about using manual memory management skills that enable the creation of C++ applications that are quicker and use memory more efficiently than Java. The Java designers eliminated all manual memory allocation and deallocation (Example Appendix 1.1) in an effort to make it easier to create bug-free code.

Example Appendix 1.1

```
int*pt = new int ;
delete pt;
```

Pointer arithmetic has been thrown out with Java (Example Appendix 1.2). Arrays in Java are true arrays and not pointers as in C++. In fact, Java uses a pointer model that eliminates the pointer syntax used in C++. This change is instituted to prevent accidentally overwriting memory because of an off-by-one error in pointer arithmetic and to prevent data corruption.

Example Appendix 1.2

```
char *na = "Bob Smith";
na++
```

Java prevents memory leaks by automatically deallocating memory. A sort of automatic garbage collection service.

Also, the memory size of primitive data types in Java is not compiler or machine dependent as in C++. Data types are fixed in size such as an int in Java is 32 bit (Table1). The Java compiler generates bytecode instructions which are efficiently translated into native machine instructions.

TABLE 1.   Java Data Types

Type	Size
int	4 bytes
short	2 bytes
long	8 bytes
float	4 bytes
double	8 bytes

You won't find a couple of other familiar constructs either. The designers of Java also eliminate two other memory management constructs. These are structures (Example Appendix 1.3) and unions. Java does not support either of these C++ syntax.

Example Appendix 1.3

```
struct name {
    char fname [20];
    char lname [30];
}
```

An objective of Java is to prevent runtime errors through elimination of common sources of errors in C++ one of which is confusing the assignment operator (=) with the equivalent operator (==). Example Appendix 1.4 contains a common error in C++ which is caught by the Java compiler.

Example Appendix 1.4

```
if (value=10)
```

If you've spent countless hours developing sophisticated multiple inheritance in your applications and are looking to port them easily to Java, then you're in for some disappointing news. Another important difference between Java and C++ is Java does not support multiple inheritance because of the complexity managing multiple inheritance hierarchies.

However, Java has interfaces that provide the benefits of multiple inheritance without enduring the confusion of multiple inheritance.

Watch out for the Java pits! Java is full of traps for C++ programmers. Java classes, for example, are similar to C++ classes. However, all functions in Java must belong to a class including main. Java requires a shell class be created for main as shown in Example Appendix 1.5. Java does not have member functions. Member functions are called methods. Therefor, main is a method, not a function.

Example Appendix 1.5

```
public class ShellClass
{
    public static void main (String[] args)
        {
                }
}
```

Strings in Java are a bit confusing. In C++, strings are an array of characters and individual characters of a string can be modified. This is not the case in Java. Java strings are similar to a char* pointer. String objects in Java are programmer friendly because string objects automatically allocates and deallocates memory which is performed by the assignment operator constructor and destructor.

Methods in Java are similar to, but not exactly the same as functions in C++. For example, there are no global functions and no function prototypes in Java. The Java compiler makes multiple passes through the code that enables functions to be used before they are defined. Furthermore, the location of a variable cannot be passed to a function because pointer and reference arguments do not exist in Java.

Some parts of Java are familiar once you've learned the Java's name. For example, Java object variables are analogous to object pointers in C++ as illustrated in Example Appendix 1.6 Java objects reside on the heap and an object containing another object's variable actually points to another object on the heap.

Example Appendix 1.6

```
//Java
MyObject obl;
```

```
//C++
MyObject* obl;
```

Methods in Java must be defined inside a class and cannot be defined externally such as in C++. Code shown in Example Appendix 1.7 will work for C++ but not in Java. Although methods are defined inside a class, methods are not automatically inline functions.

Example Appendix 1.7

```
Class Person
{
};

void Person::Raise()
{ salary *= 1000
}
```

Should you abandon C++ and move to Java? The question isn't easy to answer. Java must be given serious consideration when building an application for the Internet, intranet, or Extranet. Java's library has all the tools required to work with TCP/IP protocols such as HTTP and FTP. These routines make accessing objects using URLs across the net as simple as using the local file system.

Java is architecturally neutral because the compiler produces and object file and makes Java applications implementation-independent. These features are more relevant for Internet applications than they are for applications not designed to run on the Internet. With Java, you cannot use C++ memory management techniques to tweak every ounce of performance from the platform. This is the price paid for turning memory management over to Java.

Java's architectural neutrality really doesn't exist when it comes to multithreading. Multithreading code is the architectural neutral, but Java relies on the operating system to implement multithreading since implementation of threads differ widely on major platforms.

Will Java revolutionize programming languages and become the end to C++? Don't rush to toss out your C++ compiler yet. Java is a simpler language than C++ when used to develop Internet, Intranet, and Extranet applications. However, the jury remains out as to whether Java can mature into a comprehensive language that draws programmers away

Index